Get Smart!

Ronald James Dietel

Foreword by

Robert L. Linn

Get Smart!

Nine Sure Ways to Help Your Child Succeed in School

JOSSEY-BASS
A Wiley Imprint
www.josseybass.com

Published by Jossey-Bass
A Wiley Imprint
989 Market Street, San Francisco, CA 94103-1741   www.josseybass.com

Jossey-Bass books and products are available through most bookstores. To contact Jossey-Bass directly call our Customer Care Department within the U.S. at 800-956-7739, outside the U.S. at 317-572-3986, or fax 317-572-4002.

Jossey-Bass also publishes its books in a variety of electronic formats. Some content that appears in print may not be available in electronic books.

Library of Congress Cataloging-in-Publication Data

Dietel, Ronald J.
Get smart! : nine sure ways to help your child succeed in school / Ronald James Dietel; foreword Robert L. Linn.—1st ed.
p. cm.
Includes bibliographical references and index.
ISBN-13: 978-0-7879-8334-5 (alk. paper)
ISBN-10: 0-7879-8334-9 (alk. paper)
1. Academic achievement. 2. Learning. 3. Education—Parent participation. I. Title.
LB1062.6.D53 2006
371.19'2—dc22

2006017867

Printed in the United States of America
FIRST EDITION
HB Printing 10 9 8 7 6 5 4 3 2 1

Contents

Foreword

Get Smart! Nine Sure Ways to Help Your Child Succeed in School should be on the must-read list for parents of school age and preschool children. The book is easy to read and packed with well-grounded suggestions for parents who are striving to help their children become better learners and experience the joy of learning. The suggested ways for parents to improve the academic performance of their children are well supported by education research, and by author Ron Dietel's personal contacts with many leading researchers, involved parents, and teachers.

Dietel has written a parent-friendly book that communicates effectively without use of educational jargon. All nine ways to improve academic achievement elaborated in *Get Smart!* are grounded on solid principles derived from numerous learning studies. Parents, teachers, principals, and even students can benefit from the numerous real-life vignettes of how leading educational researchers and outstanding parents have helped their own children succeed in school.

Dietel has done a masterful job of weaving these vignettes into the nine ways he suggests to improve children's academic performance. The examples reveal some of the methods that learning researchers and involved parents use to motivate their own children, help them improve their achievement, and develop positive attitudes toward learning. The vignettes are not meant to be a set of cookbook recipes to be followed. Rather, they illustrate a rich array of successful approaches that parents can adapt to help their own children succeed in school.

Although it is natural to think of schools as the place where learning takes place, numerous examples throughout *Get Smart!* show the critical role played by parents at home. Dietel offers excellent advice on how parents can interact with teachers on the basis of his experience as a parent and as a four-year member of a school district governing board. *Get Smart!* suggests many valuable methods that parents can use in selecting a high-quality school and how they can help reinforce what their children are learning in school.

Students with high academic achievement usually have a positive attitude toward learning and beliefs about their own ability. As is true with other topics, Dietel makes effective use of actual parent-child interactions to help parents think through the steps they can take with their own children to foster development of similar positive attitudes and beliefs.

Dietel's qualifications for writing *Get Smart!* are excellent. A graduate of the U.S. Air Force Academy, Dietel holds a master's degree from the University of Northern Colorado in communications, an MBA from Chapman University, and a doctorate (Ed.D.) in educational evaluation from UCLA. His many years of work at CRESST as assistant director for research use and communications has put him in close contact with some of the nation's leading experts on learning and assessment of student achievement. He has a wealth of practical experience as a former president of the La Cañada (California) Unified School District Governing Board and as a former board member of CHILD Share, a nonprofit organization supporting foster and adoptive parents of neglected and abused children.

All parents want the best for their children. They want to encourage their children to achieve to the best of their ability. But few parents have a clear understanding of how they can improve the academic performance of their children. *Get Smart!* does not proscribe a mandatory list of steps that parents must follow; rather, it presents a rich array of research-based approaches with extensive examples for parents to consider and use as a guide in interacting with their children. I will certainly recommend the book to both my sons and their wives as a valuable resource for their interaction with my preschool and early-elementary-school-age grandsons.

Robert L. Linn
Codirector of CRESST and retired
Distinguished Professor of Education,
University of Colorado at Boulder

To my wife, Sue, and our children,
Coty and Markie

Preface

Get Smart! Nine Sure Ways to Help Your Child Succeed in School is the product of a number of events. Hired in 1991 as the director of communications at the National Center for Research on Evaluation, Standards, and Student Testing (CRESST) at UCLA, I decided to learn more about the research that our center did, so I soon enrolled in a doctorate program at UCLA's Graduate School of Education & Information Studies. Funded by competitive grants, CRESST conducts research on educational testing issues, evaluates the quality of many educational programs, and develops innovative assessments to help improve learning. CRESST is a key research center within UCLA's Graduate School of Education & Information Studies.

Not long after beginning work at CRESST, my wife and I became parents of two children, making my graduate school lessons and my CRESST work extremely relevant. We knew that the foundations of their learning in school were largely dependent on how we supported their learning as infants and toddlers. Like many parents, we committed to do whatever we could to make sure they entered school "ready to learn." At about the same time, our center was being encouraged by the U.S. Department of Education, one of our major funding agencies, to better communicate CRESST education research findings to the broader public. Couldn't we write and publish an article about our work in *Redbook* or *Reader's Digest*, they suggested? The idea inspired my first article in the National PTA magazine, *Our Children*. Meanwhile, my kids were entering elementary school and I became involved in my local school site council.

In 1997, I heard an excellent speech by Penelope Peterson, who was then the president of the American Educational Research Association. In her presidential address, called "Learning to Talk with New Audiences About Educational Research," she discussed the difficulty of getting schools to use educational research, including one instance of how "being a researcher" worked against Harris Cooper's bid for a seat on his local school board (Peterson, 1997). She also talked about trying to apply what she knew from her own education research to her children's learning, and the need to better communicate research results to many groups, including parents.

Her remarks fed an idea in my mind. Education researchers know better than anyone what works in education. Surely, just as medical doctors apply their knowledge of medicine to their own children, education researchers should apply their professional knowledge to the education of their own children, even if they aren't quite as successful in getting their knowledge into their local schools. Wouldn't it be nice to ask their advice, and publish it in a parenting magazine, or even in a book?

In the meantime, I became more involved in my local school district, serving on a local educational committee and eventually running for our school board. I was elected and took office in December 2001. Now completely immersed in education, the parenting book or *Reader's Digest* article would have to wait, if it ever happened at all. Serving on a school board, even in a small district like La Cañada Unified, and working a full-time job, was very time-consuming, in addition to my primary role as a father and husband. Eventually I managed to start on the book, drawing from my graduate school studies and interviews with education researchers in which I asked them how they helped their own children succeed in school.

As I got to know more parents in my school district, it became obvious to me that many of them had valuable lessons to share about helping children in school. Virtually all of the people who move to La Cañada Flintridge do so because of high-quality schools, excellent test scores, and the fact that approximately 98 percent of students go on to attend college. Some parents' methods were similar to those of education researchers, but many were unique—and, I believe, equally useful. Without doubt, every parent I interviewed, whether researcher or nonresearcher, had at least a few strategies that were helpful. Consequently *Get Smart!* became a combination of suggestions from both groups.

Each *Get Smart!* chapter is based on one of the nine components of the Get Smart Learning Model, a set of key learning factors drawn from research and interviews with parents, many of them well-known education researchers. The Get Smart Learning Model is also based on a fair amount of common sense, such as the idea that effort plays a critical role in student learning (see Chapter Two) and that parents can help increase student effort. However, the Get Smart Learning Model is not a scientifically proved method for improving your child's achievement. I did not split a school into two parts and randomly assign the Get Smart Learning Model to half of the parents, while the other half received nothing. So I offer the Get Smart Learning Model as a way to tie critical learning factors together, not as a stand-alone educational program that guarantees your child's entrance into the university of his or her choice.

The students described by parents in *Get Smart!* represent a broad spectrum of student achievement. A few are graduates of Ivy League colleges, and a few have learning disabilities. But the common factor is that they all have at least one parent, probably a lot like you, whose children's education is a top goal in their life.

The interviews that I conducted for *Get Smart!* took place over a period of more than three years, and since that time the children have moved on to higher grades. In some cases, they are now in college, graduate school, or the workforce. For consistency, I've generally used the ages of the children at the time of the parent interview. My rationale for this decision is that some strategies are age-dependent, although most tips should transfer across quite a few grade levels. Please accept this as a convention and not a gross mistake by my editor or me. Finally, this book is not sponsored or endorsed by UCLA, CRESST, the U.S. Department of Education or any other agency mentioned herein. All conclusions, opinions, or errors are my own responsibility.

Acknowledgments

There are many people to thank for this book. My wife, Sue, and my children, Coty and Markie, to whom I dedicate this book, are tops on my list. Sue handles the school logistics, which are many, and Coty and Markie diligently do their homework, which is far more than I ever had during my K–12 education. Sue is a breast cancer survivor, and her perseverance and effort make her a hero to me and our kids.

No one could ask for a better agent than Sally van Haitsma and her boss, Julie Castiglia of the Castiglia Literary Agency. They took a risk with a new writer, and I am deeply in their debt. My supervisors, Eva Baker and Joan Herman at the National Center for Research on Evaluation, Standards, and Student Testing at UCLA, have taught me more than I ever thought I might know about educational research. Thank you. My deep appreciation as well to Robert Linn, one of the first and finest people I met in the educational research field back in 1991. Bob is always a source of inspiration, and I greatly appreciate the excellent Foreword he wrote for *Get Smart!*

My thanks to my fellow school board members with whom I had the pleasure of serving from December 2001 to December 2005, including Andy Beattie, Virgina (Jinny) Dalbeck, Meredith Reynolds, Scott Tracy, and Cindy Wilcox. They shared with me their successful strategies with their own children. La Cañada Unified School District (LCUSD) Superintendent James Stratton was very supportive and allowed me to use several valuable district documents. Thank you, Jim. Deep appreciation goes to all of the outstanding

LCUSD teachers, administrators, school principals, and staff, who either taught my children or supported them while helping me learn more about education and schools. School people are among the hardest-working and smartest people on earth.

My thanks as well to those who reviewed my early drafts or chapters: Mary Jane Hufstedler, retired English teacher from La Cañada High School; Lani Moore, a third grade teacher from Janson Elementary School; Joan Evans, from the Los Angeles Unified School District; CRESST researcher Margaret Heritage, a former principal of Corinne Seeds University Elementary School; and Donna Elder, also a former principal of Corinne Seeds. Special thanks to parent Gayle Friedmann for her input to *Get Smart!* To the many parents who shared their strategies with me, my very deep thanks, especially to the late Harry Handler, who was also a dear colleague. I have learned much from each of you.

My appreciation to the following for their review of *Get Smart!* and their very generous endorsements: Greg Bowman, Donna Elder, Joyce Epstein, Jim Kohlmoos, and Kathy Seal.

Finally, my deepest thanks to my editor, Kate Bradford, and her assistant, Constance Santisteban, from John Wiley & Sons, Inc., who shared my vision and hopes for this book. Kate had many excellent suggestions that made me a better writer and *Get Smart!* a better guide for parents. Thanks as well to the many people at Wiley and Jossey-Bass who were so helpful during production, including Thomas Finnegan, Justin Frahm, Matt Kaye, Patrick Seitz, and Jennifer Wenzel. To all of you, my sincere thanks.

Get Smart!

Introduction: The Get Smart Learning Model

> Let us think of education as the means of developing our greatest abilities, because in each of us there is a private hope and dream which, fulfilled, can be translated into benefit for everyone and greater strength for our nation.
>
> —*John F. Kennedy*

Get Smart! Nine Sure Ways to Help Your Child Succeed in School is a bold title for a book. Why should we as parents push our children to do so much better in school—and to do so much more work? Is there no time left for being a kid? For lying in the grass and gazing gloriously at puffs of cumulous clouds?

Perhaps not. Ever since the 1983 publication of *A Nation at Risk*, the emphasis on higher achievement in the United States has proceeded at a relentless pace. Concluding that American students were rapidly falling behind the rest of the civilized world, *A Nation at Risk* spurred interest in better schools and better learning more than any previous report. *A Nation at Risk* was terse and forceful.

> If an unfriendly foreign power had attempted to impose on America the mediocre educational performance that exists today, we might well have viewed it as an act of war. As it stands, we have allowed this to happen to ourselves. We have even squandered the gains in student achievement made in the wake of the Sputnik challenge. Moreover, we have dismantled essential support systems, which helped make those gains possible. We have, in effect, been

> committing an act of unthinking, unilateral educational disarmament (1983, p. 5).

More recent impetus for better student performance comes from federal legislation, notably the No Child Left Behind Act (2002), which requires all students (including those with disabilities and English language learners) to reach 100 percent proficiency in mathematics and language arts by the 2013–14 school year. Public schools that fail to make adequate yearly progress are being placed on "needs improvement lists" and may lose federal money. Because only a handful of even the highest-achieving public schools have reached the 100 percent proficiency mark, nearly every school is expected to eventually miss their goal (Linn, 2005). With the ratcheting up of NCLB requirements, the percentage of Hawaii schools making adequate yearly progress dropped from 53 percent in 2004 to just 34 percent in 2005 (Martin, 2006). Idaho dropped 31 percentage points in the same time period. Although many schools are posting substantial achievement gains, they often cannot keep pace with NCLB's adequate yearly progress requirements. The pressure on schools and children grows.

Disappointing performance in the United States on a series of international assessments reinforces the drive for higher test scores. When scores were released from the Third International Mathematics and Science Study (TIMSS) in the 1990s, newspapers reported that American students "failed" when compared to their Japanese and German counterparts. One headline proclaimed that "U.S. Twelfth Graders Flunk International Math, Science Test"—despite the fact that TIMSS ranks nations only according to performance and that U.S. fourth grade student scores were among the highest in the world (Clowes, 1998). On the more recent *Program for International Student Assessment*, U.S. students were outscored by twenty of twenty-eight OECD countries in mathematics literacy, focusing on mathematics applied to real-world problems (Lerner, 2004). Deserved or not, international test performance and the media contribute to the perception that our schools must improve (Lemke et al, 2004).

The corporate world also regularly expresses dismay with the quality of U.S. public education; this constitutes another factor in the move for higher student achievement. "The grim reality is that even as our overall achievement inches up," said corporate icon and former CEO at IBM Lou Gerstner, "our sons and daughters remain severely handicapped by a [school] system that expects too little and then routinely rewards substandard performance . . ." (2001, n.p.).

Increased political and community pressure on schools means increased academic pressure on students, representing an even greater need for parental involvement and support of learning at home and school.

Higher university admission standards are also pushing students to study harder and score better. Ivy League universities are becoming ever more competitive (Cooper, 2002), and some public university applications are soaring despite higher tuition. For the 2006-07 school year, UCLA received over 47,000 applications for a freshman class of 4,625 students (*UCLA News*, 2006) despite double-digit tuition increases totaling more than 40 percent in the past few years. The average entering UCLA freshman has increased to a 4.27 high school grade point average. Although many educators express regular dismay with the relentless focus on achievement, the words "let them be kids" are becoming a faint echo of the past.

How can parents help their children keep up and succeed? Fortunately, a growing body of research shows that substantial increases in academic achievement are possible if parents, teachers, and students work in partnership. Researchers such as Joyce Epstein, Eva Baker, Joan Herman, Robert Linn, Robert Glaser, and Lauren Resnick have all said that student ability, though important, is not the forever factor in student success.

Research also shows that parents have a strong influence over what, how much, and how well their children learn in school. In their study of 256 California schools, Joan Herman and Jennie Yeh

(1980) concluded that "parent participation appears pivotal: it is positively related to both parent satisfaction and student achievement." Rhoda Becher (1986), on the basis of a literature review of research on parents and schools, wrote that "substantial evidence exists to show that children whose parents are involved in their schooling have significantly increased academic achievement and cognitive development." Karl White (as cited in Marzano, 2003) found that the influence of a good home atmosphere produced a test score gain as high as 42 percentile points. An extensive review of research from the Northwest Regional Educational Laboratory found that "the most effective forms of parent involvement are those which engage parents in working directly with their children on learning activities in the home" (Cotton and Wikelund, 2001, n.p.).

Mothers and fathers both contribute to their children's success, even if mothers often appear to be more actively involved. A study by the National Center for Education Statistics (Winquist Nord, 1998) found that students with a father who had a high level of involvement in their education performed better in school and were less likely to have ever been suspended or expelled. Many of the researchers and parents quoted in this book are fathers who were highly active in their child's learning.

Having both parents closely involved in a child's education makes a difference, but many instances abound of highly successful children raised by a single parent or grandparents. Figure I.1, using scores from the National Assessment of Educational Progress (NAEP), shows that a parent's own educational background has a strong impact on a child's learning. The gap between students whose parents have less than a high school education and students who have at least one parent with a college education may be as many as 30 NAEP scale points.

The purpose of *Get Smart!* is to help parents and educators create a home learning environment that supports student achievement. Parents can use many of the suggestions directly, and teachers and principals are encouraged to share many of the enclosed tips

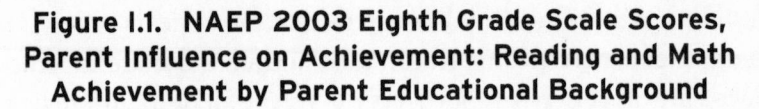

Figure I.1. NAEP 2003 Eighth Grade Scale Scores, Parent Influence on Achievement: Reading and Math Achievement by Parent Educational Background

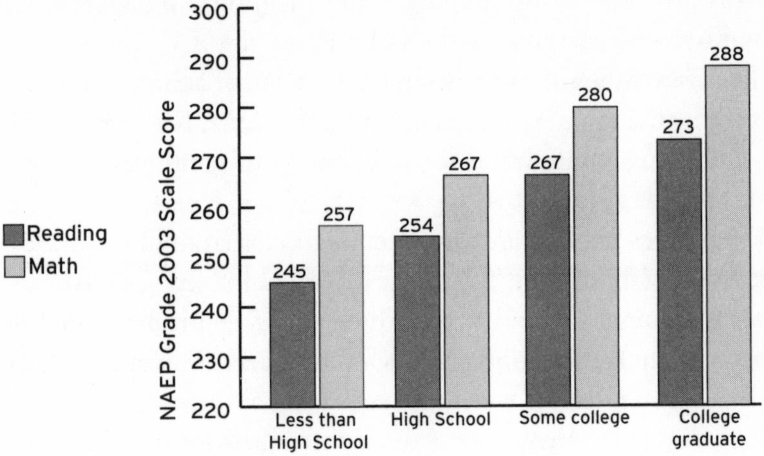

with interested parents. Older students can benefit by applying the enclosed suggestions to their own learning.

To provide a roadmap of research-based learning, I've proposed the Get Smart Learning Model, drawing largely from research funded through the U.S. Department of Education. Other key sources are syntheses of research publications, the latest of which is the National Research Council's publication *How People Learn: Brain, Mind, Experience, and School* (2000, pp. 234–235). Authored by well-known education experts, the report concluded that "children's natural capabilities require assistance for learning: Adults play a critical role in promoting children's curiosity and persistence by directing children's attention, structuring their experiences, supporting their learning attempts, and regulating the complexity and difficulty of levels of information for them."

The interviews contained in this book from researchers, parents, and educators help to support the components of the Get Smart Learning Model. Many of the parents interviewed, such as

Marilyn Cochran-Smith, Robert Glaser, and Hilda Borko, are among the most respected researchers in their fields. Others interviewed are all active parents deeply involved in their child's learning. All of the people I interviewed put education as a high priority in their lives and the lives of their children.

There are nine components in the Get Smart Learning Model: ability, effort, attitudes and beliefs, school quality, teacher quality, school learning habits, home learning habits, evaluation, and communications (Figure I.2).

I begin *Get Smart!* with three factors that often form in a child's earliest years (though crucial during all of a child's education). Described in Chapters One through Three, these are primarily *student* factors of ability, effort, and attitudes and beliefs. Recognizing that children come into this world with differing abilities, as described in Chapter One, parents can create opportunities for their children to develop and enhance their skills. The second student component, effort, makes a difference in school and in most endeavors, as

Figure I.2. Get Smart Learning Model

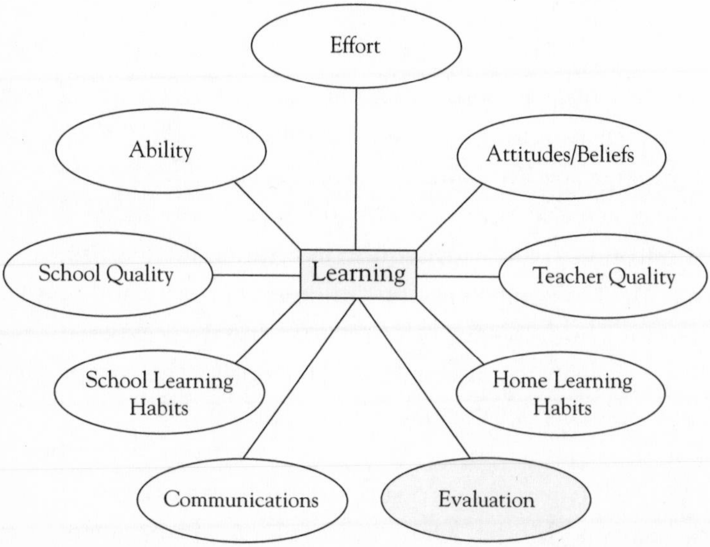

is borne out by research described in Chapter Two and our own practical experience. We can likely point to children and adults who have made the most of their abilities, which may not have been as strong as others', through hard work and consistent effort. Rounding out the *Get Smart!* student factors are positive attitudes and beliefs toward learning, described in Chapter Three, which enhance our children's abilities and efforts, completing a triad of the first components in the Get Smart Learning Model. Reinforcing each of these factors helps a child enter school truly ready to learn. For students already in school, these components and chapters improve their overall learning potential.

The middle chapters, Four and Five, address the *school* factors that are crucial for ages five through eighteen, among them school and teacher quality. Parents might select a good school, for example, by moving to a neighborhood where schools have high-achieving students, strong leadership, and excellent teachers. If we can afford a private education, we may decide that a private school with small class size is the best choice for our child. Although parents seldom have choice over their child's teacher, *Get Smart!* suggests ways to develop an effective parent, teacher, and student rapport that promotes their child's learning in school.

Chapters Six through Nine describe a set of *critical* factors in the Get Smart Learning Model: school learning habits, home learning habits, evaluation, and communications. All four components are important throughout a child's K–12 education, and each is a factor over which parents can have substantial influence. Reading to our children at an early age, for example, is a well-known method for helping our children develop their early reading skills. Listening closely, as opposed to mostly talking *at* our children, can help them overcome social and academic hurdles at school and home. Evaluation allows us to effectively monitor our children's progress, including their strengths and weaknesses. Increased availability of data from achievement tests and growing willingness on the part of schools to view parents as an essential partner in student learning has heightened the importance of evaluation in recent years. Each *critical* factor builds on both student and school components, giving your child the opportunity to succeed beyond his or her own basic ability or the contributions of a good school.

The tips throughout *Get Smart!* are intended to help any student. Appendix A, Get Smart Strategies for Students with Special Needs, has additional ideas for parents of children with learning disabilities.

Naturally, the level of parent control over all of these factors changes as children mature. Parents and teachers generally have less control as children grow older and assume greater responsibility for their own learning. Nevertheless, children are still learning throughout their school years and can make great improvements in their ability to self-regulate learning. Many of the suggestions continue to help me with my own children, who are now in high school.

Although *Get Smart!* is a model for supporting student success, each chapter is designed to stand alone. You should not hesitate to select a section or topic that is most helpful for your child; you will find useful tips on almost every page. For example, even if you have already selected your child's school you will find valuable ways to work with the school to support your child's learning in Chapter Four, "Schools That Help Children Get Smart."

I've tried to use terminology in this book that every parent will understand. Two frequently used terms are *assessment* and *multiple measures*. As used in *Get Smart!* assessment is the measurement of student knowledge, ability, performance or skills, often using a written instrument such as a test. Educational assessments are often *classroom assessments*, either teacher-developed or textbook, or *large-scale assessments* such as multiple-choice state tests. The term *multiple measures* means the use of more than one assessment or measure of a student's knowledge, skills, abilities, or performance. Educational test standards recommend that multiple measures be used whenever major decisions are to be made about students (APA/AERA/NCME, 1999) because no single assessment can precisely measure knowledge or performance.

No educational model is perfect. The Get Smart Learning Model may not necessarily include every component of a child's learning. Components shift over time and vary with students and their relationships with parents and teachers. I hope though, that this model amounts to a useful approach to all of us as we help our children reach high standards.

"Education begins at home," said dancer, actor, and director Geoffrey Holder. "You can't blame the school for not putting into your child what you don't put into him."

"I can't *make* my children learn," said parent and former school board president Meredith Reynolds, "but I can help them develop good skills and lay the foundation for their *ability* to learn."

1

MAKE THE MOST OF YOUR CHILD'S ABILITIES

> Ability is what you're capable of doing. Motivation determines what you do. Attitude determines how well you do it.
>
> —*Lou Holtz*

Every human being is born with both physical and mental abilities. Physically, some of us are stronger or weaker than others, faster or slower, more agile or awkward, and every possible combination in between. We may be strong in one trait and weak in others. Whatever our current physical abilities, we can do something to make them better. We can exercise to be more muscular or increase our endurance. We can adjust our diet to bulk up for playing football, or train ourselves to be faster on the tennis court, but only if we are determined to do so. As the quote from college football coach Lou Holtz makes plain, ability defines our capabilities, but motivation and attitude help to determine our ultimate success. We can improve our physique or physical ability, but only if we have the will to do so.

Mentally, we are born with certain abilities too. We have intelligence, which includes working memory (short-term) and long-term memory, thinking, problem solving, perception, attention, and language (Sternberg, 2002). As with our physical abilities, we may be better in one or more mental abilities than others. Can we get our mind into shape just as we can our body? The answer, according to a range of research studies, is yes. We can also help children get their mind into shape for learning too.

On the basis of a comprehensive analysis of research studies, the U.S. Department of Education concluded that "many highly successful individuals have above-average but not extraordinary intelligence," (Bennett, 1986, p. 16). "Accomplishment in a particular activity is often more dependent upon hard work and self-discipline than on innate ability," added the researchers.

In their study of eighth grade students, researchers Angela Duckworth and Martin Seligman (2005) found, for example, that self-discipline was more important than ability as measured by an IQ test. "Highly self-disciplined adolescents outperformed their more impulsive peers on every academic performance variable, including report-card grades, standardized achievement-test scores, admission to a competitive high school, and attendance," wrote Duckworth and Seligman in their research paper published in *Psychological Science*.

Shari Tishman (2000, p. 43), from Harvard's Project Zero, drew similar conclusions from her study of sixth grade students, noting that students have "abilities that they don't use or they don't use appropriately."

A major step for parents therefore is to capitalize on their children's abilities. This chapter describes *Get Smart!* learning strategies to improve your child's ability to acquire and recall knowledge, apply knowledge, concentrate, self-monitor, think flexibly, and improve creativity.

Improve Your Child's Ability to Acquire and Recall Knowledge

It was another heavy homework evening for my daughter, Markie, a sixth grade student at the time. She finished all of her math homework except for a few challenging problems at the end. It didn't take long to see her confusion. The problems were new to her, solving the perimeter with two unknown variables in two equations. With both of us worn pretty thin, I needed to motivate Markie and determine the best way to help. Complicating matters, I had no idea how she was being taught to solve such problems; nor had I done similar ones in many years. I promised her a great bedtime story if she got through the assignment. We plodded ahead and finished, but it was clear that her understanding needed reinforcement.

At bedtime and as expected, Markie called on me to deliver my story. Typically, my stories are completely off the top of my head, and this one was more so than usual. I used the bedtime story as an opportunity to help Markie visualize what we had covered earlier that evening, supporting what she already knew about perimeters combined with just a beginning knowledge of unknown variables.

I told Markie about a girl who wanted to know the size of her room. The next day, the girl was going to teach her classmates how to measure the size of their own rooms, consequently she really needed to understand how to do it. So at 9:15 P.M., we were measuring the perimeter of Markie's room, applying the day's lesson to a real situation. When we were done, Markie thanked me for another great story and hopped into bed, secure in her mind that the perimeter of her room was fifty feet.

The next evening, she told me that her math problems were all correct, which made us both feel good. I knew that Markie still needed more help in thinking through this new concept, so I sent a note to her math teacher, who reviewed the material with her.

Because this was new knowledge, Markie needed multiple opportunities and different ways to understand it. As parents, we can help our children learn by evaluating what they know or don't know, reinforce their new knowledge in several ways, and solidify their understanding by following up with a teacher.

Learning Expectations Emphasize Factual Recall

The *Taxonomy of Educational Objectives* (1956), a well-known 1956 handbook authored by Benjamin Bloom and other social scientists, defined *knowledge* as observation and remembering (recall) of previously learned information. In the taxonomy, acquiring knowledge precedes higher-order thinking skills such as problem solving, application, and evaluation (Eisner, 2000).

Nearly fifty years later, education still focuses on knowledge acquisition and retention, as reflected in many national and state education standards, including these examples:

- Knows the language of basic operations (for example, factors, products, multiplication)
- Knows that water can be a liquid or a solid and can be made to change from one form to the other, but the amount of water stays the same
- Knows the features of the major European explorations that took place between the fifteenth and seventeenth centuries
- Knows appropriate terminology used to explain music, music notation, music instruments and voices, and music performances

Such standards—in fact, most education standards—depend heavily on recall. Students must memorize "features of major European explorations" or demonstrate that they "know the language of basic operations." Similarly, most tests that students take in school measure their memory ability or ability to solve short problems. Students with a strong memory tend to perform well and students with weaker memory tend to perform less well.

Your child's classroom assignments probably confirm the strong-memory component in most learning. Weekly spelling or vocabulary words are good examples. Students in elementary school frequently receive a list of spelling words on Monday, study during the week, and take a test on Friday. Although many textbooks have been revised in recent years to incorporate more problem-solving skills that represent the higher levels of the taxonomy, most textbooks remain fact-heavy. Social studies textbooks are usually a good example of a continued factual recall emphasis.

There isn't anything wrong with knowing facts. Even advanced learning models such as the CRESST models developed at the center where I work require important factual knowledge. Research by Eva Baker, Pam Aschbacher, David Niemi, and Edynn Sato (1992), for example, has shown that prior knowledge is important for performing well on complex assessments. As I tried to do with Markie's math assignment, parents can create opportunities that support their children's ability to acquire new knowledge.

Early and frequent usage is a key method for improving memory, for children and adults. Most children take a foreign language in school, sometimes beginning in elementary school although usually starting in middle or high school. Yet few become proficient. Despite starting to learn Spanish in seventh grade under the careful teaching of Ms. Kuhl and continuing my Spanish courses through my senior year of college, I never became a fluent Spanish speaker because only English was spoken in my home and I don't use the language frequently. Most students don't become fluent in a foreign language for the same reasons. Frequent usage and support improve memory.

Help Your Child Acquire and Recall Factual Information

How can you help your child store the type of knowledge he or she needs to succeed? First, it's useful to have some measure of your child's ability to recall facts. During your reading time together, ask your young child to occasionally summarize the story that you have read so far. According to learning researcher Merl Wittrock (1990), summarizing helps students connect words, sentences, paragraphs, and concepts that are reinforced by their personal knowledge and experience.

Ask your child, What are the names of the main characters? What seems to be the central problem or conflict in the story? What obstacles is a character encountering? How do you think the story will end? I've used this process productively with both of my children and found that it allows me to informally evaluate their recall ability while conveying to them the value of memory and prediction. It also gets them into the habit of answering questions about their reading, which is an essential ability for performing well on any reading comprehension test.

To measure longer-term memory, try asking your child at dinner to tell you one thing he or she learned in school that day. Not only do you find out what your child is learning, but you can also evaluate his or her ability to recall, summarize, and express ideas. Asking about your child's learning also communicates the value you place on education.

Regardless of your child's current recall ability, you can enhance it by encouraging specific learning strategies. Three suggestions are to *write* it, *draw* it, or *simplify* it.

Writing something down gives meaning to it and creates a written record that can be referred to later. Making a note or outline can focus your child's attention on a historic event, a lesson, or a procedure, often long after he or she was introduced to it the first time. If your child has an assignment and can't seem to get started, have her write down what she remembers about the topic. It is often more than what she can remember verbally. Once she has brainstormed in writing what she knows, it is usually easy to organize and finish the remainder of the assignment. It also establishes a good habit of writing to reinforce recall.

Drawing slows us down and helps us concentrate on ideas, procedures, and relationships. Drawing may help us to recognize similar situations we have encountered and bring back information to reinforce our memory. A simple way to use a drawing is a cause-and-effect diagram. Let's say that the event is the Great Depression. Your child places the event, Great Depression, in the middle of the page, together with causes of the Depression to the left and effects to the right. Even with a moderate amount of effective instruction about the Great Depression, your child should be able to list at least two or three causes and an equal number of effects, just from memory. (Causes might include stock market speculation, lack of regulated stock trading, uneven distribution of wealth, and overproduction of consumer products. Effects were massive unemployment, loss of individual and corporate wealth, a series of new economic policies, and even a second world war.) A simple diagram (such as Exhibit 1.1) can help a child recall information, organize it, and have it become a model for future assignments.

Exhibit 1.1. Simple Diagram of Event, Causes, and Effects

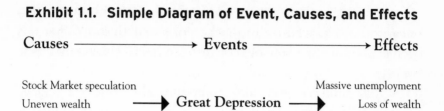

Causes → **Events** → **Effects**

Causes		Event		Effects
Stock Market speculation Uneven wealth Overproduction	→	**Great Depression**	→	Massive unemployment Loss of wealth New economic policies

Simplifying can help children understand a difficult concept or reduce an overload of information. One week in elementary school, for example, Markie had thirty-one spelling words to remember for her Friday spelling test. It looked overwhelming, given a high homework load for the week. In reviewing the words, we noticed that there were only nine unique words and that each unique word ended with an *e*. The other twenty-two words were adjectives or adverbs of the root word. This greatly simplified the recall that Markie needed to do, and she performed well on the test.

Researchers and learning experts have investigated many methods for enhancing recall. The following tips are derived from ideas put forth by Dr. Mel Levine, an expert in children's learning styles (2002):

- *Paraphrase a lesson or chunk of learning.* It is impossible to remember everything contained in a textbook or everything a teacher says in class. Paraphrasing condenses longer information into shorter bits of information. For example, in taking a note in class, your child creates a bullet point that says "1920, Woman's Suffrage." Because the class has been studying the constitutional amendments, this short phrase should be enough to jog his or her memory that in 1920 a new amendment was passed to the U.S. Constitution giving women the right to vote. It is also something that can be written down quickly, reducing the probability of losing the next important point.
- *Form associations with previously learned terms or concepts.* In kindergarten or first grade, students learn how to add. Later, teachers

use what students know about addition to help them learn multiplication, which is basically another form of addition. What was been learned about a previous concept can help a child learn a new concept.

- *Talk through a procedure*. Sometimes also known as *thinking aloud*, verbalizing information helps children remember it. Talking or thinking aloud repeats and therefore reinforces previously learned information. It can also help to exclude from a child's memory other information that is less important.
- *Establish rules*. Rules are useful because they can be applied to many situations to support memory. In Chapter Seven, I describe a four-step rule that I use to help my children solve word problems in mathematics.

Mary Ann Rafoth, Linda Leal, and Leonard DeFabo also offer a number of research-based strategies for improving memory (1993). Memory can be improved if students:

- *Classify* information into specific categories, such as placing foods into a food chain. Animals can be classified as mammals, birds, reptiles, insects, and fish. Because each category generally has similar visual features, the classifications can help students to remember the animal.
- *Self-test* to enhance memory. Flashcards or one-page summary sheets reduce the total amount of information to be recalled. They also allow frequent repetition, which supports memory.
- *Use organizational strategies* such as identifying similarities and differences in items or events. Chunking information helps to organize our thoughts, jog our memory, and express what we know to others. Cause and effect, inputs and outputs, and simple models can support children's recall.

Here are a few more examples of memory-enhancing concepts. Mnemonics are often helpful for improving memory. The rhyme, "Thirty Days Has September . . ." is a verbal mnemonic technique that many of us used as children to help remember the number of days in each month. Association with familiar objects is another useful mnemonic technique. For example, Kenneth Higbee (2001) says that you can remember a piano has fifty-two white keys by associating fifty-two with the number of cards in a deck and thirty-six black keys with the number of inches in a yardstick. According to Higbee, research indicates that even very young children can benefit from the use of mnemonics as a memory technique, and that making up your own mnemonics tends to be more successful than having somebody give you one. Researcher Robert Mislevy described what worked for his daughter:

> In early grades, one of our daughters had a hard time memorizing a lot of unrelated facts, so we encouraged her to use mnemonics. We explained that meaningful things help you to remember, but mnemonics can help you remember what is not easily connected or meaningful. One time in third grade she had to learn a large number of musicians, more than 20, plus the instrument that each of them played, so we developed a mnemonic to help. Wynton Marsalis was a famous jazz trumpet player on her list. To help her remember his name, we said that blowing a trumpet was like blowing *air into a sail* (m'air sail es). It worked.

Our memories benefit from practice. Research indicates that children who participate in challenging thinking games can develop vocabulary and strategies that help them in other situations. Reinforcement in practical situations, such as identifying the capitals of states whose license plates you see on a long road trip, may also contribute to factual recall. Give your child lots of opportunities to expand vocabulary, and learning is likely to improve.

Recall can be enhanced through a conscious process of concentration and reinforcement. For example, you or your child has just met a new person called Sabrina. Set yourself a goal that at the end of the conversation you will say, "It was nice meeting you, Sabrina." Just setting that goal is likely to lead to a process whereby you remember her name. You might use her name several times during the conversation; remember that Sabrina was the name of a television show called "Sabrina the Teenage Witch," or that you have a niece or friend named Sabrina. You set a goal, reinforce the name through repeated use, and associate the name with a visual of other people having the same name. Similar methods can help enhance a child's recall in school. Mayflower is the combination of the name of a month, May, and the part of many plants, flower. Custer's last stand occurred in 1876, a date that can be remembered as one hundred years after the signing of the Declaration of Independence in 1776.

Improving knowledge and recall ability at a young age is an important foundation for good learning habits and study skills later in school.

Improve Your Child's Ability to Apply Knowledge

On the way to school one day, Jacquey Barber's son exclaimed that the route they had just driven to school was shorter than other routes they had taken in the past. Barber, the associate director of the Lawrence Hall of Science at the University of California, Berkeley, asked him, "How do you know?"

"Well, it takes less time to get to school" he said. But Barber wasn't convinced and encouraged her son to collect evidence, using scientific methods he had learned in school.

Thus began a multimonth inquiry into finding the most efficient route to school, a practical problem in the urban streets of Berkeley, California. Barber and her son set up several driving routes in as scientific a method as possible, trying to alter just one factor each day. Her son measured and recorded distances, departure times, and arrival times, with Barber asking many questions, such as why a longer route might require less time to travel. Eventually they had scientific evidence of which route was usually the fastest, depending on their departure time. Using a real-world question, Barber supported her son's ability to apply his knowledge to a practical problem: getting to school in the least amount of time (adapted from Barber, Parizeau, and Bergman, 2002). Parents can use similar opportunities to encourage their children to apply their knowledge to practical applications.

One of the goals at the National Center for Research on Evaluation, Standards, and Student Testing (CRESST) has been to develop innovative assessments that measure students' ability to apply their knowledge. Some of the assessments require students to use factual knowledge, combine it with new information, and apply it to a specific problem. In one assessment, students are asked to read original source materials, such as the Lincoln-Douglas debates, combine their understanding of those documents with their prior knowledge, and then write a well-constructed essay on the issue of slavery. Another assessment, called a knowledge map, requires students to show that they understand the relationships between key events, not just know them as a group of disconnected facts. Most CRESST assessments require the ability to apply prior knowledge to a new situation, and in many cases solve problems in a way similar to how experts solve them. Figure 1.1 is a sample of the types of problem-solving assessments developed at CRESST that measure application of knowledge, not just regurgitation of facts.

Parents can help their children solve complex problems by encouraging them to apply existing knowledge and skills. For example, when her daughters get stuck on a tough math problem, parent Cindy Wilcox says she helps them apply what they know. "I take them back to a similar, but easier, math problem that they have previously solved, then apply the same problem-solving process to the question they can't do," says Wilcox.

In nearly all cases, the technique works. Cindy's daughters have the knowledge and ability to solve the new problem, but they sometimes need someone to help them apply or transfer the appropriate skills. Testing researcher Robert Mislevy explains his approach:

Figure 1.1. Knowledge Map Assessment

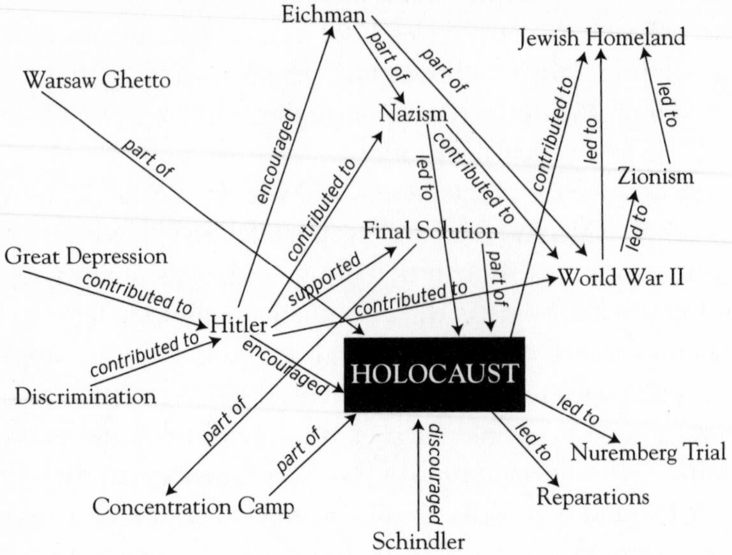

The most important way that my wife and I tried to help our girls succeed was to connect what they were learning in school to the real world, to get them to see other boxes of their life, the big idea. This was true especially on their school assignments, especially in fourth through ninth grade. For example, on a science experiment which focused primarily on procedures involving gases, liquids, and solids, we asked them three things. What are you trying to do? What are the teacher expectations? How does this connect to something in the real world, like getting gas at the gas station? We believed that seeing practical uses for science and math would encourage their effort and it did.

Here are a few more ways to help your child apply existing knowledge:

- Encourage writing, whether it is short notes, a letter to a friend or relative, or a diary. Writing builds on existing vocabulary, encourages personal expression, and helps children organize their thoughts.

- Find problems that can be solved in more than one way or that have more than one solution. Show your child a different way of solving a problem or conducting an experiment.
- Expose your child to a variety of life experiences. Visit a museum, and point out how an artist uses light, the same light that grows crops in a field, the same light that caused last year's sunburn.
- Reinforce student learning with academically focused computer games, which require your child to apply academic skills to fun activities. Spelling, vocabulary, math, science . . . all topics can be reinforced through computers.
- Play board games with your child, especially games that build on vocabulary or thinking skills. Chess has thousands of ways to win or lose and forces players to think ahead. Monopoly reinforces counting skills in young children and can be used to teach money management.

"To help our three kids improve their abilities," said Meredith Reynolds, who served twelve years on the La Cañada Unified School District Governing Board, "we involved them in a broad variety of activities when they were growing up, including art, music, and sports, both team and individual sports. We oftentimes would pick things that we didn't know much about so that it was something new for all of us, sort of like, 'What's this about? Gee, I don't know; let's go and find out.'"

Improve Your Child's Ability to Concentrate

> The ability to focus attention on important things
> is a defining characteristic of intelligence.
>
> —*Robert J. Shiller,* Irrational Exuberance

Jeff Koberstein was one of the smartest kids in Menomonee Falls East High School. He earned good grades in every subject despite taking the toughest classes and working more than thirty hours every week at JC Penney's, saving money he would soon need for college. Jeff was also a gifted piano player. Despite the fact that he had little time left for studying, he graduated second in his high school class, worked his way through college, and became a professor of chemical engineering at Princeton University.

Today Jeff is a professor and leading researcher in chemical engineering at Columbia University, where he teaches and conducts research on the molecular structures of polymers. He said that doing well in school came from his ability to concentrate for sustained periods of time. He could call on that ability for a specific, extended mental task.

Not all of us have Jeff's deep concentration. I have been known to walk the length of my house with a clear-cut purpose in mind, only to arrive at the other end and find myself distracted in my own thoughts. I blame our dog Goldie for such distractions (and a host of my other personal shortcomings), but the truth is that all of us fail to concentrate at one time or another.

School requires the ability to concentrate deeply and remain focused for a long period of time in a multitude of school subjects that may hold little interest for kids. It's no surprise that children with attention problems struggle. Unable to maintain the necessary concentration that school and life require, they are frequently on someone's "needs improvement" list. Distractions, such as a noisy classroom, which may pose few problems for most kids may further erode their concentration.

Research supports the importance of helping children develop listening skills in early grades. In one study, children who were good listeners in kindergarten and first grade became successful readers by third grade. Researchers in another study found that students who were good listeners in fifth grade performed well on aptitude and achievement tests during their high school years (Bennett, 1986). M. S. Conaway found that listening skills were a stronger factor in predicting college student failure than reading ability or aptitude (1982). Because anywhere from 50–80 percent of what we learn comes from hearing, listening is an essential component of concentration and one of the first areas in which students show problems (Rafoth, Leal, and DeFabo, 1993).

As with reading, one good way for parents to help their children improve listening skills is to ask them questions shortly after a conversation. Questions convey to children the importance of careful listening, an important school expectation. Being a careful listener yourself sets an example for your child. When my children say something that I don't understand, I summarize back to them what I thought I heard. This helps us both focus on the conversation.

Here is a list of strategies to help develop your child's concentration skills at any stage in school:

- Encourage and praise your child often for quality work on assignments or projects that require sustained focus.
- Play games that require strong concentration with your child, such as Scrabble or Othello, not just at an early age but as they grow older too.
- Emphasize to your child that good school work requires strong concentration skills at home and at school. Have your child close his eyes and listen carefully to the noises around him. What does he hear? It might be a radio, a television, or a dog barking. Does your child see how these sounds can be distracting, especially to someone concentrating? At school, suggest that your child watch how some students are able to concentrate while others cannot do it well. Encourage finding a setting that allows the best concentration. It may be a special place in the library or a quiet corner in your home. Because you can't be with your child all the time, it's important for him to develop an ability to avoid or control distractions.
- If you have an opportunity to help in the classroom, observe your child's concentration and compare it to that of other students of the same age. You can't see your child listening, but you can observe her on the computer or contributing to work in a small group setting. If you don't have an opportunity to visit your child's classroom, observe her concentration while on a trip to the museum, zoo, or any setting where other children are present.

- If your child seems easily distracted, ask the teacher that she or he be permitted to sit in the front of the classroom. Sitting in the front row means less distraction, and most teachers are happy to comply with such a request.
- Look for indicators of lack of concentration outside the classroom. Missed or late assignments, incomplete agendas, lack of note taking at higher grade levels, or dropping grades may suggest that your child's concentration needs improvement.
- If you believe that your child has attention deficit disorder or attention deficit hyperactivity disorder, by all means request a formal evaluation from the school. I also suggest that you discuss the issue with your child's pediatrician and ask for a referral to a trained psychiatrist specializing in learning disorders. If your child does have a disorder, work closely with teachers and counselors to help meet specific needs.

Not every child's concentration skills will develop at the same rate or reach the same level. I will never have Jeff Koberstein's concentration ability. Be careful to keep your expectations realistic. If you have concerns, discuss them with your child's teacher. As I mentioned in the Introduction, multiple measures should be used to evaluate any aspect of your child's abilities, including concentration.

Improve Your Child's Ability to Self-Monitor

Three children—Sammy, Jason, and Anna—are at home, applying what they learned in math class today, focusing on the correct mathematical order of operations. In today's lesson their teacher showed them that the correct order was what we see in Exhibit 1.2. To help them remember, she used the mnemonic phrase "Please Excuse My Dear Aunt Sally."

Sammy is doing his homework. Because he remembers today's classroom lesson quite well, he finishes quickly, without a single error. He recalls that they covered the same material in fifth grade, so today's homework seems pretty simple.

Exhibit 1.2. Sequence of Math Operations

parentheses→exponents→multiplication→division→addition→subtraction

Jason is moving through the same problems at a rapid rate, but in the back of his mind he thinks about his need to finish before tonight's soccer match. He gets to a question that throws him for a moment, but he applies what he recalls from today's lesson and chugs ahead. Unfortunately, this question and several similar to it are incorrect when he turns his homework in the next day.

Anna is progressing along on the same assignment when she encounters a problem similar to Jason's. She says to herself: "I'm not sure my thinking is right on this." Anna checks her answer in the back of the book and realizes that she made a mistake. She goes back to her original textbook lesson and finds an exception to the order of operations. She makes the change and finishes the problem. Just to make sure, she asks her mom, who confirms that her problem-solving method was correct. Anna finishes the rest of her math problems without error.

This simplistic example illustrates a concept called metacognition, sometimes called self-monitoring or self-regulation—being aware of our own thinking. In this example, Sammy didn't have to think about his thinking. He understood the order of operations and its exceptions so well that the work was automatic. Jason, on the other hand, thought he was doing the problems correctly. When he encountered an obstacle, he just kept plugging away, not aware of his mistake or too impatient to self-regulate his work. The third student, Anna, monitored her learning by checking her answer in the back of the book, recognizing a possible error, using her textbook to help her correct a misunderstanding, and asking her mom to review her strategy. She not only monitored her work but took steps to support her own learning.

Being aware of your own thought processes and regulating your own learning is a key ability of high-achieving students. Although even kindergarten students monitor their own thinking, most students don't develop these skills until about age eleven (Costa, 2000). Even then, it's usually a slow process. Some students and adults seldom think about their thinking. Like Jason, they act impulsively to get it done so they can move on to more pleasurable activities. If academic learning is a low priority to them, they may put forth minimum effort or avoid tasks that require deep thinking.

To encourage self-monitoring of children's thinking skills, parents may ask their child to use a *think-aloud* process while working on an assignment, as mentioned earlier in this chapter. Children simply talk about their thinking as they work on a specific task. Quite a few researchers have found positive effects from thinking aloud.

Another strategy is to ask children *probing* questions along the lines of "Why did you do that?" and "What seems to be the difficulty?" Or ask your child to explain the problem in his own words, with the goal of finding his own mistake, avoiding the same mistake in the future, and developing his own mistake-detection ability.

You will probably be tempted to use *prompting* questions. This kind of question suggests a process that a student has missed or not considered, such as "Did you check your addition?" Although such questions may lead to a quick solution, they do not seem to lead to improved learning because they don't push a child forward in self-monitoring work (Dominowski, 1998).

Evaluations of some self-monitoring training programs, such as the Strategic Content Learning Approach, have shown that these programs can improve students' problem-solving strategies, self-monitoring knowledge, and motivation (Butler, 1998). But self-monitoring training programs are rare. Here are some ideas on how to enhance your child's self-monitoring skills at home:

- At an early age, encourage your child to evaluate her own work and recognize when she needs help. If, after trying her known list of strategies, your child is still hung up, she should seek information in a book or on the Internet, or ask you, a friend, or a teacher. Research shows that higher-achieving students seek help more often than lower-achieving ones (Dembo and Gubler Junge, 2005).

• When encountering a difficult task, encourage your child to explain what she is doing and why. Ask questions about obstacles, if this looks like other tasks she has done, and previous strategies she has used.

• Avoid questions or comments that infer or lead directly to a solution. For example, "Is your multiplication correct?" is a dead giveaway that the student made a multiplication error. A better question might be, "Does the answer seem reasonable to you based on the given information?" or say that the answer is not correct, but "Can you find the error?"

• A problem may be easy for you but quite difficult for your child. Don't say "Think harder" in hopes that your child will suddenly get it. Take a deep breath, give yourself a moment, and think about how you can help your child move ahead. Alternately, switch to another problem or part of the assignment if your child is stuck on it for more than a few minutes.

• Ask your child to explain to another person the problem, a strategy for solving it, and then the solution. Having to teach a subject requires an excellent knowledge of the content and concepts (Dembo and Gubler Junge, 2005).

• Manage your child's impulse to just "do it to get it done," as Jason did in our earlier example. Many high-achieving students analyze the problem or assignment, put effort into understanding the skills needed to complete a task, know how it will be graded, and check their work. Encourage your child to develop similar skills.

Researcher Robert Mislevy described his approach:

> Another way we tried to help our daughters in school was to increase their ability to self-monitor their work. We didn't want them

> to just apply an algorithm to a math problem, or memorize facts and dates. One time when my daughter read an English story three times, trying to find an answer to a question from a study guide, she became very frustrated because she just couldn't find the answer in the book. She asked me for help and I read the story. I said, "A-ha, you're right; the answer isn't there. But the purpose of the teacher's question is to make you think, to connect ideas together. You have to infer an answer from information within the story." I encouraged her to go back, reread the story and look for clues that would help her answer the question. This helped her to connect ideas together and improved her ability to self-monitor her thinking process.

Self-regulation is not an overnight process. As with most learning, students vary at the age and depth to which they acquire this important ability. Be patient and persevering. As the writer and philosopher Napoleon Hill said, "Education comes from within; you get it by struggle and effort and thought."

Monitoring Time and Priorities

Time awareness and management is another important ability in children with strong self-monitoring skills. "Sensing when and how to get going, knowing when the process is speeding up excessively, or when it is getting bogged down and needs to be moved along," says Dr. Mel Levine, "is a key ability of good problem solvers."

Years ago as a student at the U.S. Air Force Squadron Officer School, I participated in an exercise called the "in-basket." Every officer was given an overflowing in-basket containing numerous memos, letters, and to-dos. Students were told only that they needed to work on the in-basket tasks within a specific amount of time.

When given the green light, I attacked my in basket with vigor, determined to finish every task there was to do. I went through in direct order of the tasks, top to bottom. When time was up, I had made a pretty good dent in my stack, although there were still a number of tasks I never reached. The instructor then explained that the intention of the in-basket exercise was not to see how many tasks we had completed, but to see how well we prioritized our work given a limited amount of time. The desired method was to review each in-basket task and prioritize it, such as A, B, and C, then work only on the most important tasks in the A basket. Like others, I learned a valuable lesson that serves me well today.

The next time your child has a major assignment, encourage estimating how much time it will take to do it. Your child should consider how important the task is (for example, how much will it count toward a grade?), estimate how long it might take to do a minimum job, and how much time to do a high-quality job. This also helps your child know when to start. In school and in life, the ability to prioritize work is essential.

Improve Your Child's Ability to Think Flexibly

Most of school is not too flexible. There are rules for students, rules for teachers, rules for school districts, and rules for parents. You and your children probably receive a large packet of rules just before school each year that govern everything from tardiness to the dress code. There are rules for behavior, and subjects have very specific rules (such as "*i* before *e* except after *c*", although there are many exceptions that you just need to memorize).

We encourage flexible thinking in our children, epitomized by the cliché of "thinking outside the box," but we don't often create a flexible environment for it. This is perhaps why some of our most famous inventors and artists never finished school. Thomas Edison was in and out of many schools, was thought to be unteachable, and was eventually home-schooled by his mother. Yet Edison's ability to think flexibly contributed to more than a thousand patents, invention of the light bulb, phonograph, movie projector, and many more accomplishments.

Flexible thinking is a valuable skill, especially when our children's thinking becomes blocked. Moreover, inflexible thinking can result in substantial learning obstacles. In a study of algebra abilities, Mercedes McGowen and David Tall (2001) found that inflexible thinking contributed to students' inability to reach even a proficient level in intermediate algebra concepts, despite extensive and repeated instruction. "The inability to think flexibly," concluded McGowen and Tall, "leads to a fragmentation in students' strategies and a resulting divergence . . . between those who succeed and those who do not."

My son, Coty, is often a one-way thinker. In elementary school, he was struggling with the concept of negative numbers. "How can you have less than nothing?" Coty asked. "That's a good question," I said, and told him that we use negative numbers as a mathematics tool to help us solve certain problems. Elevation is one example, I said, such as above and below sea level. We found a submarine example in Coty's textbook to illustrate negative numbers and discussed other examples of how negative numbers can help solve practical problems. Having images to guide Coty finally warmed him up to the idea that negative numbers can help solve common mathematical problems.

With a bit of creativity on our own part, we can encourage flexible thinking in our children. Draw a straight or curved line on a sheet of paper, and then ask your child to create a drawing using that initial line. She might draw a building, a stick figure, a face, an animal, a building, or a thousand other possibilities. Once she is done, repeat the initial line and ask her to draw something very different using the same line. The idea, of course, is that from just a simple beginning, many drawings are possible, with no two quite alike and no one drawing necessarily any better than another. If you are looking at a black-and-white photograph with your child, casually point out that even a black-and-white photograph has many shades of gray; it isn't truly just black and white.

Although art often lends itself to flexible thinking, any topic can be used, including math. If you are going on a road trip, each person in the family can estimate how long it will take to get to your destination. Have tools available, including a map, string, ruler, and calculator. Once everyone is done with his or her estimate, each person describes how they made an estimate. Ideally, you will have several methods ranging from how the distance was measured to inclusion of variables such as traffic delays, route, and number of bathroom, gas, and meal stops needed. Use an Internet map, and see what it estimates the travel time to be. Ask your child, "How do you think the mapmakers estimated travel time?" which likely varies among Internet sites. Compare your actual travel time with each person's estimate, both going and coming home, and with the Internet estimate. Point out that even in mathematical calculations flexible thinking is important, and one way of solving a problem may not be more accurate or better than another.

Social studies and civics can also be topics for flexible thinking. Ask your child, "Why does the world have so many forms of government? religions? political parties? Do all governments, religions, and political parties have common elements? Do they have major differences? Can we say definitively that one political party is better than another? At school, how do social groups form? Do social groups form along gender, race, and personal interests?" The key point is that flexibility exists more than they probably think, and flexible thinking can create a more flexible world.

Improve Your Child's Creativity

> Every child is an artist. The problem is how to remain an artist once he grows up.
>
> —*Pablo Picasso*

Creative thinking and school do not always go hand in hand. Many artists, notably Pablo Picasso and the U.S. photographer Ansel Adams, disliked school immensely. Although a talented painter even as a child, Picasso struggled to read and write. Adams's severe attention problems contributed to his leaving school at age thirteen, yet his creative abilities made him America's most popular photographer. Both parents and researchers consistently believe that creative thinking is important to a child's education. The American Psychological Association supports the importance of creativity in their Learner-Centered Psychological Principles, noting that a "learner's creativity, higher order thinking, and natural curiosity all contribute to motivation to learn" (APA, 1997, n.p.). Several research studies as well have found a correlation between creativity and achievement. Karnes and others (1961) found that overachieving students had higher creative abilities than underachieving students, while McCabe's study (1991) of 126 children found a strong relationship between scores on a creativity assessment and scores on English achievement tests.

Two common traits of creative thinkers are that they usually master the fundamentals of their craft at an early age and have deep subject matter knowledge. The son of a painter, Picasso created traditional paintings and illustrations by the time he was eight years old and quickly surpassed his own father in technique and style. Ansel Adams began taking his Yosemite photographs at age fourteen, and by fifteen he was honing his black-and-white developing skills at Frank Dittman's photo finishing business in San Francisco. Creativity may seem to be at odds with basic skills, but a more accurate case is that highly creative thinkers master basic skills in their youth, preparing them to spend the rest of their life exploring new ideas.

Another trait common to most creative thinkers is the ability to discipline their energy. The artist Winslow Homer, for example, produced a prodigious number of illustrations, oil paintings, drawings, and watercolors. He created more than six hundred watercolors and about half that number of oil paintings. Ida Lupino was both a prolific actress and a successful director, writer, and producer. In addition to starring in more than fifty feature films and television shows (among them "The Untouchables" and "The Fugitive," Lupino was the first woman to direct an episode of "The Twilight Zone" and was the second woman admitted to the Directors Guild of America; Maltin, 1995). Most successful creative thinkers produce an abundant amount of work and are self-motivated. They are not on the golf course or at the mall when they could be creating. Similarly, children who have strong creative thinking skills also tend to be self-motivated and less driven by external factors such as rewards (Fasko, 2000–01).

What are some common traits of families that have helped to nurture their children into highly creative thinkers? In his book *Creating Minds*, Howard Gardner (1993) analyzed seven highly creative thinkers of the twentieth century: Picasso, Sigmund Freud, Albert Einstein, Igor Stravinsky, T. S. Eliot, Martha Graham, and Mohandas Gandhi. Gardner found that, in general, the families of highly creative persons were not highly educated themselves, but they had high expectations for their children and valued learning, achievement, and hard work. Gardner noted the importance of "positive models in childhood of a creative life," and a "special relation to one or more supportive individuals." Einstein said that "curiosity is a delicate little plant which, aside from stimulation, stands merely in need of freedom."

Parents can develop an environment that supports their child's creativity. As with most aspects of learning, give your child many choices in activities and model the behavior that you desire to see. Although my daughter has never been a prolific writer, during Christmas vacation at age thirteen she picked up her computer and started to write a story about two star-crossed lovers in a medieval setting. Perhaps coincidentally or not, I was completing this book at the kitchen table; or maybe she was motivated by her recent school study of Romeo and Juliet. Whatever the motivation, Markie wrote almost nonstop, and I praised her from first draft to final version, being careful not to criticize or offer my own ideas about how the story should go. This was her creative writing and I was thrilled to see her internally motivated to do something she had never done before. Forcing her to do a similar project would never have been successful.

Parents have to provide time for creative projects, which may mean sacrificing other activities or controlling existing time, as with limiting video games, television, or Internet surfing. School breaks during the year are other good opportunities. Research by Joseph Renzulli (1992) indicates that the deeper a child's interest in a subject, the greater a child's creativity in that subject. Other ways to support a child's creative thinking are to introduce him to creative people, whether individuals you know or through museum visits, music and theatrical performances, and art shows. Enrolling your child in an extracurricular program matching his interests and encouraging imagination is another way to promote your child's creative thinking ability.

Most children ask many questions; this presents an excellent opportunity for parents to support their creative thinking. The next time your child asks a question, instead of saying the answer, you might suggest, "Let's find out together." Then guide, not direct, your child to discover the answer whether it is from a book, on the Internet, or through a simple experiment. The goal, of course, is to encourage the learning process while simultaneously supporting creative thinking.

Andrea Terry, former president of a local PTA, explained her approach to giving children an environment that nurtures their creative abilities:

> Children frequently see our compliments as an expression of our love, not as a true measure of their talents. Consequently it's often difficult for parents to convince their children that they have creative abilities. As a parent of two daughters now in senior high school, my experience has been that if someone else compliments them, they are more apt to believe it. So, you put them into situations where they will get these strokes. For example, you put their artwork up where it will be noticed by those coming into the house. You ask them to design your holiday card. You have their favorite picture made into greeting cards. You enter their work in the school PTA Reflections contest where all kids are honored for participating. You sign them up for art lessons because the art teacher will tell them they have talent.

Some other suggestions are to find fun teachers and classes that nurture their creativity. Local community centers usually have classes in everything from pottery to photography. Museums have classes. Some colleges have summer programs for kids in middle and high school too.

Notice what your children like to do and find a way to expand it, even if they buck you some. Their resistance is usually nervousness due to not feeling confident about their creative skills yet. You have to explain that there will always be people who are better at this or that than they are . . . but they will be better than a lot of people too. We all have different styles and tastes, and need to appreciate that in each other's work. We need to teach them that the process is important. What we enjoy, like art, feeds the soul. We teach our children that feeding our soul . . . our creativity is important throughout our lives. It is where we find joy and meaning. Our creativity will grow and meander into other parts of our lives as a result.

"Nurture your child's curiosity and creativity," advises Hasmik Avetisian, an early elementary educator at UCLA's Corinne Seeds University Elementary School. "Recognize that your child is an individual with a set of specific needs, feelings, and abilities that are different than your own, and different from other children."

Ability then, is the first component of the Get Smart Learning Model. Whatever its starting point, children can improve their physical, creative, or mental abilities, but as Lou Holtz says, it is then effort and attitude that determine just how far a person will go.

2

ENCOURAGE YOUR CHILD TO MAKE THE EFFORT

> Perhaps the most valuable result of all education is the ability to make yourself do the thing you have to do, when it ought to be done, whether you like it or not; it is the first lesson that ought to be learned . . .
>
> —*Thomas H. Huxley (1825—1895)*

Denise's story, presented here, is an excellent example of how parents can help their children increase their motivation and the effort that they put into school.

> One of my children doesn't generally excel at school, could really do without it, doesn't care to read, and has been socially immature. She sits right between two sisters who are GATE [gifted and talented education] students who are in advanced math classes.
>
> In helping her to study one night for a social studies test, I realized that she was very good at memorizing. She was also very good at grammar and spelling. I told her she needed to work with her strengths, while acknowledging and improving her weaknesses. I told her that it used to drive me crazy when I was a child because I had a sister who could write a paper in one night, absorb information like a sponge and also be the class president and homecoming queen. I realized that my brain didn't work like hers. I needed to put more effort into things. I needed to study every night for several nights; I needed to rewrite my notes into a more condensed form for memorization; I needed to write a paper with a lot of lead time and add in time for rewrites.

> I didn't like competition; I preferred to work hard and be acknowledged for my efforts, not run for offices. I told her that I became an excellent student, earning a 4.0 one semester in college and graduating cum laude. I found my niche.
>
> My daughter realized that she, too, needed to put a little more effort into things as well. We developed a way for her to study for social studies tests. She wound up getting an A. And she even received an honor roll award for her last semester at school.

Denise's actions serve as a model for parents whose children may not be putting forth their best effort in school.

First, Denise recognized that a problem existed and decided there was something she could do as a parent to help. Unfortunately, many parents believe that there is little they can do to improve their child's motivation, shrugging off obvious problems until a crisis hits. They may presume that their child will improve on his or her own. In some cases, parents blame the teacher or school for their child's lack of motivation.

Second, using her own personal experiences, Denise helped her daughter see her strengths and weaknesses and then helped her apply her strengths to increase her social studies grade. Success can be its own reward, and in school grades can help build self-confidence and lead to greater effort.

Finally, Denise developed a plan, which included working with her child's teacher and getting a tutor. She monitored her daughter's progress and praised her when her classroom assignments, and eventually her final grade, improved.

Many university studies show a strong relationship between effort and achievement. Barbara McCombs (1991), from Denver University, who has studied student motivation for more than thirty years, found that student motivation has a stronger impact on achievement than any other school factor. Further, high motivation leads to improved self-regulation, which helps children become better learners, according to researchers Harold O'Neil and Jamal Abedi (1996).

Following Denise's example and research evidence, parents can help increase their child's effort through a number of Get Smart! learning strategies:

- *Know your child's baseline*. What are his strengths and weaknesses? What is your child's current achievement level? Help your child apply his strengths to those areas of school that will benefit him the most.
- *Help your child understand what counts in school*. Though we want students to perform well on all schoolwork, their efforts must adapt to teacher and school requirements. This means understanding teacher grading systems, prioritizing work, and applying different amounts of effort at key times. Parents and students sometimes need to ask their teacher to clarify important learning goals, assignments, and tests.
- *Encourage persistence and planning*. As Thomas Edison said, "The trouble with other inventors is that they try a few things and quit. I never quit until I get what I want!" Both children and adults have a tendency to begin projects on a strong note but then lose momentum as other priorities take over. Our failure to persist is often because we initially failed to realize the amount of work involved, did not develop a plan, or became distracted. Parents can help their children develop persistence by encouraging them to make a plan. Work in stages, so that your child sees frequent progress and a reward in sight. Set the example of getting your own work done before a due date. Encourage saying no to activities or people who distract your child from the goals. Monitor your child's progress and reward with praise.

In his dissertation, Douglas Jackson (1998) studied some fifteen motivational factors and their relationships to student grades in science. The strongest relationship to grades was industriousness, "persistence in working hard, often at the expense of fun or recreation," said Jackson (1998, p. 30). Jackson also found a high relationship between grades and a mastery orientation. Mastery-orientation students go beyond good effort and seek challenging problems, according to

Jackson. Motivated by internal rewards, they want a sense of accomplishment and learn for the sake of increasing their own knowledge and abilities, not for an external reward such as a grade or praise from a teacher or parent. "Mastery-oriented students," said Jackson, "regard lack of effort as the major cause of failure and increase their effort when faced with task difficulty or failure." (1998, p. 107).

In a separate study, University of Colorado researcher Haggai Kupermintz (2002) compared a variety of motivational factors to achievement on both multiple-choice and short-answer science tests. Kupermintz found that among the strongest relationships to achievement was effort. Students with high effort also had higher science grades and a strong belief in their ability to do well on the test.

"Hard work when you're in school or college," write James Banner and Harold Cannon, "is like a wise investment: its capital grows, its interest compounds, and its dividends pile up" (1999, p. 11).

Research by Carol Dweck from Columbia University supports the value of a belief that positive attitude and effort, not smarts, is a key component to school success. Dweck and Claudia Mueller (Dweck, 2000) conducted six studies of students who were praised for their work on a specific set of problems. Some were lauded for their intelligence and others for their effort. Those who were praised for their intelligence, says Dweck, "became so invested in looking smart that they became afraid of challenge." When students were praised for their effort, adds Dweck, they put forth even greater effort on the next more challenging task than did children praised for their intelligence.

The lesson for parents and teachers is to praise effort, not intelligence. "Effort praise," says Dweck, "seemed to give students a more hardy sense of themselves as learners, a more healthy desire for challenge, and the skills to cope effectively with setbacks."

"We praise our three children a lot when they put forth strong effort," says parent Karen Mathison, "regardless of a grade or the result. I ask them how it feels to do well and encourage them to realize that effort results in better performance in whatever they do." According to Mathison, better performance produces a good internal feeling for her children and further reinforces a positive belief in their own abilities.

Effort is the outcome of several processes, as further described in the remainder of this chapter, the primary ones being motivation, persistence, and efficiency. By gently influencing each of these factors, parents can help their children produce the effort that they need to succeed in school.

IMPROVE YOUR CHILD'S MOTIVATION

> By motivation, I mean not only the desire to achieve but also the love of learning, the love of challenge, and the ability to thrive on obstacles. These are the greatest gifts we can give our students.
>
> —*Carol Dweck (2000)*

Parents are often searching for ways to enhance their children's motivation, and for good reason. All of us probably know someone who has achieved great success because of being highly motivated, not necessarily possessing unusually high intelligence or talent. Sometimes we call these people overachievers because their performance exceeds our expectations and those of others. But how do we build a base for high motivation in our children?

According to researcher Jere Brophy (1987), motivation to learn can be acquired "through general experience but stimulated most directly through modeling, communication of expectations, and direct instruction or socialization by significant others, especially parents and teachers" (pp. 40–48).

In other words, parents should be motivated learners themselves. Show your child that you enjoy what you do, either through your work or through a hobby in which the child might participate.

Encourage exploration and the desire to learn new things. If your child asks 100 questions, answer 101. Communicate high but realistic expectations, tell your child that he can reach his goals, and give your child the constant support and encouragement that he needs. Surround your children with other motivated learners and yourself with positive, motivated friends.

"We helped our youngest daughter stay motivated by encouraging her to take control of her own learning," said University of California, Davis researcher Ann Mastergeorge. "Instead of us e-mailing the teacher when she had questions, we encouraged her to do it herself so that she would develop her own ability to get help and her own responsibility for getting that help."

Here is an approach from researcher Jamal Abedi, a leading specialist in assessment of English language learners:

> We learned that telling our kids to work harder often produced the opposite effect. What seemed to increase their motivation and effort was to encourage them to associate with friends who were positive influences both academically and socially. We subtly encouraged our daughter, for example, to associate with motivated students, knowing that in high school, friends often have greater influence than parents. We encouraged our children to take more challenging classes, where they met friends whose parents had similar values to our own. We didn't promise our children a reward in advance for getting a certain grade or scoring high on a test. We rewarded them for good performance, such as taking them out for a nice dinner, but only because it was something that they had earned.

Here are some other research-based suggestions to encourage motivation in your children.

- *Establish value.* Subjects that interest students are by their nature more motivating than subjects in which students have little interest or see little value. In a series of Stanford University studies, researchers found conclusively that students had higher achievement on science tests when they had a stronger interest in science. "When learners personally value what they are learning," says Richard Clark from the University of Southern California, "they choose to get involved and persist over time" (2005, p. 90). Giving students at least some choice of what they learn and control, says B. J. Zimmerman (1994), leads to higher motivation.

- *Use novelty*. "The more that learners are convinced that the important elements of a learning task are novel to them, the more mental effort they will invest to succeed," says Clark (2005). When an assignment is routine and not challenging, Clark adds, research shows that students don't try as hard.
- *Set goals*. Deborah Stipek, dean of Stanford University's School of Education, says that student motivation is higher when assignments are defined in specific, short-term goals that can assist students in associating effort with success (1988). Many students, especially younger children, need an immediate payoff to keep their motivation level high.

Several years ago, I videotaped teacher Charlotte Higuchi in her early elementary classroom. Although most of her students were from low-income families where parent involvement was not always high, Higuchi's students were some of the most motivated I had ever seen. In one of her lessons, Higuchi had her students develop their own scoring criteria for writing. Not only was this a novel exercise to the students but they had choice in the criteria and valued the process because they knew that what they developed would be used for the rest of the year. Thus students had *choice* by selecting the criteria, a *novel* assignment in the criteria-setting process itself, and *value* in the activity because it would be used in an upcoming assignment and others during the year. The combination of factors contributed to high student motivation and strong classroom participation.

How can parents use a similar method to instill high motivation at home? James Raffini from the University of Wisconsin at Whitewater suggests that when possible students be allowed to decide when, where, and in what order to complete homework assignments. In addition to increasing a child's motivation to work on assignments, choice also expands student independence, a major goal itself. Parents may still have to monitor the quality of a child's work and its completion.

Early childhood educator Hasmik Avetisian advises parents to let their children do as much as they can for themselves as is appropriate for their age. "When a parent does something for their child that they can do themselves, they take away a learning opportunity."

When UCLA researcher Noreen (Reenie) Webb tried to be the math teacher to her two daughters in middle school, she met resistance. "My daughters have reached the point where they don't want their parents to see all of their schoolwork," said Webb, "so I don't micromanage their assignments. When they are about halfway through a major project, however, I try to get them to see where they are, what is left to do, and how long it will take. Then they can structure their own time. They have become very good at that, and it makes them more responsible than if I set up and manage their whole schedule."

Positive feedback can also help instill greater effort and persistence in students. "Point out their strengths by reminding them of their successful mastery of components of the skill," Richard Clark advises.

A parent's goal is to see his or her children internalize their motivation, which in most cases produces high achievement and a feeling of success. As Lloyd Dobyns and Clare Crawford-Mason (1994, p. 86) said, "The only lifelong, reliable motivations are those that come from within and one of the strongest of those is the joy and pride that grow from knowing that you've just done something as well as you can do it."

Improve Your Child's Persistence

> If I had to select one quality, one personal characteristic that I regard as being most highly correlated with success, whatever the field, I would pick the trait of persistence. Determination. The will to endure to the end, to get knocked down seventy times and get up off the floor saying, "Here comes number seventy-one!"
>
> —*Richard M. DeVos*

Like an Energizer battery, persistent people just keep going and going. The same trait frequently applies to successful students.

In a well-known research study, Harold Stevenson and James Stigler (1992) found that Japanese students were much more persistent than American children when confronted with an unsolvable math problem. American children would quit while Japanese children kept searching for an answer. Perhaps not surprisingly, Japanese children outperform American students on most international education assessments.

In their book *Discovering and Exploring Habits of Mind,* Arthur Costa and Bena Kallick (2000) put persistence at the top of their list as a characteristic "displayed by intelligent people in response to problems, dilemmas, and enigmas . . ." Although Costa and Kallick don't claim that persistence is more important than other learning traits, research and our own experience suggest it is a key to success in school and in life.

As with most human characteristics, persistence can be taken to an extreme. On a Boy Scout trip to Red Rock Canyon, Coty and I visited a tunnel excavated through solid rock by William Henry Schmidt. For thirty-eight years, "Burro" Schmidt dug a tunnel in the California desert that led only to another side of a small mountain. At one point, he spent five years digging in the wrong direction. Persistence becomes useful only when applied to a productive task, said John Dewey, but doing something only because you started it and without a clear-cut purpose is obstinacy.

Researcher Richard Clark says that students' attitude and interest have a direct, strong influence on whether they complete a specific project and how well they do it. An important strategy to keep students on track and persisting is to connect their "personal goals and interests to course goals." Clark's suggestions include clear communication of course goals and the risk of not achieving them, pointing out previous student success in reaching similar goals, and high teacher-to-student interaction. Clark's suggestions apply primarily to teachers, but parents should help their child by regularly connecting school subjects to student interests, especially those subjects of less interest to the young person. If your child loves space exploration to the exclusion of most other subjects, connect those other subjects to space—the history of space exploration, fiction books about space, key figures in space exploration, and use of mathematics in space. Almost any interest can be connected to more than one subject.

Parents can help their children develop persistence by helping them understand its components: staying with a task over time even when confronted with challenges, a low level of distraction from outside sources, knowing when to get help, getting help, and finishing the task.

Here are some specific suggestions to help your child develop persistent learning habits:

- *Praise your child* when he or she is persistent during school and nonschool activities. Make your child aware that children and adults demonstrate differing levels of persistence and that persistence contributes to good learning. If your child gets stumped on a problem, suggest that he or she explore different ways of solving it.
- *Encourage your child* to read about key figures in U.S. and world history, most of whom were persistent throughout their lives. Helen Keller overcame enormous physical impairments of deafness and blindness to become a well-known author. World-famous cy-

clist Lance Armstrong persisted through a battle with cancer to win more Tour de France competitions than any other person in history. Gandhi persisted in his belief that nonviolence was the right means to win independence for India until his vision was fulfilled.

- Most important, *model persistence* in your own life. Show and talk about persistence in your work, hobby, and volunteer activities. Parents usually have more contact with their children than anyone and thus have the greatest opportunity to model persistence and other important learning traits.

Improve Your Child's Efficiency

> There are only two qualities in the world: efficiency and inefficiency, and only two sorts of people: the efficient and the inefficient.
>
> —*George Bernard Shaw*

Adults seldom maximize their own time efficiently, so it should be little surprise that children are often unskilled in developing and applying efficiency in learning. Nor should we necessarily expect or desire high efficiency in children. Learning is, after all, about trial and error, disconfirmed hypotheses, and at least sometimes taking the path less traveled. Nevertheless, as school workloads increase, students are being confronted with the same need to efficiently manage their time as adults are. Increasingly, students need to set and prioritize goals, avoid overcommitment, and apply their time where it will maximize their learning.

Set and Prioritize Goals

Students with specific, challenging goals outperform those with general, easy, or no goals, according to CRESST research conducted for the Office of Naval Research. Although children set goals for themselves all the time, such as to make a new friend, become an actress, or defeat a rival basketball team, the goal may be unrealistic, they may not have a plan to reach the goal, or they may not have the necessary support from others to attain it. Parents need to work with their children and teachers to define and attain goals until their children become adept at their own goal-setting and monitoring.

Parents take different approaches in helping their children set and prioritize their school goals. One size does not fit all. Here's how Karen Mathison helps her three children set reasonable goals for their grades. "At the beginning of the semester," says Mathison, "I sit down and discuss each subject and what grade I think my children are capable of earning and what grade they think they are capable of earning. We reach agreement and then I provide them support to reach that goal." Mathison also helps her children become responsible by working with them to develop planning strategies so that assignments don't become overwhelming. "One of the key benefits to detailed planning is that my children know exactly what has to be done and when it is due," adds Mathison. "This reduces their stress level, improves their efficient use of time, and helps them perform well in school."

Some guidelines for helping your children set goals that will increase their efficiency in school:

- Set high goals, but not so high that they are unattainable.
- Make sure goals are of appropriate duration (younger children usually need to see results faster and usually require more frequent feedback).
- Develop a plan to attain the goals.
- Have coordinated support from parents, teachers, and others.

Avoid Overcommitment

Both children and adults frequently struggle with priorities in their lives. We know however, that having no priorities, the wrong ones, or too many of them can result in little accomplishment that is worthwhile. Parents, though well intentioned, often allow children to participate in too many activities, which can prevent them from performing well in school. Some parents worry that they will miss some key talent or interest of their child ("If my child doesn't start at a young enough age, she will be doomed to mediocrity"). The result can be an overwhelmed child and parent.

"Limit your kids' activities to one or two per week per season," says Elaine St. James in her book *Simplify Your Life with Kids* (1997), a suggestion we have implemented in our own family. Every time we are tempted to violate St. James's suggestion, we remind ourselves that our children and the two of us suffer if their schedule is too full. For us, education has always been the highest priority because we believe it will be more lasting than sports or other programs. School is not the same as it was when we were growing up, and in general, students have more homework and more choices in activities. Without a sensible limit in nonschool programs, school efficiency is likely to suffer.

"If you know your child is overinvolved in extracurricular activities, just say 'no' to some of them," suggests recently retired teacher Mary Jane Hufstedler. "My daughter played three sports: volleyball, basketball, and softball. I was very happy about her involvement in team sports because I believe students learn a lot from being on a team. However, when she also wanted to try out for cheerleading, I said 'no.' I felt she would be spreading herself too thin. As adults, experience has taught us that we can't do everything we'd like to, and I think we owe it to our children to pass that knowledge along."

"If I know that my children are overcommitted," says parent Karen Mathison, "we talk about how to prioritize their work and activities. Let's say that a test is coming up on the day after a big extracurricular activity. My kids and I discuss the possible options and consequences. Then I let them solve it. They have developed enough responsibility to know when to choose the option of missing the extracurricular activity and concentrating their effort on the school assignment."

Using Time Efficiently

If there is one given during your child's school years, it's the amount of time that your child has available in which to accomplish all that there is to do. If there are two hundred days in a school year, there are two hundred days in the school year available to *all* students. However, the decisions that students make about *how* to use that time vary greatly. Students can take notes, read, study, exercise and make quality use of their school hours, or they can daydream, distract others, and waste much of the opportunity that school offers. Most of us probably remember students who did plenty of the latter in school, which was reflected in their grades and eventually in their careers and personal lives. We may have done a fair amount of it ourselves.

One way we can encourage efficient time use at home is by setting an example. Shut the TV off and apply yourself to a worthwhile activity. It may be an activity with your child at school, volunteer work, going back to school yourself, or engaging in a serious hobby. You make yourself a better person and model the type of person you would like to see your child become at the same time. If possible, involve your child directly in what you are doing and let your child see you set goals and timelines. The concept that you are your child's best teacher by setting an example is paramount.

Efficiency also applies to managing schoolwork. Parents can help their children by pointing out that certain assignments, tests, and even specific test questions count more than other assignments, tests, or test questions. The sooner they learn such differences, the more quickly they will know to apply time and effort where it counts the most.

In their study of 249 university students, Ranjita Misra and Michelle McKean (2000) found that effective time management reduced academic stress. They suggested that students take time management courses, which could enhance efficiency. Check to see if your school offers a study skills course. A number of free online courses are available that are worth investigating. At a minimum, have your child maintain a day timer or large calendar to list key milestones such as the beginning and end of quarters, all assignments, known test dates, and a specific study schedule prior to a large assignment or any test. The study schedule should spread out the work into reasonable chunks, and for any major assignment or test set an appropriate time for a final review. If your child is regularly cramming the day before a test, she is most likely not using her time efficiently and creating unnecessary stress on herself and on you. If your child is too young to maintain her own calendar, then do it for her and explain its purpose.

In the Get Smart Learning Model, motivation, persistence, self-discipline, and efficiency are the key components of effort. The value of effort to success has been summed up by the saying, "The harder I work, the luckier I am."

3

HELP YOUR CHILD DEVELOP CONFIDENCE AND A POSITIVE ATTITUDE TOWARD LEARNING

> Chances are, if you can envision something, you can also achieve it.
>
> —*Adam Urbanski*

Look at the successful people you know. Do they have a positive attitude and believe in their own abilities? If something needs to be done, do they do it even if it's something they don't want to do? Did successful students you grew up with have a similar mind-set?

For me, the answer is yes to all three questions. Successful students usually have a positive attitude toward learning and believe in their own abilities to learn. Parents can contribute to their children's positive attitude, like the parents of recent UCLA graduate Armen Donigian.

"As a young child in Iraq, my mother helped me learn to read," said Armen, "by reading many books to me and telling me many stories, especially fables."

His dad helped Armen develop his math skills and confidence in solving difficult problems. "At a very young age my Dad would quiz me on my multiplication tables in the car and played chess with me almost every night," said Armen. An engineer, Armen's father would make up interesting math problems for his son to solve at home.

When Armen was just ten, the Gulf War brought U.S. missiles down on his Western Baghdad neighborhood. His parents fled to neighboring Jordan. Like many immigrants, his parents hoped to make their way to the United States and start a new life. But Jordan would not allow Iraqis to attend their schools, so Armen went without formal education for the next three years, including nine months in France. Eventually his family was granted immigrant status to the United States, and Armen faced the daunting challenge of learning a new language and entering a new school, having missed more than three full years of education. But the preparation his parents had given him contributed to his positive attitude and self-confidence.

"By the time I started seventh grade in the United States," said Armen, "I felt confident in my math skills because of the help my father gave me when I was younger. I quickly picked up the English language, even by watching TV."

Armen graduated from UCLA with nearly all classes in advanced mathematics and computer science. Like his father, he became an engineer and was immediately hired by Lockheed Martin, with offers from other major corporations.

I know Armen will make a positive mark on the world. He is a reminder of the key role that parents play not only in our learning but in our becoming good people. He also shows that belief in one's own ability is important for high performance. As former first lady Rosalyn Carter said, "You have to have confidence in your ability, and then be tough enough to follow through." This chapter will show you how to help your child increase self-confidence and develop and keep a positive attitude toward learning in school.

Help Your Child Become Self-Confident

Research supports the link between self-confidence and achievement. A study by Angela Haydel and Robert Roeser (1992) at Stanford University showed that students who lack confidence in their ability to succeed—a trait sometimes called learned helplessness—perform lower on tests, regardless of the type, than students with higher confidence. Helpless students, according to the authors, have high test anxiety.

"One of the things that I did," said researcher Ann Mastergeorge, "was to take photographs of my daughters and put them on their science and math books. I wanted them to have positive attitudes toward those subjects, which historically have been dominated by men, and to see themselves as competent in both math and science," she added.

"We also told our daughters that sometimes in school you have to jump through hoops," Mastergeorge admitted, calling it the trajectory of education. Life has a lot of hoops in it too, so encourage your child to maintain a positive attitude even when it seems to make little sense.

Researcher Reenie Webb felt her twin daughters were better writers than they thought they were. Instead of suggesting herself that they enter a writing contest, Webb asked her daughters' language arts teacher to be on the alert for such opportunities. Webb felt that her daughters would probably be more likely to participate if their teacher expressed confidence in their writing skills rather than hearing it from her as a parent.

It wasn't long before the language arts teacher found a contest that matched her daughters' abilities. The teacher encouraged both of them to enter a Martin Luther King writing contest. They did and placed second and third at the school district level. This initial success increased the girls' self-confidence in their writing and encouraged them to enter another contest. The new one, focusing on a wildlife refuge, improved their writing skills and further reinforced their belief that they were good writers.

In some cases, a student's attitude toward school may be influenced by personality. Denise (whom we met in Chapter Two) used a particular strategy to increase her daughter's self-confidence and make her feel more comfortable in school: "My daughter was quiet and a bit withdrawn, so I got her more involved in activities that were good for her self-esteem and were also opportunities to meet other girls. She is involved in Girl Scouts and National Charity League. These groups encourage volunteering, helping others less fortunate, and socializing with other girls. All of this will, over time, not only help others but will help my daughter grow in confidence, compassion, and abilities. These are all attributes that will help her in school and for the rest of her life."

Help Your Child Develop a Positive Attitude Toward Learning and School

Many of the researchers and parents I interviewed for this book said they enhanced their children's positive attitude toward school by finding learning opportunities outside the classroom, usually promoting their interests. For researcher Hilda Borko (who was 2003–04 president of the American Educational Research Association), it was having her son attend a nationwide computer camp, which supported his strong interest in computers. Researcher Robert Glaser and his wife, Sylvia, went to museums as often as possible and had deep discussions with their children about what they saw, such as why dinosaurs were not on earth anymore.

"Another thing that I did was to talk about my work with our daughters," said Glaser, who usually traveled once a month to various parts of the country. He told them that he went to help people, and his daughters became curious about his trips and the cities he visited. "That supported what they were learning in school," said Glaser.

"In high school, our daughter was involved in a United Nations UNICEF project," said researcher Jamal Abedi, "which built her positive attitude toward learning, helped make school more fun for her, and developed the type of values that we think are important."

"Like other parents of our generation, we provide many opportunities to learn to our daughters," said Ann Mastergeorge, "and they know that they have a family who will help them. We tell them that if you have an opportunity, then that is a gift and you must use it."

Expressing your own values about education to your children is also important. "To promote my [third grade] daughter's positive attitude toward school and learning, we talk about why math, science, reading, and writing are important in life," said Suzanne Lane, a past president of the National Council on Measurement in Education. "She also knows that these skills are ones that my husband and I use in our own professional lives," added Lane, who developed a series of performance-based mathematics assessments in the 1990s. "I think that she already has an idea about the years of education that my husband and I have had, and that it will promote her positive attitude toward school and learning." Both Lane and her husband have doctorates and are professors at the University of Pittsburgh.

What to Do If Your Child Falls Short

Keeping your child's attitude positive is even more important if his or her work falls below his or her ability.

"Don't criticize your children when they bring home a bad grade," suggests Eckhardt Klieme from the University of Frankfurt, in discussing his approach with his two children. "Talk with your children," says Klieme; "show them that you are interested in their thinking, not just achievement."

Many children already know when they have come up short. Consequently, reminding them of their low performance may do little good. Tell them that this is just one test or one grade; you have confidence that they will do better the next time. How can you help? On tests, for example, review the test with your child and find out the cause of the low score. It could be a lack of effort, but it may also be improper preparation, lack of understanding key material, or the test itself including material not well taught in the classroom. The key goal should be to develop a plan for improvement, not to push your child to the point of losing self-confidence.

One possibility is to ask the teacher (or better, have your child ask the teacher) if your child can retake the test or redo the assignment. Most teachers are well aware that the ultimate goal of education is learning content or a skill, not just a grade. Giving a student a "D" or an "F" on an assignment or test and not following up with some remediation or review almost guarantees that the student will not understand the subject matter or skill. This sends a hidden and often unintended message that learning this particular content isn't essential to the child's education.

Parents should realize that classroom tests or assignments are not a perfect measure of student knowledge or effort. Classroom tests for example, are often scored as a percentage correct of all questions, without considering the difficulty of the test and without accurate comparison to other student performances. Again, talking to the teacher is more productive than a tongue lashing.

Help Your Child Learn How to Learn

"We tried to help our daughters always maintain a positive attitude toward school and learning," says University of Maryland researcher Robert Mislevy. "We explained to them that the purpose of school is really to learn how to learn," he adds.

Mislevy told his daughters that every assignment was a learning experience, even a poorly designed one. The real world is like school, he told his daughters: "Not everything [in school] is perfect, so try to be positive and look for learning opportunities in everything you do."

Here are more tips to increase your child's belief in his or her own academic ability. As Thomas Edison said, "If parents pass enthusiasm along to their children, they will leave them an estate of incalculable value."

- *Praise much more than you criticize*. We have all seen the example of the screaming coach on the sidelines who motivates through intimidation and fear. Though players might exert some additional effort in the short run, the long-term effect can be a demoralized player who quits because of not meeting the coach's expectations. Emphasize what your child does understand and help your child to learn what is not understood.

• *Point to your child's previous successes.* If your child experiences failure or hasn't met her own standards, let her know that all great people have had failures, usually more letdowns than successes. As Winston Churchill said during the darkest hours of World War II, "Success is nothing more than going from failure to failure with undiminished enthusiasm."

• *Step back, let your child do the work, and increase his self-confidence.* It's hard to let your child make mistakes on schoolwork when you could step in and help. But if you help too much, your child may become dependent on you or others. Suggest ways that your child can improve his work, but let him do as much as and the best that he can do.

• *You can't help your child when she needs you most if you aren't there.* Be there for your child's successes and failures, and promote her self-esteem and positive attitudes. Michael Josephson, founder and president of Character Counts, says that he has yet to meet anyone who looks back on his or her life and wishes that he or she had spent more time at the office (2005).

• *Encourage your child to take calculated risks and challenges.* A calculated risk is not one so great that it almost guarantees failure. In encouraging her sons to take on new challenges, researcher Diane Steinberg tells her sons that "practice makes perfect." When you first try something, you may not be very good at it, but practicing improves your skills. When one of her sons first started karate, for example, he became discouraged because other kids were better than he was. But with her encouragement and his practice, he improved substantially. He is now in the advanced karate class, enthusiastically working toward his black belt.

"My husband and I have tried to instill confidence in our daughters by encouraging them to take reasonable risks and learn from mistakes," said Ann Mastergeorge. "We told them about risks we had taken in our own lives," she added, "how we learned from mistakes and how risks helped our careers."

Her efforts seemed to work. When her older daughter found a mistake in her math textbook and pointed it out to the teacher, she was the only student to do so despite the fact that other students were similarly baffled. Her teacher confirmed that indeed the textbook answer was wrong.

More Tips to Keep Your Child's Attitude Positive

School board member Cindy Wilcox says that she kept her two daughters' attitudes positive with several strategies. "If my kids thought that they were weak in spelling or any challenging subject, they would lose confidence," said Wilcox, "so in some cases I would buy them more time." For example, in second grade Wilcox negotiated with teachers the number of spelling words that her daughter needed to get right. A second strategy was to help her children with tasks they had not yet mastered, such as typing. "They type a paragraph, then I type a paragraph," said Wilcox. "The idea is to not overwhelm them, to realize that some tasks are a low priority compared to others, and that for most children mastery doesn't come right away. For example, some kids can just naturally spell and never struggle; that's maybe one-third of the kids. The middle third struggle on occasion, and another third perform poorly and quickly develop a negative attitude about not being good spellers. I wanted my daughters to be successful, so we focused more on reading, less on spelling. Some parents think that because their other child or other children can do high-level work, all kids can. They fail to see that kids have very different abilities."

Children sometimes are weaker in one subject than another. There may come a time when everything you try doesn't seem to work. To encourage your child to keep a positive attitude toward school or toward a specific subject, it may be necessary to repeat a class. If other strategies have not worked and your child is developing an I'm-not-smart attitude, then taking a course again may be the best thing to do. As former high school English teacher Mary Jane Hufstedler explained, "My daughter took algebra in eighth grade and was passing the class, but as the year went on I realized she did not really understand the material. She took the diagnostic test at the end of the year and qualified to go on, but I knew that it would be a struggle for her, so I insisted she repeat the course in ninth grade. Surprisingly, she was not upset but agreed that it would be a good idea. As a result, she got A's in the algebra class next year, understood the material, and developed confidence in her ability to do math."

Holding a child back in grade is a much more serious issue and a substantial amount of research shows that retention may produce only short-term improvements and have substantial long-term emotional impacts. If you think that your child should repeat a full grade or if a school makes that suggestion, meet with all of your child's teachers and the school principal.

Building a child's self-confidence and keeping his attitude positive toward school are two key components of the Get Smart Learning Model. The support that you give your child on these important factors will help him succeed throughout his school years and well into his life.

4

SCHOOLS THAT HELP CHILDREN GET SMART

America's future walks through the doors of our schools each day.

—*Mary Jean Le Tendre*

Finding a good school should be like finding the right house for your family. For a home you probably develop a list of criteria: affordability, distance from work, number of bedrooms, quality of schools, size of yard, the factors that best meet your family needs. You check Websites and hire a realtor to show you homes, visiting each one, always looking inside, sometimes more than once. You likely spend many hours making this important decision and hopefully find a house that meets most of your criteria.

But do we put the same amount of time and effort into finding the right school for our children? Yes, we probably check school report cards, which offer test scores on every public school in the nation as required under the No Child Left Behind Act. (For more on using a school report card, see Appendix B.) We talk to other parents. But do we actually visit the schools we are considering? Do we meet with the school principal, visit classrooms, and talk with teachers and parents at the school?

If you are like most parents, the answer is probably no. Despite the fact that our children may spend six or seven hours, five days a week, at school and that the quality of the school makes a substantial difference in student achievement, most of us make this important decision without visiting the schools our children will attend.

Even if the schools you are considering have an outstanding reputation and high test scores, I urge you to visit them before you make your final decision. Research shows that high-quality schools can contribute substantially to your child's success.

"The average student who attends a 'good' school will have a score that is 23 percentile points higher than the average student who attends a poor school," says researcher Robert Marzano (Marzano, Pickering, and Pollock, 2001).

Although the criteria for a good school differ with a child's needs and parents' perception of those needs, key factors stand out. Ron Edmonds, one of the early leaders in school quality research, found that school leadership, high expectations, emphasis on basic skills, safe and orderly environment, and frequent monitoring of student progress were the most influential school factors on student achievement (as cited in Marzano, 2003). Other researchers have found the same factors important but have also concluded that parent involvement was highly influential on achievement. Teacher quality in these studies was not considered a school-controlled factor, but research and common sense clearly show its influence on achievement.

This chapter describes a set of features that you can use to evaluate school quality as supported by research:

- Teacher quality
- School leadership
- School programs
- Safety and discipline
- Parent involvement

The chapter also discusses why community is important to your child's learning and suggests other critical school-quality factors to consider. Some of these components may be evaluated through a school report card, but many are best evaluated by visiting schools and talking to parents, teachers, and school leaders. To help guide your visits to classrooms, Appendix C includes a classroom observation checklist developed by researcher Margaret Heritage, a former inspector of schools in Great Britain and former principal of Corinne Seeds University Elementary School at UCLA.

Teacher Quality

Research and practical experience yield solid evidence that teacher quality is the school factor with greatest influence over student achievement. A research study by Linda Darling-Hammond showed that teacher preparation and certification were the strongest factors of student achievement in reading and mathematics, regardless of student poverty level (Darling-Hammond and Loewenberg Ball, 1998). A CRESST research study analyzing student achievement on a challenging performance assessment showed that years of teaching experience and whether or not a teacher had a degree in the subject being taught were critical school components influencing student achievement (Baker and others, 1999).

"Effective teachers appear to be effective with students of all achievement levels," said researchers who conducted a study of more than one hundred thousand students across hundreds of schools (Sanders and Horn, 1994). "More can be done to improve education by improving the quality of the teacher than any other factor," they reported.

The importance of teacher quality was not missed by the authors of the No Child Left Behind Act, which requires that a high-quality teacher be in place in every classroom in the nation. At a minimum, teachers must have full state certification and "must not have any requirements waived on an emergency, temporary, or provisional basis" (Boehner, 2004). Here are a few guidelines on evaluating the quality of teachers at your child's current school or a prospective school.

• *Experience and expertise*. On school report cards, look for a high percentage of fully certified teachers, and in middle and high school look for teachers with a degree in the subject they are teaching. Also look at the average years of teaching experience of teachers at the school. By themselves, these are general indicators and do not guarantee teacher quality. But a low level compared to other schools may be a warning sign.

• *Student assignments*. Research by Pamela Aschbacher (1999) and Lindsay Clare Matsumura (2000) and others (Clare Matsumura, Garnier, and Pascal, 2002) indicate that the quality of classroom assignments is associated with higher-quality student work and higher standardized tests scores, even when student background factors are considered. You won't have access to finished student assignments from children other than your own, but you can find student work prominently displayed on the classroom walls in nearly all elementary schools and also in many middle and high schools. With the permission of the school principal, visit classrooms and look at the assignment quality as well as assignments that students are doing at the time of your visit. Is the work challenging? Does it cover a range of topics reflected on the state standards? Does it show a variety of student abilities? Naturally, work posted on the wall tends to reflect what the teacher believes is students' best work, so try to observe what students are doing at their desks or in small groups at the time of your visit.

• *Teacher-student interaction*. High-quality teachers monitor student work, offer effective feedback to students, and give them many opportunities to engage in discussion, according to researcher Ann Mastergeorge (2000). Evaluate these factors as you visit classrooms.

Principals usually send visiting parents to teachers who they consider the best in the school, so also talk to other parents and attend a PTA meeting or school site council meeting. Teacher, principal, and parent interaction can give you excellent insight into the cooperative spirit among these important groups.

School Leadership

While conducting an evaluation of a teacher professional network at an urban middle school several years ago, I witnessed firsthand a leadership struggle between a new school principal and the teachers. The principal was attempting to institute some modest reforms to improve student learning, an initiative funded through a foundation grant. One of the senior teachers who had taught at the school for many years resisted and was supported by most of the other teachers. The relationship between the principal and the senior teacher reached such a negative point that learning was seriously undermined in many classrooms. In one class, I observed an English teacher droning on for the entire class period while leaning up against her desk. Meanwhile, the children sent notes to each other or otherwise ignored her lesson. There were a few reform-minded teachers at the school, but most sided with the senior teacher and were confident that the principal would eventually quit. Sure enough, when I followed up the next school year, the principal had moved to another school just as expected, and the school reform was quite dead. As Adam Urbanski, president of the Rochester (New York) Teachers Association, says, "Real change is real hard" (1994).

School leadership is important, and I encourage parents to consider the vision set by the local school board, district, and school as an important (but frequently overlooked) component of school quality. An obvious factor to review is the longevity of the superintendent and school principals. Far too often, school superintendents and principals leave their job after only a few years, frustrated by the high demands or lack of support from parents, teachers, and their school board. School boards are often accused, rightly or wrongly, of micromanaging the school superintendent and district staff, preventing the superintendent from implementing a shared vision for better schools. Frequent turnover of school principals means that teachers, parents, and students must adjust to new ideas and different expectations. As happened during my school reform evaluation, teachers may develop a wait-and-see attitude toward a new principal, knowing full well that they will likely stay at the school many more years than any school leader.

By itself, longevity does not equal good leadership. Principals and staff are lost to competition, especially in hard-to-fill positions. Ineffective principals, superintendents, and school board members should be replaced when conditions warrant. Here are some school leadership factors to consider:

- *High expectations.* One area of common agreement backed by research is that schools, principals, and teachers firmly believe all children can achieve high standards and then give children the support they need to reach those goals. High standards for all students has become a mantra in most schools, but a good principal, superintendent, and school board can help to ensure that students receive the instructional opportunities according to their needs. Instructional leadership is, in my opinion, the most important quality that a principal brings to a school. A principal may be a wonderful communicator or a strong advocate for students, but if she is not involved in establishing high standards, supporting teachers to meet student needs, and monitoring instruction, her impact on student achievement and school goals may be modest at best.
- *Vision.* Good school leaders have a vision for their school and communicate it clearly to parents, teachers, and students. They almost always have at least one substantial school improvement that they successfully implement in their first few years. Lily Ogden, former principal of La Cañada Elementary School, for example, successfully brought the Safe Schools character education program into my children's school, eventually spreading it to our district's two other elementary campuses.
- *Decentralization.* In his book *Making Schools Work*, William Ouchi (2003) develops a reasonable argument that decentralization of budget and management control to individual schools increases school quality. Several cases support his theory, particularly when

an effective principal is given substantial freedom in controlling hiring and the school's budget. Deborah Meier, for example, was given great freedom to develop new schools in East Harlem, the lowest-performing among thirty-two New York school districts. The greater autonomy, combined with Meier's vision, produced a group of new schools serving the most disadvantaged children. Shared decision making contributed to East Harlem's rising student achievement such that by 1987 the district outperformed at least half of the other New York districts (Mondale and Patton, 2001). Central Park East Secondary School, for example, sent 90 percent of its students to college.

School Programs

In the 1980s and 1990s, the *Nation at Risk* report spurred many schools to try a host of new programs and reforms, often with little impact. In some cases, schools took on too many new programs or switched from one to another without giving the first enough time to work. Today, schools tend to be more cautious; parents are likely to find that school reforms focus primarily on student achievement. Good school programs adapt to a broad range of student needs and offer a level of differentiated instruction (that is, providing different instruction based on children's specific needs), recognizing variations in student abilities and learning styles. High-quality public schools have curriculum, assignments, and tests that are tied closely to the state standards. Private schools are much more diverse but should still have learning standards that form the framework for their curriculum and that are communicated to parents.

Parents of students with special needs or English language learners should carefully evaluate the programs offered by prospective schools. Many private schools, for instance, are not equipped to handle students with moderate to severe disability, whereas public schools are required by law to serve every student who legally resides in its borders.

A school or district Website should contain the basic information about the school curriculum and its programs that will help you decide if this school is a good match for your child. If your child has special interests or special needs, they should factor into your choice. When visiting a school, talk to the principal, several teachers, and parents. Here are some school quality factors based on research to help guide your decision:

- *Opportunity to learn*. Students are unlikely to master what is not taught in the classroom, or what is not taught effectively. In addition to experienced teachers, parents should look at the length of the school day, length of the school year, and total classroom minutes as indicators that sufficient time is available for students to learn. If total instructional minutes are not reported, the school calendar may give a good indication of the number of instructional days in the school year. Teachers should have professional development days that support improved teaching.
- *Challenging courses*. Schools with many advanced placement (AP) courses are usually rated higher on state academic performance scales than those with few (Choi, Seltzer, Herman, and Yamashiro, 2004). At San Marino High School, one of the highest-performing schools in California, 90 percent of juniors and seniors take and pass AP courses, compared to a 21 percent rate in Los Angeles county overall (San Marino High School Report Card, 2004).
- *Monitoring*. Researchers Pam Sammons, Robert Marzano, Jaap Scheerens, and Roel Bosker have found that when teachers effectively monitor students and give them high-quality feedback, their achievement increases (as cited in Marzano, 2003). Based on a comprehensive review of more than forty papers and studies, Paul Black and Dylan Wiliam (1998) found that students who received effective feedback through high-quality classroom assessment moved from being average students to the top 35 percent of students overall. Consequently, a quality school has an effective assessment program, which gives feedback to teachers who use data to help students individually and collectively. Feedback to students is in-depth, specific, timely, and leads to improvement.

• *Instructional materials*. High-quality schools have plenty of instructional materials—textbooks, libraries, and technology—that contribute to the school program and to student achievement. Former *Los Angeles Times* reporter Richard Colvin found substantial differences on his visits to seven public high schools in the Los Angeles area. "In some cases libraries are full of books and students; in others, libraries are a wasteland. If you see a row of copies of *The Old Man and the Sea* that haven't been checked out in fifteen years, that tells you a lot" (Lewis, 1999, pp. 41–42.). However, just having books, computers, and other materials is not enough. A good school knows how to effectively *use* what it has, tries to get more of what it needs, and integrates supporting materials into curriculum and learning. Teachers and school principals are constantly on the lookout for new resources and opportunities.

Technology

Several years ago I was visiting a second-grade classroom and watched students as they rotated among work centers. At the computer workstation, a young girl was trying to answer a multiple-choice geography question that was far beyond a second-grade level. After a long time thinking about the question, she guessed at an answer, which was wrong. Clearly, the software program was not matched to her grade level or tied into a current lesson. The computers were being used just to give the children something to do, which occurs too often in classrooms. During the time of my visit, the teacher attended to the more immediate needs of seventeen other children and did not check on the students working on the computers. Technology should be tied to a lesson plan and support specific instruction. Otherwise it may just be filling up time.

Eva Baker, the 2006–07 president of the American Educational Research Association and a UCLA learning and assessment expert, has analyzed technology extensively in schools. "Without a doubt," says Baker (1999), "school use of technology is increasing rapidly as new and intriguing products—both software and hardware—arrive on the market. But just as we have learned with every other innovation in education, impact doesn't come simply because one has or hasn't purchased the new approach or tool. Rather, it matters how we use the innovation; how it connects to serious, internalized goals of the organization and the people in it; and how other parts of the system learn to support its effectiveness."

Many schools can and do use technology and support materials effectively. When visiting Stevens Creek Elementary School in Cupertino, California, in the early 1990s, I videotaped fourth grade students using advanced technology (for that time) to create digital portfolios of their California mission projects. At UCLA's Corinne Seeds University Elementary School, not only do teachers and students develop technology fluency in early elementary school but former principal Margaret Heritage and technology director Sharon Sutton worked with teachers to develop a technology assessment, evaluating how well students have learned the technology skills defined in their school learning standards.

Having stuff, even the right stuff and the right amount of stuff, isn't enough. In evaluating school quality, be sure to look at the *use* of instructional materials and technology when you visit classrooms.

Safety and Discipline

The thirteen deaths from the 1999 Columbine High School tragedy, as well as other school violence cases, have emphasized that safety and discipline can break down at any school. In such cases, the tragic consequences go far beyond student learning. But in hundreds of other cases across the country each year, subtler forms of safety and discipline lapses create a school environment that inhibits learning. Not surprisingly, research has confirmed that a safe and orderly learning environment is a critically important component of student achievement. Research by J. Ron Nelson (Nelson, Martella, and Marchand-Martella, 2002) showed that a comprehensive schoolwide program to prevent problem behaviors can increase student performance while reducing discipline problems. In a group of elementary schools in the Northwest, Nelson and colleagues found that a schoolwide behavioral intervention and support program produced significant improvement in reading, language arts, mathematics, spelling, science, and social studies achievement. In addition to improved achievement, formal disciplinary actions declined and teachers felt that the program improved their ability to work with difficult students.

A high-quality school has a social skills or character education program that addresses problems of physical and verbal conflict, bullying, and substance abuse. As with any education program, social skills or character education may be poorly designed or implemented weakly, making the program little more than a name. Any program needs regular attention and adequate resources or its impact will be limited. Most social skills and character education programs are not evaluated regularly to determine their effectiveness, so finding out if your school's program works may be difficult. Check the discipline rate, talk to parents, and visit the school to judge for yourself. Listen closely to see if children are talking and acting appropriately. Sitting in the school office for a few minutes during the school day may give you an opportunity to witness the number of students who are coming in to be disciplined or who exit from an assistant principal's office after their discipline has been meted out.

Ask the school principal about the external security program and emergency preparedness program. Do children receive training about possible threats to their personal safety, both human and physical? When did the school last test its emergency procedures? Does it have a regular drug and alcohol awareness program? Even though virtually all principals will say that they have an active safety program, ask the principal when the last drill or training took place to determine if the program is more than in name only. Ask also if they have written procedures. As always, visiting more than one school gives you a better comparison on any of these factors.

Parent Involvement

"Active engagement of family members," say researchers Margaret Wang, Geneva Haertel, and Herbert Walberg (1997), "is associated with improved student achievement; increased school attendance; and decreased student dropout, delinquency, and pregnancy rates." Just having the love and support of a single family member can increase children's resilience, they add, mitigating against adversity. Participating in school management teams, being involved in parent-development workshops, providing tutoring, and assisting teachers in classroom or after-school activities are all examples of helpful parent involvement activities.

Data from the National Center for Education Statistics firmly back parent involvement in school as a link to student success (NCES, 2001). The NCES study found that:

- Both a father's and mother's school involvement is associated with a higher likelihood of students getting mostly A's.
- The school involvement of a father in a two-biological-parent family is associated with a lower likelihood of students ever repeating a grade.
- The school involvement of a mother in a mother-only family is related to lower odds of a child ever repeating a grade.
- The school involvement of a mother is associated with a lower likelihood of sixth through twelfth grade students ever being suspended or expelled.

In this study, a high level of parent involvement was defined as a parent who participated in at least three of four school activities offered by most schools, such as a general school meeting, a parent teacher conference, a school or class event, or volunteering at school.

Researchers from Johns Hopkins University (Epstein and others, 2002) have developed a framework of six types of parent involvement in schools. On the basis of their criteria, parents might use a number of factors to evaluate the quality of parent involvement at a potential school or their current school:

- Accurate and easy-to-understand information about the school goals, curriculum, and programs that support student learning
- An active parent organization, advisory council, or parent involvement committee
- A volunteer program that encourages parents to help in the classroom or at the school
- Regular school-parent communications such as newsletters or e-news that link all families with parent representatives
- Parent conferences at least once each year and frequent opportunities for parents to learn about their child's progress
- Homework that requires students to regularly share with their families what they are learning in school

School report cards may cover some of these factors, but most can be determined only by visiting schools and talking to teachers, school leaders, and parents whose children are enrolled there.

Community Is Important

Despite our fast-paced world and high mobility, many parents still find the quality and involvement of the local community important in their selection of a school. "Having been a parochial school student myself," said Scott Tracy, the La Cañada school board president and father of two children, "I decided I didn't want my kids to attend a private school because I wanted them to be part of the community, which draws on a wide group of children." He and his wife Mary selected a small public school district because their daughters' friends would be just minutes away and because he and his wife would have the opportunity to know other parents very well.

Virginia (Jinny) Dalbeck selected public schools in La Cañada not just for the quality of its schools but because she wanted to be involved in her daughters' education. "You can have influence as a parent in La Cañada, which is much more difficult in a large district," said Dalbeck, who has served on our school board for more than ten years. A small district and community allowed Dalbeck and Tracy, both dedicated community volunteers, to be a key part of important school district decisions, including budgets, school facilities, and programs.

Other Important School Quality Factors

The quality of facilities, before- and after-school programs, and a school's use of data to improve learning are a few other school quality factors to consider.

Facilities

Unfortunately, many state and local school districts have been unable to furnish the necessary school maintenance and facilities for their students, especially in urban areas. For years, the Los Angeles Unified School District, with more than seven hundred thousand students, has had to transport many thousands of them far outside their local school neighborhoods because of a lack of school buildings in those areas. Superintendent Roy Romer and the Los Angeles City School Board have made improved school facilities a top priority. They are in the midst of a massive building campaign to alleviate these problems, but many L.A. (and other American) schools remain overcrowded or poorly maintained. In 2003, the *Miami Herald* reported some forty-four thousand uncorrected safety problems in Dade County schools as part of a special report on crumbling schools and cramped classrooms (Pinzur, 2003). In California, the conditions of many schools had deteriorated so badly that a lawsuit, *Williams* v. *California*, was filed in May 2000 against the state to give students safe and clean facilities. The problems included vermin infestation, nonflushing toilets, leaky roofs, noisy classrooms, and mold (Asimov, 2003).

Although some states and school districts are seeing a drop in student enrollment, the NCES predicts a substantial increase in student enrollment, which will in turn continue to place pressure on school facilities. "Total public and private elementary and secondary school enrollment reached a record 54 million in fall 2001, representing a 19 percent increase since fall 1988," according to the NCES study (Gerald and Hussar, 2003, p. 5). "Between 2001 and 2013, a further increase of 5 percent is expected, with increases projected in both public and private schools."

Enrollment growth combined with aging school buildings and inadequate government funding make it difficult for many school districts to maintain adequate facilities. Parents should consider the practical if not the possible academic impact that school facilities may have on their child. When visiting a school, ask yourself if this school is an inviting place. Look for cleanliness, adequate space, and up-to-date technology. Like many other California communities, our district passed several school bonds in recent years to improve the deteriorating conditions in our schools. Good facilities don't come without a cost, so expect to pay something extra in property taxes, rent, or tuition for schools in good condition.

A growing link between nutrition and student learning has focused attention on the quality of food served in school cafeterias. "Good nutrition is linked to learning readiness and academic achievement, decreased discipline problems, and decreased emotional problems," according to the American Dietetic Association, which cited improved test scores for those students who participate in a nutrition-based School Breakfast Program (Briggs, Safaii, and Lane Beall, 2003). Cafeterias are an easy place to look for school quality. When visiting a school, ask yourself if the cafeteria is an inviting dining experience with nutritious food and a variety of healthy selections. Are the staff friendly, and is order maintained without a repressive approach? Ask the principal about programs or instruction that encourages children to eat nutritious food.

Before- and After-School Programs

The percentage of American children under the age of eighteen with a mother working outside the home rose from 39 percent to 62 percent between 1970 and 1990, according to the federal departments of education and justice (Schwendiman and Fager, 1999). As a result, the need for before- and after-school programs has risen dramatically, but the quality has not always kept pace with the demand. Just having a before- or after-school program is not enough. Here are some factors that parents may want to consider in deciding if a program meets their needs and those of their child:

- Does the program have adequate hours to cover a parent's working time, usually 7:00 A.M. to 6:00 P.M.?
- Are there qualified, caring staff? To attract quality caregivers, employees need to be paid a competitive salary.
- Is the space adequate, clean, and well maintained?
- Is there a quiet area for homework, and staff with appropriate knowledge and ability to assist students?
- Does the program have clear goals and regular evaluation? For example, our district has a committee that participates in an annual evaluation of our before- and after-school program, meeting three times a year to review program goals and results.
- Is there a supportive relationship between school and before- and after-school staff? Frequent communication is important.
- Does the program teach and reinforce social skills and character development? Ideally integrated with the regular school's social and character development curriculum?
- Is there a reasonably low staff turnover rate?

Visiting the program during its busy operating hours will help you make this important decision.

Use of Student Data to Diagnose Strengths and Weaknesses

The widespread availability of powerful software programs combined with the increasing availability of student data systems has given schools a valuable tool to analyze student data and do something with them. The Quality School Portfolio developed by CRESST, for example, makes data analysis available to every school with Internet access. But as with other aspects of technology, just making a tool available doesn't mean it is used successfully. Our center's research shows that many schools' use of data is hindered by not having trained people who know how to use data appropriately or by frequent staff turnover.

If you want to know if data are being used successfully at a school, talk to teachers and parents to see if the information is helping to inform instruction—or if it reaches the teacher at all. Teacher conferences should be informed not just by your own child's results but by comparison to schoolwide averages. The other question is what, if anything, teachers do with the data. Knowing that a child has low spelling or math performance doesn't necessarily result in a clear-cut improvement strategy. Teachers and parents usually need to work in partnership to create a specific plan that works in school and at home.

Magnet or Charter Schools, Private Schools, and Home Schooling

Although public schools are still the predominant educational setting in the United States, variations have become prevalent in recent years, including charter and magnet schools. A charter school operates independently from many of the educational mandates required at regular public schools. Administrators and teachers usually agree to a performance contract, frequently promising to raise student achievement in exchange for substantial administrative freedom from school district and state requirements.

Magnet schools, on the other hand, are usually public schools that focus on teaching a specific subject, or several related subjects (for example, technology, science, math, and even medicine and law). A key attraction of the magnet school is that it is committed to a specific emphasis in education that may align well to a student's strengths or interests. In many cases, a magnet school's focus is attractive to a parent's desired career for their children.

However, the quality of both magnet and charter schools remains quite variable; parents should employ the same method they would use to evaluate other public or private schools in considering a charter or magnet school for their child. Fancy school names may reflect the creativity of the school's leadership more than the quality of the school itself. Charter schools may not have online school report cards, so they can be more difficult to compare to noncharter public schools or to other charter schools. However, test scores are still usually available, if not on the school Website itself then by checking an independent source, such as www.greatschools.net. For magnet schools, parents should be able to find the same accountability information, including school report cards, that they can find for a traditional public school.

Private schools may well be an appropriate choice for your child, although tuition can exceed $15,000 per year. Comparing private and public schools is often difficult because private schools do not administer state tests, frequently differ among themselves in the type of test given, and usually report far less school quality information. Private schools generally have printed literature, which parents may find useful, but such information may be more promotional than an accurate report of school quality.

So how do you compare a private school to a public school or another private school? A case study of sixteen private and public schools suggests that, as in public schools, the social and economic background of the parents is highly related to student achievement (Rothstein, Cornoy, and Benveniste, 1999). In the absence of comparable online report cards and test scores, the educational and economic background of parents is a strong indicator of private school quality; a higher level of parent education and income at least suggests a better school. Otherwise, the same factors that were discussed for public schools (teacher experience and certification, school leadership, school programs, safety and discipline, parent involvement) are all still important. Is the school showing at least modest improvement each year on its test scores, so that this year's students in fourth grade mathematics are a bit higher than last year's fourth grade students? If you are considering a private high school, what percentage of students go to college, how many AP classes are taken and passed by students, and how do students perform on the SAT or ACT? But since this information is not always so readily available from a private school as from a public school, it's even more important to talk with many parents, meet with the school principal, and visit classrooms. You might also find helpful information from schools that typically feed into private schools.

"When our daughters reached eighth grade," said researcher Robert Mislevy, "we talked to them about having a choice for high school. We explained to them that in some high schools kids can get by without much effort, which is not what we wanted or expected from them. We said that private schools were a possible option. Both of our girls wanted to go to the public high school where most of their friends were going. We were fine with their decision but made it clear that we expected them to study hard, and they did."

Researcher Diane H. Steinberg explains how she chose University Elementary School (UES), a private school for her two young sons:

> After visiting several private schools, we selected Corinne Seeds University Elementary School for a number of reasons. UES has children from many different backgrounds and focuses on educating the whole child by addressing the social, emotional and academic needs of its students. Other schools we visited focused primarily on academics, and children sometimes were forced out if they didn't keep up. Prior to making a primary school decision, we went to a school presentation for prospective families, toured the whole

school, talked to parents whose children attended the school, and observed classrooms. UES fosters a love of learning by educating the whole child, which was more important to us than a school that had the highest test scores, even though UES students do well overall on standardized tests. In fact, when my husband asked the principal at the time, Margaret Heritage, about the UES test scores, she said that if test scores were a high priority for us, then UES might not be the best choice. UES also works with parents if their children have problems or a special need. Parents are involved in many school activities and are welcomed into classrooms as volunteers.

Home schooling may be another possible option for your child. Research by Larry Rudner at the University of Maryland indicates that home-schooled children usually perform in the upper 50th percentile on tests, although demographic factors appear to have a strong influence. Home schooling requires of at least one parent both the time and the expertise to teach their child full-time. This requirement can be problematic when a child reaches high school and subjects become more complex. Further, the parent-child relationship needs to be one that makes home schooling a viable option for both parent and child. If today's homework sessions are strained, home schooling is unlikely to reduce the tension and become a positive learning experience.

Improve Your Current School

If you are not happy with the school your child currently attends, don't resign yourself to thinking that you can't make it any better. Parent participation does make a difference. As a school board member, I've seen small groups of parents raise money to build a new science center, get the city to put in a new sidewalk to improve student safety, and clean up the campus. As elected representatives, and because they have the interests of children at heart, school boards do listen to parents, in my experience. The same is true of school principals and administrators. Granted there are exceptions, but I think that few people stay in education without wanting to make a contribution and improvement. Schools and districts often seem to move at a glacial pace, but making your voice heard in a positive way and at the right time can help your school make significant changes.

Which individual you approach about school improvements varies with the specific issue. A majority of concerns should begin with your child's teacher or teachers, especially those that directly involve your child's learning. But if those issues concern your child's teacher, where should you turn? My advice—and you will find this also written in many teacher contracts—is that you should still express your concern to your child's teacher. The teacher will eventually be brought into the picture, and it is a professional courtesy to talk to him or her early. Most issues are quickly resolved at that level, either through a clarification between teacher and parent or in an actual change on the teacher's part. If this isn't successful, then by all means talk to your school's principal, or an assistant principal if this person has authority over teachers. If that still doesn't resolve your concern, contact a school board member or your district superintendent. Superintendents appreciate the opportunity to resolve issues before board members become involved, and as with any professional it is courteous to resolve issues at the lowest level.

On the other hand, board members are elected to represent you, your child, and your community; consequently, don't hesitate to contact them. There are no specific rules on when to take an issue to a board member or to the full school board (and board members are contacted on virtually every issue there is). I offer a few suggestions based on my four years' service as a board member.

Issues that involve just you and your child should in most cases be handled by the teacher or the school principal. If this doesn't work, then I would move up the chain to the district office and contact the superintendent if necessary.

If you need clarification of a policy, your school principal or superintendent can be helpful; this administrator usually has many years of experience in the field. Board members are also a good resource as they should have a copy of their school board policies and school regulations. Sometimes board policies and school regulations are available on your district Website. You should also consider contacting board members about new ideas or improvements that you have, although school principals and district staff are ideally your first contacts. Any of them should be able to tell you if the idea has already been tried, if a similar program is in place, or who the person or school group is that you should contact. District staff or the school board may solicit parent input on a broad number of issues, including school budgets, facilities, or curriculum programs. Your district Website or local newspaper is a good source of information for school board public hearings, the dates and times of regular meetings, special workshops, or newly formed committees that may need additional members or public input.

Effective board members help to answer questions from any constituent; if they don't have the answer, they will find or guide you to the information you need.

School board members may be a good source of information about the quality of their schools, especially in the key differences among the schools they serve. They should be extremely familiar with their school programs, and though they may not be an unbiased source of information they certainly are worth contacting when making a decision about a school. You should be able to find the name, e-mail address, and phone number of a school board member on the school district Website, or by calling the school district office.

A Final Note on Finding a Good School

Even if you already know where your child will go to school, visiting before your child is enrolled prepares you to make the next few years a successful learning experience. Recognizing the learning differences between children, Donna Elder, former principal of UCLA's University Elementary School, says that "the best school for your child may well be different than the school for another child." Consequently, gathering information helps to ensure that your child's school is a good match to his or her needs.

Looking at both private and public schools, researcher and professor Reenie Webb shared with me how she found a high-quality elementary school for her three children:

> After visiting both public and private schools in the Westwood (California) area, my husband and I made a conscious choice for our children to attend a public school. Our choice was made after meeting with school principals, visiting classrooms, and talking to other parents at each school. Our criteria for a good school included student engagement in learning, evidence that the curriculum covered a broad and interesting variety of topics represented by classroom work on the walls, and high-quality school buildings and facilities. I wanted to know, for example, that the kindergarten rooms had a homelike learning environment, soft places for children to read, and many age-appropriate books.
>
> We were also looking for positive interpersonal relationships among students, especially those from different backgrounds. The diversity of the student population at Westwood (more diverse than it is now) and the fact that students seemed oblivious to each other's backgrounds were impressive.
>
> I also looked for and found a rich curriculum, one which didn't overly focus on single subjects but exposed children to many different learning opportunities, including music, arts, and opportunities for children with exceptional skills.
>
> Another important school quality factor was the amount of assistance that the teacher had in the classroom. Our son, now a freshman in college, entered school before California reduced most K–3 class sizes [student-to-teacher ratio] to twenty to one, so knowing that the teacher had classroom assistance was important. Strong parent involvement was also essential to us, and we found many involved parents at Westwood Elementary. There were always parents around at school and tons of activities for parents to be involved in. There was good school-home communication, although we didn't appreciate the extent until later.

"I always visited the schools my children attended before they were enrolled," said researcher Marilyn Cochran-Smith. "I met with the school principal, with teachers, and visited classrooms.

"Parents should imagine their child in that class," said Cochran-Smith. "Will it meet their needs? I never based my opinion about a school on what others said; I based it on what I saw when I actually visited the school. What did I feel was the right school for my child's needs?"

"My view is that kids will be fine in many schools," said Meredith Reynolds, "if their parents are supportive, if they have good friends, and live in a stable community." When she was growing up, Reynolds moved thirteen times but says that her parents "placed a lot of value on education and expected me to learn."

5

BECOME A PARTNER WITH YOUR CHILD'S TEACHER

> Teachers–whether teaching physics, literature, or arithmetic–thus lose a bit of themselves in their students while helping them lose themselves in their subjects.
>
> —*James Banner, Jr., and Harold C. Cannon*

Teachers have truly made a great difference in my children's education. When our daughter, Markie, was eight, my wife and I became concerned about her reading. She didn't like to read, wouldn't read on her own, and preferred picture books to any book with text. Our son, Coty, on the other hand, was a prolific reader. For him, learning to read was easy, and even today he reads a new book every week.

My wife and I had done what the reading research told us to do. We read to our children from infancy, made reading materials available just about any place we went, and visited the library every week. Beginning in third grade, we required an hour's worth of reading every night. When we realized that our efforts weren't working for Markie, we had a conference with her teacher. The teacher moved her to a seat close to the front of the classroom, and we enrolled her in the school's reading intervention program.

That summer, Markie's state reading scores arrived and were well below her math scores. A meeting with her new teacher in the early fall led to a second diagnostic reading test. The results helped to identify Markie's reading problem as a tendency to skip words or lines. A school reading specialist recommended that Markie use a reading ruler as she read. Her classroom teacher, Mrs. Burke, suggested that we let Markie read easier books. She explained to us that it wasn't so much what Markie read but that she was reading, building her vocabulary, and having more confidence in her own reading ability. She also suggested that we find books on subjects that Markie liked, to increase her motivation to read.

We did everything her teacher suggested, and it wasn't long before Markie had read all the Harry Potter books—an impossible accomplishment just a year earlier. Following Mrs. Burke's advice was one of the best things we ever did to improve our daughter's chance of future success.

Research and practical experience tell us that teachers are the most important school influence on student achievement. Here are key findings from a diverse number of research studies (Darling-Hammond and Loewenberg Ball, 1998):

- Teacher expertise—including teacher education, experience, and test scores—is the greatest factor in achievement, according to an extensive study by Ronald Ferguson. The teacher effect was so strong in Ferguson's study that achievement differences between black and white students were nearly all explained by differences in teacher quality.
- Data from the National Assessment of Educational Progress, also known as America's Report Card, show that reading achievement is higher when students are taught by fully certified teachers who have a higher level of education.
- A 1996 review of sixty studies found that teacher quality, along with small schools and smaller class size, were strongly associated with high student achievement.
- A study of schools in New York City indicated that teacher qualifications accounted for 90 percent of the variation of student achievement between low- and high-quality schools.

Some of the key factors of teacher quality are high standards and expectations of students, subject matter expertise, teaching experience, and the quality of feedback that teachers give to students.

Constructive feedback from teachers, including deserved praise and specific suggestions, helps students learn as well as develop positive self-esteem. The contribution that a teacher makes to a child's character development, reinforcing parent's efforts at home, is another factor to look for.

Student assignments are a good indicator of high-quality teachers. Is the assignment interesting? Does it appear to support important student learning and challenge your child without being overwhelming? Are the instructions clear, and do they include an explanation of how the work will be scored and how much it counts towards your child's grade?

Effective teachers often use hands-on learning to engage students and are able to adjust their teaching for a variety of student learning styles. They know how to use technology as an instructional tool, incorporate it into their instruction, and help students improve their technology skills. High-quality teachers also get along well with other teachers, use novel teaching methods, and love teaching and students.

But having a quality teacher is not a guarantee that your child will reach maximum potential in school. Parents still play a critical role. This chapter describes three ways that you can partner with the teacher and support your child's learning at school, including how to:

- Be an active school parent
- Establish a quality relationship with your child's teachers
- Find flexible solutions to problems that may occur

Be an Active School Parent

Many of us grew up in an era of little parent involvement in schools. Our parents made sure we had a lunch, got to school on time, and did our homework. They attended major school events and parent-teacher conferences, but for the most part there was an invisible boundary between home and school that only children crossed.

The boundary started to change as a growing body of research pointed to the importance of parent involvement in school. A research review by Diana Hiatt-Michael from Pepperdine's Graduate School of Education and Psychology, for example, showed that "teachers' efforts to involve families [in school] promote better student attendance, higher graduation rates from high school, fewer retentions in the same grade, increased levels of parent and student satisfaction with school, reduced negative behaviors, and most notably, higher achievement scores on reading and math tests" (2001, p. 1).

With so many positive outcomes as a result of parent involvement, schools have formed new partnerships aimed at bringing teachers and parents together. Consequently schools today are frequently alive with parents helping in the classroom, raising money through special events, or participating in a variety of school committees. Many parents, especially those with children in elementary school but also in middle and high school, have found that they have something valuable to contribute to their child's education not just at home but at school as well. Being in the classroom helps parents make a contribution to the school while fostering a child's learning.

"One of the ways that I stayed connected to my daughter's teacher in fifth grade was to volunteer every week for a writers' workshop," said researcher Ann Mastergeorge. "I emphasized to the class and to my daughter how I made many changes to my own writing, emphasizing how important revision is to the writing process. That was very powerful."

Mastergeorge brought an unpainted and unvarnished chair to the classroom every week and would sit in it when she was working with the children. "This is the writer's chair," she would explain. Each child got to sit in the chair and write his or her name on it. "That was very motivating for them," said Mastergeorge, "to be authors and to sit in the writer's chair and write their names on it."

As children get older, parental opportunities to be directly involved in the classroom are fewer. But even in seventh grade, Mastergeorge was helping her daughter's science teacher, instructing a lesson about the brain, based on her work at the MIND Institute in California.

"I believe it's really important to stay in touch with teachers," said former math teacher Jody Priselac, "so I volunteered in schools a lot. It was one way that I knew about my children's progress.

Here are some additional suggestions to develop a positive relationship with your child's teachers, and to help you become an active school parent contributing to your child's learning.

Make Yourself Visible to Teachers

Attend back-to-school nights, open houses, local school site council meetings—whatever gets you seen by teachers. In some cases, I have sent an introductory letter or e-mail to my children's teachers at the beginning of the year, just to let them know that my wife and I will support their teaching at home. I have yet to meet a teacher who didn't respond warmly. Like you, teachers are at their office (the school) during the day, so it may mean that you need to take some time away from work to meet them. You probably take off work if your plumbing is broken and someone has to be at the house. Our children's education deserves at least that much commitment.

If both parents are working, attending every school function and visiting teachers on weekdays might be a challenge. But many supervisors understand the value of strong parent involvement in a child's education. Check to see if your state has a law similar to California's Family-School Partnership Act. This law allows parents, grandparents, and guardians to use up to forty hours of vacation, compensatory, or personal leave each year to participate in school functions. I've taken many vacation days in order to be at my child's school or district, and it's always been worth it.

Check your school's newsletter or Website frequently, and show up at any event that gives you an opportunity to touch base with your child's teacher, experience firsthand what's going on at the school, and show your child that what is being done in school is important to you. School board meetings are usually held in the evening or late afternoon, and though attending them won't put you into contact with your child's teacher it will increase your knowledge of what is happening in curriculum and instruction across your school district.

Always Attend Scheduled Conferences with Teachers

UCLA's University Elementary School considers parent-teacher conferences so important that they schedule three meetings each year. If your children are past the age of regularly scheduled parent-teacher conferences, consider requesting one. If your teacher agrees to it, have your child attend the meeting. As teacher Charlotte Higuchi once told me, "The conference is, after all, about the child!"

Teachers and children provide plenty of evidence of how things are going in school. Like many parents, you may have a hard time keeping up with all the assignments, artwork, tests, and other artifacts that make their way into your child's backpack and agenda. Review your child's work regularly and use the information to enhance your teacher-parent collaboration.

Stay Involved

The presumption that you can buy a house in a good school district and then expect teachers and the school to take care of the rest does not guarantee success. It's like buying a high-performing mutual fund and never looking to see if it's still the big winner it was when you bought it. By the time you realize that your child has a problem, your child may have lost more than can be gained back.

". . . The main reason to create partnership [between parents and schools] is to help all youngsters succeed in school and in later life," says Joyce Epstein, director of the Center on Families, Communities, Schools, and Children's Learning (2002). "When families are involved, students hear common messages from home and school about the importance of attending school, staying in school, and working hard as a student."

Establish a Quality Relationship with Your Child's Teachers

Teachers serve a number of masters: children, parents, a principal, a superintendent, a school governing agency, the public, a state, and even the federal government. That teachers cannot serve all of these masters equally well at all times may seem obvious. But parents can pose a unique challenge to teachers because they have the most at stake: their children are either too young or presumed to be too young to fend for themselves. Sometimes parents are not on their best behavior, criticizing schools for factors far outside of their control or for trying to make improvements that take a long time to implement or fall by the wayside completely.

Some parents have excessive expectations for schools and teachers, which may lead to conflict. This is especially true of parents who seem to believe that no teacher is quite good enough to bring out their child's many gifts, or that every issue is a big one. Deborah Meier explained the dilemma from a teacher's perspective in her book *In Schools We Trust* (2002, p. 45). "It's no wonder that for many teachers, parents are a source of acute distress and discomfort," wrote Meier. "Even if 90 percent of students' families love you, the fact that the other 10 percent do not is not just a passing inconvenience but an endless wound that never quite heals, and that still aches sometimes even years afterward." Meier points out that parents go to bed every night believing that they have only one opportunity to get a good education for their children. If they make a mistake, there is no second chance.

If teachers are unsure about their relationship with parents, parents are equally unsure about their relationship with teachers. Some parents frequently challenge their child's teacher; others hide their concerns, afraid that they are stepping across the hidden line that protects a teacher's domain. In fact, parents tend to be unsure about their entire relationship with schools in general, creating a hazy trust. They often keep their views about what they perceive as a school or teacher shortcoming to themselves, afraid that they will be seen as pushy, or that they are wrong. Some parents fear that if they complain the teacher or school will take reprisal in a subtle or more direct form against their child. Doing nothing becomes easier than doing something, but it doesn't serve the student or educational system and allows issues to fester.

Researcher Hilda Borko, whose work concentrates on teachers' professional development, explained a dilemma she faced with her son's teacher in elementary school: "My son had a teacher who was not a good match for his learning style or personality in the third grade. Although I talked to the principal, I should have been more forceful in requesting that he be transferred to a different teacher. By the time I made an official request to move him, it was too late in the school year. The lesson I learned was that you have to be proactive when problems arise."

Hasmik Avetisian, a veteran teacher from Corinne Seeds University Elementary School, shared with me some suggestions on how parents can establish a quality relationship with their child's teachers before problems occur:

- *Trust your school and teachers.* Like you, your child's school and teachers want the best for your child. Let your child's teacher know that you trust his or her experience and will reinforce school learning at home. Be able to let your child go.
- *Share information.* Let your child's teacher know what you think is unique about your child, his or her gifts, and any special needs.
- *Advocate for your child.* Talk to your child's teacher about what you think your child needs in school, especially if you feel those needs are not being met. But also hold your child accountable for his or her own learning and behavior.

Almost all parents have at least one concern with a teacher at some point in time. Even teachers who have their own children in school have occasional concerns with their child's teachers. What to do when problems arise? Here are a few suggestions.

Find Flexible Solutions

If your child is self-motivated and performing well in all of her school classes, you may have little need to advocate on her behalf. But most parents find themselves at least occasionally concerned about some school issue. No one can tell you exactly when or how to talk to your child's teacher about a problem, but communicate your concerns. If you are particularly upset about an issue and it doesn't require immediate action, consider waiting overnight before sending an e-mail or making a phone call. You want to give yourself a chance to approach the teacher constructively. Then, when you do write or call, make it clear that the purpose of your contact is to find out more than what you already know, not to make an accusation based on what might be unreliable information.

E-mail is a great way to communicate with teachers, but be careful. I've seen e-mail messages pass from one person to dozens of other people across a school district. E-mail messages are also more likely to be misinterpreted if the tone is unclear. If the issue is serious, a face-to-face conversation may be best. Most teachers will furnish their preferred contact method during back-to-school night. If not, just ask.

Knowing when or how to step in is not easy. Reenie Webb, who conducts research on mathematics and science learning in cooperative groups, found an approach that worked for her son and that taught her something about working with teachers:

> In middle school, our son had a math teacher who was not doing an adequate job, so we talked with the teacher about what we could do to help. Some of the things we tried were supplemental math materials, special lunchtime sessions with the teacher, and private tutoring. While we have occasionally expressed concern about whether our kids were learning what we thought they should be learning, our focus has been to help our children develop coping and learning strategies in school that would help prepare them for the real world. At the same time, we learned how important it is to be alert to our children's progress and potential shortcomings in instruction.

If your child is not getting the help she needs in school and a transfer is simply not possible, then you need to look for alternatives, says former teacher Mary Jane Hufstedler.

"My daughter had the same teacher in fifth and sixth grade," said Hufstedler. "Unfortunately, that teacher did not understand math very well and did very little math instruction. As a result, my daughter did not learn some of the basics of math, which haunted her clear into college. If your child is not getting proper instruction from his or her teacher, you must find another source of instruction." You may be able to help yourself; if not, consider hiring an older student as a tutor or finding a tutoring service in your area.

Sometimes parents enter a school year having heard concerns from other parents about a particular teacher. Those concerns may or may not be accurate. "You need to start a new year trusting the teacher," said Meredith Reynolds, "and encourage your child to get the help that they need."

"I remember in first-grade when my daughter had to write a report about animals," said Scott Tracy, "and we thought it was way beyond what any first-grader could do. The teacher required the kids to write an extensive report, to create effects, and she kept saying to parents, 'Trust me, this will work out.' Sure enough, it was everything she said it was. It was enabling for all the kids, and a good learning experience, which our daughter recalls fondly more than a decade later."

Parent and former school board member Andy Beattie says that he took advantage of every opportunity to have good conversations with his three daughters' teachers, trying to be proactive and not reactive. If there was a problem, he or his wife, Kim, would meet with the teacher, multiple times if necessary, and if that didn't resolve the problem they would talk to the principal.

Eckhardt Klieme, from the University of Frankfurt, shared with his two children videotapes from the Third International Mathematics and Science Study showing teachers teaching mathematics. "What my children could see is that not all teachers use the same instructional methods and that some methods and teachers are more effective than others," said Klieme. Most of his children's math teachers used a thoroughly traditional, one-step method of teaching math, which was normal and accepted in German schools.

"Seeing other teachers and other instructional methods helped my children to reflect on teaching in a new way and to know that differences exist in teaching quality," said Klieme. "That helped them to realize that they [as students] play an important role in their own learning."

Veteran second grade teacher Tracy Hughes offers suggestions for parents on how they might successfully communicate with their children's teachers:

- Ask or share anything, whenever the spirit moves you. It will diffuse and solve any issues or questions that you may have, but . . .
- Prioritize; don't die on every hill.
- Make sure the teacher knows your child and is made aware of any special needs that your child may have.
- Consider short notes or e-mail to the teacher for simple questions; phone calls or longer notes if it is a major, complex, or long-term issue; and then conferences if the issue is still unresolved.

Hughes adds that a problem or issue left unexpressed serves neither you nor your child. "Don't be afraid to advocate for your child," advises researcher Marilyn Cochran-Smith, a professor at Boston College whose daughter had special needs. "Let them know that you have knowledge that is important for your child's learning. Even for an education researcher, I had to work very hard to give my opinion when in a room of special education experts. An IEP [individualized education program] meeting can be very intimidating. I listened, but I also advocated for what I thought my daughter needed."

When children move into high school, parents typically have less contact with teachers. This is natural because students are encouraged to take more responsibility for their own education.

Consequently, parents may need to develop other help strategies if problems arise. Researcher Jamal Abedi explains what happened with his daughter:

> In ninth grade, our daughter had a math teacher who just didn't seem to like her. When Sarah asked for help, the teacher would put her off quite abruptly, saying that she was busy. We explained to Sarah to not take it personally. It was not her own personal shortcoming. At first, we were going to talk to the teacher, but Sarah asked us not to, because she thought it would be more difficult for her in class. We told Sarah that if we didn't talk to the teacher she needed to be responsible for getting help when she needed it. We advised her to ask more questions in class and be the first person in line to talk with the teacher after class. Sarah followed our advice and it paid off. She learned when and how to get the help she needed independent from us. It also built up her trust in us because we let her resolve the problem herself.

"Parents must be willing to listen to teachers and vice versa," says third-grade teacher Lani Moore, parent to two children now in college. "If parents are forthright—say, that there is a home issue going on in the child's life—that really helps the teacher to assist the child."

Most teachers welcome parent input. Like Hughes and Moore, they want to see every child in their classroom succeed. Parents who provide information and politely share concerns are almost always successful in having their voice heard and in making improvements that benefit their child.

6

SUPPORT *GET SMART!* HABITS AT SCHOOL

> One can never consent to creep when one feels an impulse to soar.
>
> —*Helen Keller*

Rising expectations for schools and students have pressured children to become responsible for their own learning at an earlier age. Even before the No Child Left Behind Act increased accountability requirements on schools and students, a survey by Education Week (2001) reported that:

- Almost eight in ten teachers said the curriculum was "somewhat" or "a lot" more demanding of students.
- More than six in ten teachers said the expectations for what students would learn were "somewhat" or "a lot" higher.
- More than six in ten teachers said students were writing more; nearly half reported students were reading more.

Here's how one fifth grader's parent helped his child take charge of her own learning when she wasn't doing it herself:

> Our daughter was encountering challenges with math factors in fifth grade, and her textbook wasn't helping my wife and I to explain it to her any better. We told her to seek extra help from her math teacher. The first week went by, and when we asked her if she sought help, she said yes, but that her math teacher was now teaching reading intervention on the day when students could usually get extra

> help. Trying to get her to take charge of her own learning, we pointed out that she could have requested a different day or time, stayed in at recess, whatever would work for her and her math teacher. She eventually found an agreed upon time, had several review sessions on math, and received an A for the quarter, raising her grade from a C earlier in the year. Moving her grade up has made her feel more confident in math. It's now her favorite subject. More importantly, she knows that she has to help herself in school.

This student represents thousands of children whose success in school depends not on innate ability but on gentle nudging from others, usually parents or teachers. Without encouragement at the right times, it is easy for a child's potential to remain unfulfilled. In some cases, the child may even drop out of school.

This chapter covers *Get Smart!* learning habits in school that will serve a child throughout life. The tips include how to form good habits early in a child's education, set high expectations throughout the school years, teach a child to get help when it is needed, help a child improve listening skills, develop a child's study skills necessary to succeed in school, and other ways to promote good learning habits.

Start Early

A growing body of evidence points to the value of establishing an early foundation for successful learning. A comprehensive review of thirty-six studies of early childhood programs by Steven Barnett at Rutgers University (1995), for example, showed positive short-term effects of early childhood programs on intelligence and long-term effects on school achievement, grade retention, special education placement, and social adjustment. Some of the students showed an almost-immediate boost in IQ of eight points, attributed to the early learning programs. "Preschool programs can mean the difference between failing and passing, regular or special education, staying out of trouble or becoming involved in crime and delinquency, dropping out or graduating from high school," concluded Barnett.

Early childhood teacher Hasmik Avetisian at UCLA's Corinne Seeds Elementary School describes a number of ways in which parents can build a foundation of learning at an early age that helps their child well into the school years:

- Make sure that your child has a healthy environment. Provide good nutritious foods, plenty of water, fresh air, outdoor play, and physical activities like swinging or jumping rope to develop his or her overall motor skills.
- Treat ear infections and other health conditions quickly. If left untreated, they may lead to more serious problems.
- Make many materials and activities available to your child, such as building materials, puzzles, paper, pencils, markers, easels, paints, dress-up clothes, and books. Make everything easily accessible.
- Provide structure, routine, and positive reinforcement of good behavior.
- Teach your child social behaviors, such as how to initiate play, enter a play situation, and resolve conflict.
- Talk to your child about whatever he or she wants to talk about: feelings, questions, what makes him or her happy or sad, how to cope with anger.
- Hold your child accountable for his or her behavior. If behavior is inappropriate, discuss what your child should do the next time. Explain consequences.
- Don't act out of your own anger; you are your child's model in life.
- Hug your child often. Hugging helps to develop trust and intimacy.

Children are sometimes given more power than they know how to use appropriately, adds Avetisian, which may lead to problems in school. Know when it is time for your child to make a decision and when it is time for you to make a decision.

Set High Expectations

Parenting style and expectations are strongly related to student achievement, according to a study of more than sixty thousand families by Xitao Fan and Michael Chen (as cited in Marzano, 2003). Parents who set expectations that are neither too lenient nor too authoritarian and who encourage a partnership with schools tend to have children who do better in school (Rosenau, 1998). To set high expectations for your child, first understand the school's expectations. One concerned parent sent me an e-mail: "I am looking for a Website that will give me some information as to where my child should be academically after she is done at the end of her school year. For example, she is in the second grade . . . what will she be learning this year? Or what would she have learned or been taught by the time she completes second grade?"

This parent was asking a question that all parents should ask, but too few do. My advice to her was to review the state standards for each subject that her child was taking. Those standards strongly influence what is taught and tested in the classroom. Educational standards are available on your state department of education Website and are sometimes distributed at school. Or visit www.edstandards.org/standards.html for links to standards in all fifty states. Reviewing your child's textbooks and other instructional materials will furnish more detail about this year's curriculum. Above all, ask your child's teacher.

Encourage Your Child to Take Rigorous Classes

A key factor in learning is the rigor of the courses that students take in school. Research by Kilchan Choi and Edward Shin (2003) shows that in addition to performing better in school, students who take more challenging courses are better prepared for college. In general, children should be encouraged to take classes that challenge their intellectual abilities and lay the foundation for future learning. Jody Priselac, a former high school math teacher who has taught teachers at UCLA, explains her approach in this vignette:

> My parents immigrated here from Italy, and the whole focus for me growing up was doing well in school and going on to college. I think that influenced a lot of how I was with my kids. There was no doubt that my children, in my mind, would have very rigorous academic courses. When my kids asked "Should I take Advanced Placement (AP) Calculus or not?" the answer was "Yes, you should." There were times when they could have choices. One of my older sons was more interested in humanities courses, so his choice was "I'd rather take AP English than AP physics" and that was OK. They both were in music, yearbook, and sports. I would not give them the option to drop math—they had to take math all four years in high school. Even when they said "I only need three years of math to get into college," it didn't matter. I just felt strongly that they needed to have math and the sciences.

Both of Jody's sons went on to four-year colleges; one at UCLA and the other graduated from Claremont College in California and enrolled in graduate school at the University of Wisconsin.

Naturally, students should not be pushed to take classes they are likely to fail or that may put too much pressure on them. When her son was a senior in high school, UCLA Professor Reenie Webb's son took four advanced placement courses at the suggestion of his counselor. "It was terribly hard," said Webb. "He pulled C's in calculus and physics his first quarter. Although he made it through the year with better grades, and was accepted by all the University of California campuses that spring and several prestigious private universities, I don't know if it was worth it, because it literally killed his interest in pursuing science," said Webb.

Webb added that this experience was a valuable lesson for her two younger daughters, now in eighth grade. "We will look very carefully at taking too many AP classes when our daughters get into high school," said Webb.

"I didn't try to overwhelm my kids in the classes they took," said Meredith Reynolds, "like taking four or five advanced placement classes in high school. If they were going to take an advanced placement class, it should be something that they were passionate about because it was going to require a lot of extra work."

Reynolds also allowed her children to have choices about the classes they took. Taking AP environmental science because a child has a strong interest in the subject is better than taking an advanced placement course in which he or she has little or no interest.

"We encouraged our daughters to take certain classes like Spanish in middle school," said parent Andy Beattie "because we felt the courses were important to their education, but we tried not to be overly aggressive." He and his wife, Kim, encouraged their daughters to take the highest track that the three of them (both parents and child) felt was appropriate. In high school, these included both AP and non-AP classes. When they got to college, they were well prepared, said Beattie, because of the courses they had taken and the quality of teaching.

Parents and students should ask themselves what will be gained and given up by taking any specific program or course. "Very few students," says Reynolds, "can do everything equally well."

Stress the Importance of School Attendance

Not surprisingly, research shows a clear relationship between school attendance and student performance. In a study that examined which students were on track to attend one of the ten University of California (UC) campuses, Choi and Shin (2003) found that attendance was a major factor. Students in the first semester of the eleventh grade were at the greatest risk of dropping their UC eligibility because of excessive absence. Poor attendance, alcohol and drug use, disciplinary problems, and dropping out of school are frequently linked. A University of Tennessee study (1996), for example, found that 23 percent of high school dropouts had been addicted to drugs at some point in their life, and 55 percent of dropouts reported being drunk in the last month.

Despite my own school district's high attendance rate of more than 95 percent, parents sometimes keep their children out of school in order to extend their vacation or take one that is convenient for all of them. In one case, a parent lobbied our school board for a weeklong break in February so that he and other families could take a ski vacation. In another case, a parent allowed his child to miss school for a week because airfare rates to Europe were just "too low to pass up." Missing a few days of school might seem trivial, but I believe it sends the wrong message to students. Keeping children out of school for reasons other than illness may mean that they are not exposed to important concepts or have to work hard to catch up on missed assignments. That isn't fair to them, regardless of the educational value of the trip. Students may have a substitute 5–10 percent of school days, further reducing their best instructional opportunities. In states such as California, schools are funded according to their attendance rate; consequently, keeping a child out of school has a negative impact on a district's budget. Every day in school is important to our children's success.

Teach Your Child to Ask for Help

All students need help at some point in their education. Maybe they don't fully understand a concept, or they miss a key day of class. They may think that not understanding a few ideas is OK or that they can catch up by reading the textbook or talking to a friend. Even adults have a difficult time knowing when they have spent appropriate time and energy solving a problem and when to ask for help.

"Getting help isn't an easy thing for kids to do," said Harvard Professor Daniel Koretz. First, a student has to recognize he or she doesn't understand an important topic or idea or has missed a key point. Second, adds Koretz, a student has to be motivated enough to get help, which also means knowing that not understanding a topic will have some negative future consequence, such as a lower score on a test.

There may be an instructional reason students don't understand a topic or learn a specific skill. The teacher may not have covered the topic in enough detail, or the teaching method didn't match a student's learning style. Some children for example, learn better when a concept or skill is visually represented; they need to see it to understand it. It is important for students to feel comfortable asking the teacher to explain points that they don't fully understand.

"We encouraged our kids to ask many questions in the classroom," said Reenie Webb, "pushing the teacher to clarify her expectations or instruction."

"Although we had a lot of contact with our daughters' teachers" said Andy Beattie, "we encouraged them to go to the teacher for help even in their younger years of school so that getting help became a good habit."

"I always told my children that teachers want kids to ask questions; they want students who are willing to go the extra step to find things out rather than waiting," said Jody Priselac.

If her kids finished an in-class assignment early, says Priselac, she encouraged them to go up and tell the teacher that they were done and then say, "Is there anything I need to do next?" Or if they didn't understand an assignment or concept, rather than not do the work or wait until it became a problem they should go to the teacher and say, "I don't understand this; can you help me?"

"The other thing that I would tell them is to always be prepared with the question, not to just say this doesn't make sense to me, but to be specific about what you don't understand," said Priselac. "Rather than just saying 'I can't do it,' say 'This is really hard because I don't understand how to add unlike fractions,'" she added.

Being ready with a specific question helped Priselac's children clarify in their own minds what they didn't understand, and it helped the teacher know what concept or principle they were missing. It also communicated to the teacher that her children were putting forth strong effort and were serious about learning, traits she admired as a former math teacher herself.

"We encourage our eighth grade daughter to ask questions at home and in school," said Ann Mastergeorge. At the dinner table Ann or her husband will ask, "How many questions did you ask today in school?" "Her teachers say that our daughter is letting them know when she doesn't understand something," adds Mastergeorge, "and has the confidence to ask questions in class."

Finally, encourage your child to ask questions of and get help from other students. Your child probably has at least one friend at school who seems to get it all, and good friends are usually willing to help each other. Perhaps next time, your child will be returning the favor.

Help Your Child Develop Listening Skills

Multitasking is a buzzword referring to an individual's ability to do more than one thing at the same time, like driving a car while talking on a cell phone and sipping a cup of coffee. But as with driving and talking on the phone, when it comes to listening and learning, research shows that multitasking is not a great idea. When John Sweller visited our center a few years ago (2004), he described research showing that even the simple process of taking notes—something encouraged in school—distracts our concentration considerably. Too many inputs or outputs at the same time produces what psychologists call "cognitive overload."

A research review by Nancy Mead and Donald Rubin on listening and its impact on achievement lead them to conclude that "the abilities to listen critically and to express oneself clearly and effectively contribute to a student's success in school and later in life" (1985, n.p.). Annabel Fawcett (1965) created a series of exercises to improve listening skills of fourth to sixth grade students and found that teaching listening skills improved student listening comprehension, while Sara Lundsteen (1965) found that teaching listening skills to fifth and sixth grade students improved their listening more than a year after their instruction and that these students applied what they learned about listening to nonschool activities.

In school, overload occurs every day: announcements blaring over a loudspeaker, students talking in the middle of a teacher's presentation, hunger pains from not eating breakfast that morning, or daydreaming. If what children are expected to learn barely reaches them in the first place, they will not be able to recall the information at a later date. Listening skills are critical to high performance and equally important both in school and later in the working world.

Effective listening often means being able to avoid or tune out distraction. One main reason children with attention deficit disorder have difficulty in school is that they often hear everything. Unable to tune out the noise, their brains are constantly overloaded. High-achieving students, on the other hand, are usually very good at identifying and screening out unwanted sounds or avoiding distraction in the first place.

One of the best ways to help your children develop their listening skills is to ask them questions about something they read, saw, did, or heard. If you are reading to them, stop occasionally and ask about what you or they have just read. Doing so helps them to understand the value of recall, a key school expectation. At the dinner table, ask them one thing they learned today. Make them aware of distractions to listening. At home, praise them when they listen to you attentively and are able to repeat back key ideas or make a good summary of a book, a television show, a movie, or a vacation. Your goal is to make good listening a habit. Here are some other listening tips:

- Model effective listening by being a good listener yourself when your children or your spouse is talking.
- Discourage your children from interrupting or talking over other people, including peers and adults.

- Point to others who are good listeners (students or adults) as examples.
- Have your children close their eyes and cup their hands over their ears to amplify all the sounds in front of them. What sounds do they hear that they didn't before? Suggest to them that we can control what we hear by tuning out unwanted sounds or distractions.
- Mention to your children your own flaws in listening. Do you stop listening to a friend, for example, to mentally prepare something that you want to say?

Help Your Child Learn Effective Study Skills

Under the right conditions, improving student study skills can substantially increase learning (Gall, Gall, Jacobsen, and Bullock, 1990). In particular, if motivation is also in place, students who get in the habit of using the skills described next will generally be better learners than students who do not.

Take Good Notes

Whether it is for a lecture, a field trip, or a science experiment, taking notes helps students recall and retain information. Notes also help students know what the teacher has emphasized in the classroom, and consequently what will be tested. Students should date notes, keep separate notebooks for each class, and if time allows review and revise notes the same day they are taken.

Learn the Big Ideas

Most school topics have fundamental concepts, principles, equations, theorems, or turning points. All living organisms contain water. Distance = rate × time. The Declaration of Independence was a turning point in U.S. history. Teachers emphasize the big ideas, which are very likely to come up on tests, so encourage your child to recognize and learn them. If a child doesn't get the big ideas and major concepts, getting less important material may be of little value. Most textbooks state big ideas quite clearly (frequently in an end-of-chapter summary), as should your state standards. Being able to express the big ideas in an essay or a short answer can be helpful.

Think in Threes

Three is a powerful number. A triangle has three sides and three points combining to form a sturdy geometric shape. Presentations and essays often have three main points because this is usually the number of main ideas that an audience can easily remember. Reading, writing, and arithmetic are three key subjects; a play usually has three acts; the three main powers of the Axis nations in World War II were Germany, Japan, and Italy. Past, present, and future are three ways to approach an essay. A three-circle Venn diagram can be used to graphically display events, subjects, and causes and effects that are partly separate but also partly overlapping. Many ideas or subjects can be effectively expressed in threes, so encourage your child to think and express himself in threes on assignments, essays, and tests.

Learn from Small Group Discussion or Experiments

Research by Robert Slavin, Noreen (Reenie) Webb, and others shows that collaborative work can be effective under the right conditions. Usually in a small group, at least one child understands more than others in the group and can help the others learn. Seat partners may be another good way to learn from other students. Remind your child however, that sometimes a student who seems to know actually doesn't, and this may lead the entire group astray. If in doubt, your child needs to ask the teacher or consult another reliable source.

Use Teacher Feedback Effectively

High-quality feedback can help improve a student's performance, especially if the feedback clearly states how well a student's work meets the criteria of the assignment and what might be improved. However, with twenty to forty students in each class, teacher feedback may not be specific enough or in adequate detail to help a child improve the work. As with most aspects of school, encourage your child to ask the teacher for better feedback, or contact the teacher yourself. Then help your child use the feedback constructively.

Review Instructional Materials

You and your child may at times feel overwhelmed with the amount of instructional materials you receive from school, especially in higher grades. Keep it organized. At back-to-school nights, pay close attention to class requirements, test and quiz schedules, syllabuses, and grading criteria. Review this information at least every few weeks. If the class has written assignments, ask for scoring rubrics that might be used during the entire school year. In some cases, your district will have a standard scoring rubric; in a few cases, a teacher or school may make available the anchor papers of a particular assignment. Anchor papers are anonymous, scored samples of student work reflecting a specific grade on a completed assignment, such as a term paper.

Use Learning Tools

There are hundreds of learning tools to help a child succeed in school. As mentioned in Chapter One, flashcards, mnemonics, and sample tests can all help a child meet the demands of heavy memorization. Only a few students are truly gifted enough to retain just about everything they see and hear, so most parents I know use whatever works best for their child. The homemade vocabulary quiz in Exhibit 6.1 is just one of dozens that my wife and I have made to support our children's learning. Quizzes of this kind are easily created in just a few minutes. Older children can make up their own flashcards and quizzes.

Other Ways to Promote Good Learning Habits in School

Encourage your child to be responsible for as many of the preceding points as is appropriate for her age *and* her ability. By middle school your child should be regularly asking the teacher to clarify assignments, provide clear feedback on their work, and request extra help when necessary. Middle and high school students might also ask for scoring rubrics or samples of other work that received a specific grade, if those materials are not already available from the teacher. As always, remember that children mature at different rates, and the process of taking control of one's own learning is just that: a process. It doesn't happen overnight.

Getting over a Slump

Some children encounter a slump in their motivation level, frequently in middle school. Several researchers whom I interviewed encountered the same situation with their own children. "My kids were both pretty motivated," said Harvard researcher Dan Koretz, "but my son did hit an eighth grade slump, where he simply wasn't too interested in school. We limited his television time, but pretty much it was a phase that he was passing through."

For other parents, a slump may be more serious, as Jody Priselac, executive director of UCLA's Center X, described, which may require deeper intervention:

> We had a short period of time when my younger son didn't want to go to school, and it was very trying. We worked closely with his teacher to figure out what was going on and get him reengaged in

Exhibit 6.1. Example of a Parent-Made Test: American History Vocabulary, Eighth Grade

1. Set up by the London Company; 50 acres of land given to colonists who paid their way to Virginia: ____________________

2. Businesses formed by a group of people who jointly make an investment and share in profits and losses: ____________________

3. Legal document written by Pilgrims to specify basic laws and social rules of the colony: ____________________

4. Made restricting religious rights of Christians a crime: ____________________

5. First written principles of government created in the United States: ____________________

6. Colonists who received free passage to America in exchange for working without pay for a certain number of years: ____________________

7. Trading networks in which goods and slaves moved among England, North America, and West Africa: ____________________

8. A minister who did not like the leadership in Massachusetts and wanted the separation of his church: ____________________

9. Suggested that people did not need clergy to know God: ____________________

10. Colonial Virginia's elected assembly: ____________________

11. Attack against American Indians and colonial government of Virginia: ____________________

12. Crops that farmers grow mainly to be sold for profit not personal use: ____________________

Bacon's Rebellion	Headright system	Cash crops
Fundamental Orders	Anne Hutchison	Triangular trade
Maryland Toleration Act	Mayflower Compact	Roger Williams
Joint stock company	Indentured servants	House of Burgesses

> school. The teacher said that he would get the work done really fast and then be very bored. She started giving him some roles and responsibilities. She started to have him read to other kids or do different little jobs. And she gave him extra books to read. Working with the teacher started turning things around. He got busier in school and became involved in other kinds of activities. The communication with the teacher and making her aware of what was going on was very helpful because she had sensed the same problem. Working together helped get my son back on track.

As with many aspects of education, no one size fits all, so parents need to develop a way that works best for their child if a slump occurs.

Your Own Positive Attitude Toward Your Child's School

I've already stressed the importance of parents having a positive attitude toward learning, but you should also have a positive attitude toward your child's school, even if there are aspects you don't like. There are dozens of things to test a parent's patience, such as excessive fundraising or not hearing back from a teacher in a timely manner. While serving on our school board, one parent complained to me, other board members, administrators, and parents about so many issues that I finally asked her why she sent her children to school in our district if we weren't doing anything right. Having a lack of confidence in your school often spills over to your child and may negatively affect the positive learning attitudes you have worked hard to instill. Although your school is probably not perfect, be supportive about it to your children.

Set Your Own Limits

We can hardly expect our children to not watch TV in excess, spend hours playing video games, or send dozens of instant messages to friends daily, if we don't model good behaviors ourselves. With the large number of electronic gadgets available today, it is easy for adults to become isolated at home. Limit your own television hours, Web surfing, music listening, or video game playing. Spend more time reading, exercising, or being actively engaged in a hobby that might involve your children.

Avoid Unnecessary Interruption to Meaningful Activity

Control your own life instead of allowing others to control it for you. If you are doing homework with your children or having dinner with your family, don't allow interruption. Let the phone or doorbell ring. Distraction at the wrong time can throw you and your children off task.

Keep up the Learning at Home

It was long theorized that learning outside the home had a positive impact on student achievement (Vygotsky, 1982–1984; Piaget, 1959), and recent research has confirmed this belief. During a 2001 study of 505 middle and early high school students, a research team found that students with an enriched informal learning environment outside the home significantly outperformed a group of similar students who had substantially less of it (Gerber, Cavallo, and Marek, 2001). The performance difference on a scientific test of reasoning ability was more than 35 percent.

"Learning *outside* of school positively impacts learning *inside* of school," says researcher Ann Mastergeorge. Her family's vacations and free time are filled with learning, including camping, plays, museums—anything to do with learning outside the classroom. The day I interviewed Ann, she, her husband, and their ninth grade daughter were preparing for a trip to Costa Rica to learn about the rain forests. Every family has opportunities (which need not be expensive, or time consuming), but we have to take advantage of them. Researcher Diane Steinberg explains her strategies:

I use resources in my community and when I travel to further my sons' interests for teachable moments. At home, we try to provide both of our young sons many enrichment opportunities: the Getty Museum, the California Science Center, the Los Angeles County Museum of Art, the Page Museum at the La Brea Tar Pits, and the Los Angeles Natural History Museum. The outdoors too is a wonderful classroom. Almost anything can be a learning experience. I bought my youngest son an inexpensive bug vacuum, and he uses it to sweep up live and dead bugs in order to examine them. Because he likes rocks, we gave him a pocket rock identification guide, which he uses to identify the many rocks that he finds. There was a colony of frogs in a pool of water behind our house. We collected tadpoles and frogs from the colony and brought them to share in each of our children's classrooms. After some research, we set up the perfect habitat for Pacific tree frogs with the help of our children and their classmates. Then the children in both classes watched the tadpoles develop into frogs. The classes released the adult frogs into a stream at the end of the school year. These types of activities complement what our children learn at school, where they provide many hands-on science experiments and experiences. Working closely with their school, my sons are developing a true love of learning.

7

SUPPORT *GET SMART!* HABITS AT HOME

Education is not the filling of a pail, but the lighting of a fire.

—*W. B. Yeats*

During his visit to UCLA, Eckhardt Klieme from the University of Frankfurt said that Germany sees the same effects of social and economic background (socio-economic status, or SES) on student achievement that occur in the United States. That is, students whose parents have high income or education level show substantially greater achievement in school. Research shows this SES effect in Germany, says Klieme, but "it doesn't tell us *why* it is important. We need to know what it is that high SES parents do at home that helps their children perform well in school."

The professor's personal example with his own children, however, may help answer the question. When his children were very young, Klieme went to a half-time position so that he could spend more time with them. Much of it was spent going to museums or taking long nature walks, which he enjoyed as much as his children did. Like most parents, he spent a lot of time reading to and with them.

Although most parents may not in economic terms be able to reduce their working hours as Klieme did, his approach supports an increasing body of research showing that early childhood education can contribute to student achievement for many years into school. According to the National Center for Early Development and Learning, high-quality child care has a lasting impact on children from any background, but it plays an even more important role for at-risk children (Bailey, 2000).

This chapter describes Get Smart! home learning strategies to improve your child's skills in reading, writing, mathematics, science, and history–social science. Also offered are tips to help your child with homework, organization, test preparation, tutors, and other at-home learning strategies.

Reading

Because it is the fundamental skill for every subject in school, reading is the most crucial ability that parents must nurture in their child, beginning at a young age. Research has consistently shown a strong relationship between reading skills and such subjects as social studies, writing, and science. Research by Jamal Abedi at the University of California, Davis, shows that students with strong reading skills perform better not just in reading comprehension but also in other topics, including mathematics (Abedi, 2004).

"My advice to parents is to read to your kids as much as possible when they are young and all the way along," says Marilyn Cochran-Smith, author of the book *The Making of a Reader*. Be a role model, have lots of books and magazines in your home, and readily in their reach.

"I read with my kids out loud until my oldest was in high school," said Laurie Candelora, a math tutor and parent to three grown children. "They really enjoyed it and so did I. They would ask me, 'Aren't you going to read tonight?' It really instilled a love of reading in my children."

"The time to stop reading to your child will vary from child to child," Cochran-Smith said, "but basically keep reading with and to them until you reach the point where you are slowing them down . . . when they are way ahead of you."

Reading comprehension is one of the most frequently assessed skills on state and college entrance tests; consequently parents should evaluate their child's comprehension by occasionally asking questions when reading together. For fiction books, ask: "Who is the main character? the hero? the villain? What is the main conflict? What are smaller conflicts? What obstacles does the hero have to overcome? What do you think will happen next? What do you like about the book? What is the theme, the moral, or the lesson of the story?" (Warning: don't overwhelm your child by asking all these questions during a single reading session! Pick a few, and be careful not to lose the fun of reading together.)

Reading helps to expand a child's vocabulary—another frequently assessed skill in the early grades. Some researchers even assert that reading is the only way students expand their vocabulary. Encouraging children to read aloud helps them become better readers. Crossword puzzles can help your child improve her recognition of words.

When my children were in early elementary school, my wife and I established 8:30 to 9:30 P.M. as a reading hour for them. It became an excellent habit and now continues into high school. Coty is a voracious reader—even picking up medical encyclopedias to read when he runs out of other books. We also encourage our children to devote an equal amount of time to reading as to watching television or playing video games. At least several parents I know prohibit television viewing except on weekends, or they use television as a reward, not as something to do to fill time.

Television can be used positively if you link what your child is watching to something he is learning. When my kids are watching movies (*Titanic* was a recent example), I try to make a comparison to books, reminding them that movies and books have heroes and villains, suspense and structure. Like a book, the quality of a movie begins with the quality of the screenplay, both created by writers. The goal is to encourage children to put more effort into their own writing and foster their love of reading.

When students are young, they typically read fiction, but as they enter middle school (and certainly in high school) informational nonfiction books become increasingly important. Information-based reading or reading for content is usually related to a specific purpose, such as fact gathering for a school project or simply building interest in a subject. Students frequently use informational books to write an essay, compare points of view, or integrate new knowledge with prior knowledge. Parents can help their children develop information-based learning, says former English-language arts teacher James Stratton, who is now superintendent of the La Cañada Unified School District, by reading nonfiction books and magazines to their children when they are young, especially in topics they are interested in learning. How to care for a pet, a career that interests your child, or a magazine article about a favorite personality are just a few examples. My wife makes sure that our son and daughter have subscriptions to quality teen magazines, with a combination of fiction and informational text. My sister-in-law found a Bible written in a contemporary teenage magazine style that my kids find fun to read.

Parents can also help their children learn how to use a table of contents and an index to find information. Show them how to use a dictionary, an atlas, and an encyclopedia. Children who understand how to find and use information are likely to make more efficient use of their time and learning. Point out that it usually isn't necessary to read a complete nonfiction book when the purpose is to find specific chunks of information. Skimming is fine for certain purposes. Instill in your child that the purpose of reading—for example, creating a summary, writing a compare-and-contrast report, or reading for pleasure—often reflects what and how you read. Internet-savvy children today are often well ahead of their parents in their ability to find and use information to support an assignment or project. If they aren't, help them.

Here are some research findings about reading that parents should know (Bennett, 1986).

- The amount of reading that parents do with their children contributes to their early reading ability.
- Phonics helps children learn to read. Phonics instruction uses the knowledge that a word is a group of individual sounds, and these groups are used to form the millions of words in a language.

Research by Reid Lyon, Barbara Foorman, and David Francis has garnered substantial evidence that phonics-based instruction helps children learn to read (Foorman and others, 1997).

- Children learn vocabulary better when the words they study are related to familiar experiences and to knowledge they already possess.
- Hearing good readers read and encouraging students repeatedly to read a passage aloud helps children become good readers.
- Reading for comprehension requires most students to read material multiple times.
- Children get more out of a reading assignment if the teacher precedes the lesson with background information and follows it with discussion.

Here are several techniques that education researchers and parents have used to help their own children develop or improve their reading ability.

"I taught my daughter to read using the SWRL [Southwest Educational Regional Laboratory] reading program," said education evaluator Floraline Stevens, who at the time was a kindergarten teacher in the Los Angeles Unified School District. She credits the research and phonics-based SWRL program for helping her daughter to read by age three, adding that she always scored in the 90th percentile in reading on her standardized tests in school. (See Appendix F for more information about the SWRL reading program.)

"We enrolled our daughter in a quality preschool program at a young age," said Suzanne Lane, a past president of the National Council on Measurement in Education. "We made sure that we read to her every day and that she had the opportunity to explore age-appropriate books on her own. We were well aware of the reading research, which shows the positive impact that reading to your child has on a child's reading ability. Even though she is reading well herself, we continue to read to her and let her see us reading. We try to have a reading period for all of us every day in which we are all engaged in our own reading material."

School board member Scott Tracy explained how he and his wife (today an elementary school teacher) helped their daughters learn to read at any early age:

> My wife and I did a lot of reading out loud with our two girls when they were very young. As they got older, we read many story books. Each night would be a new chapter, something for them to look forward to the next time we read. That made it exciting, and they really were involved in reading. We used flashcards to help them learn their letters plus word recognition and phonics cards because we felt that that would support their reading ability. I asked my daughters questions when they were reading, not just about what they thought but involving them in the process of how words are formed into a sentence or paragraph. To support their early learning, we would point out words on billboards or other places we happened to be. By kindergarten they were well on their way to becoming good readers.

Robert Glaser, a learning and assessment researcher at the University of Pittsburgh, said that he and his wife used role playing to support their daughters' reading and interest in literature. "Whoever read a book would pretend they were the author and describe the book to the whole family," said Glaser. "Then the rest of the family would question them about it. 'Why did you write this book? How did you develop this character? What did you think about one of the characters?'" Glaser credits the role-playing method to research conducted by Margaret McKeown and Isabel Beck. He believes it helped his daughters become better readers, increased their reading comprehension, helped them understand the structure of a book, and made them better writers.

Writing

The National Assessment of Educational Progress (Lutkus, Daane, Weiner, and Jin, 2003) shows that only 28 percent of fourth grade students have attained the proficiency level in writing. In eighth grade, the proportion of students reaching that level is just 31 percent. But writing is a crucial skill throughout a child's school years, and in most careers. To help students become better writers, most schools teach students to begin writing even before they can read. The Center for the Study of Reading at the University of Illinois found that teaching both reading and writing at the same time leads to improved reading performance (Atkinson and Jackson, 1992).

Parents can help their children improve their writing skills regardless of their current level. A few years ago while on an airplane to Chicago, I sat next to a mother and father who were actively helping their children learn to write. The four-year-old girl was writing her name, encouraged by her mother. After a short time, the mother and daughter drew artwork together as the father worked with the young girl's twin and the couple's seven-year-old son. The thirty-minute effort helped to pass time on a four-hour flight, while increasing the probability that their children would develop strong writing skills. Parents can similarly use what might be television or electronic game time, to help their children practice their writing.

Here are some other tips to help your child become a good writer.

Take Advantage of Opportunities to Write

My wife keeps a list of relatives and friends who give our children a gift at birthdays or holidays and makes sure that our kids write a thank-you note to them. In addition to being the right thing to do and a good lifelong habit, writing a note is one more chance to encourage writing. Parent Karen Mathison explains: "Beginning when my children were very young, we talked about the old cliché, 'It's the thought behind the gift that counts.' So if someone took the time and effort to send him or her a gift, then the right thing to do is to write a handwritten thank-you note; otherwise, they could not accept the gift. Over the years they have grown to appreciate this trait and actually expect it of others," adds Mathison.

Writing to friends, taking a few notes on a family vacation, or simply writing down items on a grocery list are a few ways to encourage your child to write. A useful gift for your child is a journal, which encourages them to write regularly. Suggest that your child write a letter to a pen pal, or to the fan club of a movie star or popular singer. Your child could start a newsletter on a favorite topic. Some children find it easier to write on a computer, so give your child frequent computer access. Software such as the commercially produced Storybook Weaver can encourage very young children to write and develop stories as they go.

Useful Writing Tips

Everything that a child writes has a purpose; it may be to inform, persuade, review, or offer an opinion. If your child isn't clear about the purpose of the writing assignment, help her figure it out. With no clear purpose in mind, writing is surely unorganized and weak. "On writing assignments," said Robert Glaser, "my wife, Sylvia, and I would ask our daughters to discuss their essays: 'What is your main point, and what is the purpose of this essay? Every essay has to have an objective.'"

Knowing whom you are writing for is also important, because it helps a child adapt the writing to the background of the reader. "We asked our daughters to think about the audience," said researcher Robert Mislevy. "What do you already know, and how can you write for that audience? In helping our children learn new concepts, we often did a lot of scaffolding on the first questions; then they could take over. We could see that they were making progress over time."

Scaffolding usually consists of asking questions that help a child organize his thoughts. As Mislevy points out, an excellent way to begin is to ask your child what he already knows about a topic. When faced with a writing assignment, many students begin by going through their books, notes, or other information sources. Instead, have your child brainstorm what he already knows. Brainstorming makes a child use memory, saves time from digging through a large quantity of information, and reinforces in your child's own mind that he probably knows more about a topic than he thinks.

Among the types of writing that your child will do in school are short and long research reports, book reports or reviews, and persuasive essays. In school, especially in the earlier grades, writing is often formulaic. Teachers frequently give quite specific instructions about how to write an essay, and students are expected to follow it. One classic grade school format is the five paragraph model: an opening paragraph introducing a key point or theme and three key ideas, followed by three paragraphs describing each central idea, and a concluding paragraph that summarizes or repeats the unifying theme presented in the first paragraph. The same writing formula can even be applied to the writing portion of the SAT that is taken by students in high school.

Most teachers like to see a lot of detail, which means they want to see a child write more, not less. If a child doesn't write very much, it may look as though she doesn't know much—which may be exactly correct. The grade could reflect the quantity of writing as much as the quality. Encourage your child to write a lot. In writing, it's always easier to trim down during the editing process than to add new material at the end, especially if pushing a deadline.

Finally, whereas children may need to take a break from writing, too many breaks can produce loss of concentration and even an unfinished or overdue assignment. Encourage your child to stay with the writing until a substantial chunk of it is completed, just as most professional writers do. As a screenwriter once told me, a good writer keeps his or her posterior affixed closely to the chair.

Appendix D presents a specific method to help your child write a short paper.

Overcoming Writing Challenges

Sometimes a child may be effective at expressing herself verbally but have a difficult time putting words to paper or into a computer. If your child is having trouble getting a writing assignment started, try letting her dictate the story or her ideas to you. In many cases, just getting thoughts down is a good beginning, which can then be structured and expanded into a longer paper. Make it clear that you are glad to help now, but that you expect her to polish the work. Independence, not dependence, is the ultimate goal. If your child just can't manage the assignment at all, then contact the teacher, who may have strategies that can be used in the classroom to help your child do the assignment.

Encourage Use of Story Devices

While in the U.S. Air Force, civilian film editor Don Housholder taught me the value of "bookending" a story: concluding a film with a shot or scene that takes the viewer back to the beginning. During the middle part of the story, the viewer forgets about the beginning but reaches an a-ha moment when the writer brings the viewer back to the beginning, often resolving the main conflict at the same time. Motion pictures such as *Citizen Kane*, *Doctor Zhivago*, *Gandhi*, and *Titanic* are good examples of screenplays with strong story bookending. Other story devices include foreshadowing, flashback, and metaphor. In the movie *It's a Wonderful Life*, Jimmy Stewart grabs a loose knob on the railing to the stairs of their drafty, old home on several occasions. The loose knob is a symbol of Stewart's hectic life, too busy to fix a simple household problem. On a deeper level, the doorknob is a metaphor for all that Stewart gave up in his life in order to put his values first, living in a fixer home because he refuses to cave in to the conniving Mr. Potter, who offers to make Stewart a rich man if he will sell out the Building and Loan.

More advanced fiction writers may be capable of incorporating flashbacks into their stories. Flashbacks are a well-known method of jumping back to an earlier time to reveal an important event that advances the main story or reveals an important aspect of a character. The popular television series "Lost" uses many flashbacks to reveal important events in its characters' background that contribute to the present story. Story devices can make your child's paper stand out from others.

Connect Writing to a Child's Interest or Knowledge

Parents can use everyday objects, experiences, or topics to encourage their children to write. Old photographs may serve as the basis for writing about the family tree, or a child's own baby shoes may encourage him to write about the first thing he can remember in life. It is easier for children to write about topics of interest to them than topics of interest to others. Even an assignment that seems dry can be made interesting if you connect the subject to something your child enjoys.

For example, in sixth grade Markie had a writing assignment about Plato—not necessarily a subject of great interest to a twelve-year-old. In reviewing the materials she had collected about Plato, I noticed a story about Gyges, a shepherd in the service of the king of Lydia. In one of his dialogues, Plato wrote that Gyges removed a gold ring from the body of a dead man and placed the ring on his own finger. Gyges discovered that when he turned the ring, he became invisible, but by doing so he also became wicked. With the ring's power, he seduced the king's wife, plotted with her the murder of the king, and took over his kingdom. Plato's story illustrates the dark side of human nature if left uncontrolled.

When I asked Markie if this story sounded familiar, she said no, so I asked her if it might have any relation to any movies she had seen. The light bulb went on: *Lord of the Rings*, where the ring similarly opens up the dark side of human nature to anyone who puts on the ring. Markie wrote her essay, suggesting that the author of the *Lord of the Rings*, J.R.R. Tolkien, might have used Plato's ancient story as the basis for his own masterwork. She made the point that Plato's dialogues are still influencing writers today. She received a good grade on her essay. More important, the assignment and the few minutes of help that I gave her should encourage her to look for similar connections in the future.

Mathematics

Mathematics remains as much a defining ability for students today as it was when most of us were in school. In her study of eighth grade students, researcher Anne Howe found that mathematics and reading skills were the best predictors of science achievement (1996). According to Howe, "Students who lack [math and reading] skills are not likely to succeed in science even in activity-centered classrooms" (n.p.). In a separate study, graduate student Jacob Seiler found that students who took higher-level mathematics courses significantly outperformed students from lower-level mathematics classes in both chemistry and physics (2004).

Unfortunately, many students still become math-phobic when they encounter mathematics concepts they don't understand, sometimes developing a belief that they aren't good in math. But strong quantitative skills can mean the difference between getting a good job or not. On occasion, I interview UCLA graduate students applying for research assistant jobs at our center. In most cases, the students we hire have stronger math skills than those not hired because quantitative skills are in short supply despite many years of emphasis on math. In K–12 education, math teachers too are usually in high demand because not enough students major in college math. Consequently, helping children develop strong mathematics skills during their K–12 years is especially important to a future career.

As with other subjects, parents play an important role in helping their children succeed in math. As Eckhardt Klieme's children grew older, for example, he helped them understand the importance of mathematics by solving real-world problems together. "I also tried to help my children prepare for their math tests," says Klieme, "by doing a math review, which often included their friends." His daughter is now pursuing higher-level mathematics on her own initiative.

"Anything parents can do to help their children experientially is helpful," says Laurie Candelora, who tutors dozens of children at all levels of mathematics. "I read of one parent in a shoe store," said Candelora, "who used the opportunity to help his young child understand classification methods, showing how shoes were placed into categories—men's, women's and children's—and of course how they were classified into different sizes and styles. That helps develop a young child's ability to classify everyday objects and observe both quantitative and qualitative differences. Take the opportunities to talk about how math is used in the real world wherever you are, such as the mall, the hardware store, or the doctor's office," Candelora added.

"One day, one of our daughters was studying fractions," said Robert Mislevy, "and asked, 'What's the point of this?' I explained to her that fractions have many practical applications. To show her that they did, during the next two weeks we used fractions on various food recipes. If the recipe called for one-third of a cup of milk for four people, how much milk is required for eight people? for sixteen? That helped her to understand the value of what she was studying in school."

Board and card games can also help children learn mathematical concepts. When she plays the card game War with her four-year-old grandson, Candelora asks him questions such as, "How much more is your six than my four?" Asking simple questions helps him understand not just number values but differences between those values.

Here are some other suggestions on how to help children develop useful math skills.

Encourage Precision

Many math mistakes are from lack of precision, not necessarily because students don't understand how to solve a problem. Common mistakes include failing to read the problem correctly, missing a key calculation needed to arrive at the right answer, errors in signs or parentheses, and rushing through a problem. Lack of neatness is another difficulty, causing children to add the wrong numbers in a column, for example. Help your kids by encouraging them to read their math problems correctly, be patient and neat, and always check their work. There is (usually) no extra credit for being the first one done.

Make Sure They Understand the Question

Another frequent math error is misunderstanding what the problem asks a student to do, especially in word problems. If your child reads a problem and can't seem to get started, it may mean that he doesn't understand what the problem is asking him to solve. Here is a simple method that can be especially helpful for word problems, adapted from a method my children learned in second grade and that can be applied all the way through high school. I call it the RIES method: Read, Information, Equation, and Solution.

> Luis has seven green marbles and eight red ones. Liliana has nineteen green marbles and four red. How many more red marbles does Luis have than Liliana? How many marbles do they have altogether?
>
> 1. *Read the question*. "How many more red marbles does Luis have than Liliana?" "How many marbles do they have altogether?" Rereading the question, not the full problem, reinforces in your child's mind the variable that she must find or the problem that she must solve. What is not known in the problem? What do you need to find? What type of operation seems appropriate? This problem has two questions, and writing the questions down can help your child remember that she needs to solve two problems, not one. I have my kids *write* the question down, not just read it. This way they can come back and make sure they answered the question, not just solved an equation.
>
> 2. *Information*. Your child should write down the key information given in the problem. Luis has seven green marbles and eight red ones. Liliana has nineteen green marbles and four red marbles. This restates what is known. If the operation is not clear from step one, writing down the information given in the problem can help.
>
> 3. *Equation*. Combine the given information into an equation. Step one, rereading and writing down the question asked in the problem, usually helps determine the type of operation required to

solve the problem. "Altogether" frequently means addition. "How much more" or "how many more" usually means finding a difference between two numbers, and thus subtraction is the typical operation.

Equation for first question: 8 – 4 = ?
Equation for second question: 7 + 8 + 19 + 4 = ?

4. *Solution.* Now your child should be able to solve the problems. Most teachers and tutors encourage children to write down what they do for each step, so that the student or teacher can retrace their thinking process. Neatness helps to avoid simple mistakes.

Not all problems require every step to be written down, but the RIES method or a similar one can help on longer problems or where a child is learning new concepts. My kids still find this method helpful in middle and high school because it can be applied to almost any word problem. Use whatever method works for your child. If a teacher suggests that your child employ a specific method, you should generally use it instead of one of your own or one from a book. Consistency in the home and the classroom supports student learning and helps avoid comments like "But Mom, Mrs. Garcia told us to do it this way!" Also, schools and districts frequently use the same methods across various grades; consequently, using their preferred method—even if it differs from how you learned the same concept or skill as a child or in college—is generally better. On the other hand, if your child is pretty fluent with the teacher-provided method, showing your child that mathematics problems can be solved in multiple ways is valuable.

Make Sure Your Child Understands the Underlying Concepts

Having to explain *what you know* and *how you know it* helps to ensure conceptual understanding, not just memorization of a formula. "Parents can't assume that kids understand concepts," advises veteran teacher Lani Moore, "even if they can do a problem correctly."

Ask your child to explain how he solved the problem or how he might solve it another way. When your child is stuck on a difficult problem, it is often a conceptual misunderstanding. As Cindy Wilcox mentioned earlier, take your child back to a similar problem that he can solve, ideally a problem that builds up from a concept that he understands. If he can't solve $X - 7 = 12$, then go back to $19 - 7 = X$. Teachers often say that for them to teach a concept to their class they have to understand it very well themselves. If your child can easily explain a concept or how he solved a problem, he probably understands it. If he hesitates quite a bit or the explanation is not adequate, he may need reinforcement.

Robert Glaser applied his own learning research to helping his daughters understand math and science, not just to do assignments. "What do you know already about a particular question or assignment? What are the principles involved in the problem? How can you represent the problem?" asked Glaser. He would also ask them how an expert approaches a problem and how one part of a problem is connected to another part as well as to finding a solution. "I tried to get them to see that how they represented a problem correlated to how well they could solve the problem," said Glaser.

Try Using Supplemental Materials to Support Math Learning

Your child's textbook and classroom materials may be adequate to support math learning, but you may find supplemental materials helpful. Commercially developed home software programs can shore up math concepts that your child is learning in school, although be cautious of extraordinary claims that guarantee increased grades or better test scores. Don't expect a software program to teach your child everything needed to know about any subject, including math.

Some textbooks differ in their sequencing of math principles or try to cover so much material that students become overwhelmed. Consequently, some students might learn better with another textbook than the one used in class, although it will take a proficient parent or tutor to blend learning between two textbooks. A broad range of supplemental math workbooks may be available at bookstores that specialize in teacher's supplemental products. The Internet is another option.

Jody Priselac explained a supplemental program that she used for her children:

> When my kids were growing up, I was providing professional development for teachers using what were called math replacement units. These units included a series of engaging problem-solving activities for teachers to use with students. The units focused on developing understanding and getting beyond procedures. I tried these units out with my kids before I used them with teachers. My boys loved them because they were so different from the usual memorizing multiplication tables and practicing formulas that they were doing in their math classes. The units helped my kids make sense of math, they were fun to do, and it was something we did together. I think that these activities helped my sons develop into very strong math students.

See Appendix F for information about the UCLA Mathematics Project.

Help Your Child Succeed in Science

Because much of the achievement focus in recent years has concentrated on math and English–language arts, many policymakers, educators, and parents have had concerns that science and history–social science would receive less emphasis in schools. Research confirms that what gets tested gets more instruction, and that what isn't tested gets far less emphasis. For example, Brian Stecher, Hilda Borko, Sheila Barron and others (1999) found that in Kentucky, because math was tested in fifth and eighth grade, teachers spent substantially more time teaching math in those grades, while spending less time teaching reading, writing, and science.

Science has managed to maintain its own as a key subject taught in schools thanks to international assessments, some state assessments, and a long-term belief in the value of science to our nation. This interest will be strengthened as the No Child Left Behind Act requires that states receiving federal education funding must test children in science at least once in elementary, middle, and high school by the 2007–08 school year.

Parents have many opportunities to help their children develop strong science skills. Ask your child *why?* and *what?* about the things they *observe* in nature. Why do birds sing? What causes the tide in the ocean? Why is the sky blue? At home, why does water turn to ice in the freezer but not in the refrigerator? Why is the upstairs of the house usually warmer than downstairs? Encourage your child to make *predictions*, like a scientist. If the moon is full tonight, what will it be in one week, two weeks, a month from now? Why? What will happen if we put two identical pumpkins on the front porch, one uncarved and one carved? How might they be different in just a few days, and why? Will the changes differ if the pumpkins are in the sun instead of the shade?

The National Science Teachers Association suggests that parents promote scientific thinking by encouraging their children to *classify* objects into groups. Rocks, soils, household foods . . . just about anything we observe can be placed into a category. People, for example, are of differing cultures, ages, heights, weights, and genders. Clothes may be sorted into color, size, style, and type.

When friends or relatives are looking for a birthday or gift list, suggest a subscription to *Discovery*, *Smithsonian*, *Air and Space*, or *National Geographic* magazine. Many science magazines have versions for younger children (*Discovery Kids*, *National Geographic Kids*), and some have online versions. If you live near a science museum, visit it often and consider a membership that regularly sends a publication to your child. In the Southern California area, our family enjoys the Los Angeles Natural History Museum, California

Science Center, San Diego Natural History Museum, and San Diego Air and Space Museum.

If you don't live near a science museum, remember that science is wherever you are, all the time. Take your child on a short or long field trip, and ask questions about what you see. Encourage him to take a camera for photographs of his favorite observations, or take notes about what he sees. Middle school science teacher Hilary Gregg says that cooking is an excellent way to support children's learning about science. Most kids love to cook and simultaneously learn about measuring, changes in substances, and how to be safe when working around heat. "The kitchen is almost like a mini-laboratory," said Gregg.

Help Your Child Succeed in History-Social Science

History–social sciences is a topic frequently left out of state testing, but the subject still receives substantial attention thanks to college entrance requirements and strong emphasis in state standards and schools. Many colleges require two to three years of high school courses in history–social science; most schools, educators, and parents still expect their children to have a solid grasp of American and world history. There are many ways for parents to help their children succeed in history–social sciences.

Share with children their family history from old photo albums. Read about historical figures with your young child during reading time together. Include historical figures or events in your bedtime stories, and talk about relatives who may have been a part of local history. Encourage grandparents and relatives to share their past with your children, and talk about who was president when they were growing up. Celebrate and honor our special historical dates, from Pearl Harbor to Martin Luther King Day. Watch the History Channel together. Take your child to historic Civil War battlefields. Go to see movies that are based on true historical events. Make it a habit to visit your library and pick out books about historical figures. Magazines too can promote your child's interest in both U.S. and world history.

Like science, history is all around us, so talk about history with your children often. If your child is interested in a craft, sport, or special activity, encourage learning about its history at your local library or bookstore. While on vacation, make it a rule to visit at least one major historical site. Going to a state capitol is an excellent opportunity to learn about both state government and history. If you have an opportunity to visit Washington, D.C., contact your congressperson or senator's office for a personal tour of the U.S. Capitol building. The Smithsonian museums are free and within reasonable walking distance to many of our national memorials and monuments, plus the White House. It is one thing to read the Declaration of Independence or U.S. Constitution in a history book but a far more moving experience to view the actual documents in the National Archives.

Support your child's knowledge of history by suggesting that a writing assignment focus on an important historical event or character, ideally one that is tied to the child's own interests. If your child loves space, for example, he could write a story about Neil Armstrong, Sally Ride, or the history of the Space Shuttle. He might write about a family military hero, or a relative who served the community as a teacher, or a volunteer who helped others less fortunate. All of these can be excellent school projects with a historical theme to them. Every year, one of our local schools has a project called the VIP, which requires sixth grade students to research and report on a key person in that child's life who is at least sixty-five years old. Students learn about their family heritage or the contributions of senior citizens and gain a substantial appreciation for history during the project.

Encourage your child to learn about the local town's history, or key people to interview for a story in the school or local newspaper. Integrate the learning across topics by studying local geographic or climate conditions and how they might influence current decisions about land use issues or the environment. On history assignments, make sure your child has the tools needed, which might include an atlas, encyclopedia, Internet access, and library books related to the topic.

Get Smart About Homework

In his book *What Works in Schools*, Robert Marzano mentions four studies that show a substantial relationship between homework and student achievement (2003). None of the studies shows that a high amount of homework produces greater achievement than a moderate or low amount, but they indicate that students who regularly receive and do homework generally perform better than those who don't receive or do any. Test scores from the National Assessment of Educational Progress show that homework has a positive influence on achievement in high school, although less effect in elementary school. Homework can also be a useful way for parents to evaluate their child's learning. "Our daughters' grades helped my wife and me know how they were doing in school," said Robert Mislevy, "but looking at homework was more useful. We could see how they would approach or solve a particular assignment."

Let's turn to five important topics about homework: teacher homework guidelines, the quantity of homework, the parent-child homework interaction, the homework setting, and homework independence.

Teacher Homework Guidelines

Teachers are usually very clear about their homework assignments, and a growing number are using Websites to post assignments and homework guidelines. Teacher Websites should increase exponentially in the new few years. Back-to-school nights are valuable for understanding homework expectations and requirements. Veteran teacher Tracy Hughes, while presenting at a National PTA convention, encouraged parents to clarify homework-related questions at the very start of the year (2004):

- "Is there certain homework due on particular nights? Should I be looking for any special forms to complete?" Hughes and the other second grade teachers in our district require parents to cover several mathematics standards with their children each week. A parent feedback form is due every Wednesday to the teacher explaining how the homework went.

- "Are there any graphic organizers or other suggestions that can help me help my child with homework?" Hughes and many teachers have developed graphic organizers to help with specific assignments. Exhibit 7.1 is a sample of a graphic organizer I created for writing an essay. (See also Appendix D, Tips on Writing a Paper.)

In late elementary school (and almost always in middle and high school), students have more than one teacher, sometimes as many as five or six. Consequently, your child (and often you) may face a challenge in coordinating homework assignments between teachers who all have their own requirements. Though most teachers regularly meet as a grade-level team to coordinate assignments, conflicts and questions can occur. Encourage your child to communicate regularly with teachers about homework assignments, monitor homework as necessary, and if problems occur then contact the appropriate teacher.

Quantity of Homework

The quantity of homework can be an issue for students and parents, especially in middle and high school. On some days, students may have little or no homework, while on other days it may be overwhelming. A few years ago, I participated in a review of our school district homework policy because some parents were complaining about the amount of homework. Having concerns that my own children's homework was on the heavy side, I was surprised to find that parents were almost evenly split on the amount of homework their children were receiving. About one-third of parents felt there was too much homework, a nearly equal number felt it was about right, and the final third felt it wasn't enough. Not

Exhibit 7.1. Sample Graphic Organizer: Writing a Paper

This graphic organizer is based on a paper written during a five-night timeframe, but can be adapted to the length of available time.

DAY 1	*DAY 2*	*DAY 3*	*DAY 4*	*DAY 5*
Report Type ____________	Clarification ______	1st Draft ___	2nd Draft ___	Final Draft ___
Purpose ____________ ____________ Audience ____________	Brainstorm Facts Fact 1 Fact 2 Fact 3 Fact 4	Revision ___	Format ___	Final Proof ___
Length ____________ Due Date ____________	Research Fact 1 Fact 2 Fact 3 Fact 4 Fact 5 Fact 6 Fact 7	Format ___	References ___	Parent Check ___
Resources ____________	Outline ____________	Mechanics ___	Title Page ___	Revised Final ___
Clarification Yes/No Needed		Style ___	Glossary ___	TURN IN! ___

surprisingly the outcome was that the amount of homework remained about the same.

There may be large variation in the time children need to complete the same homework assignment. Some subjects may challenge them more than others. Occasional or even frequent breaks from homework may keep your child's energy and attention at a good level. You might try a small reward such as a favorite snack for getting through a particularly difficult assignment. I have found that teachers are extremely open to adjustments in the amount of homework that a child has to complete if they are spending an excessive amount of time on it. Children differ and have their own needs. They are not us, not their brother or sister, and perhaps not the kid next door who might speed through homework effortlessly.

Tracy Hughes says that parents should follow their district guidelines, realizing that the length of time it takes a child to do homework is often dependent on his understanding of the material and his own ability. Hughes suggests that parents view district guidelines as an average for a week but always discuss with the teacher homework that takes the child an excessive amount of time.

Parent-Child Homework Interaction

Although she has tutored hundreds of students in her career, Laurie Candelora said it was hard to tutor her own children. "Your own children want to please you so much, and want you to be proud of them. And you have such an emotional investment in seeing them do well that communications can break down in frustration, and result in anger and tears," said Candelora. Parents need to be patient and step away when necessary.

Candelora advises students to get through their most challenging homework first, when everyone is still fresh. Parents should maximize listening and minimize talking, she adds, and admit that they are not perfect and have experienced difficulties as well.

Here are a few suggestions to keep your parent-child relationship positive during homework sessions:

• Review your child's material first, make sure you understand the assignment *and* the content, and *then* provide assistance if necessary. Trying to teach your child something you don't understand can be a quick way to frustration for you and your child. With math assignments that I know will be difficult for one of my children or where I am rusty, I often do the entire assignment by myself before I try to act as a tutor.

• Proceed at your child's ability, not your own. Better to do fewer math problems, write a shorter essay, or select an easier book report assignment than to lead your child to a path of stress and possible failure.

• Avoid the temptation of doing an assignment for your child simply because you can do it faster or better. Remember that their pace may not be your pace and that their quality, especially at a young age, probably will not be your quality.

• Use someone else for support. Sometimes your spouse or an older child has a better homework rapport with a younger child than you do. Don't be afraid to step away and let someone else take over.

Fostering Homework Independence

A key point in a child's learning maturation process is when he becomes independent of his parent's assistance for homework. As with most aspects of learning, this point happens at widely divergent times and is probably well outside a parent's (or teacher's) prediction ability or our potential to control. Here are how some researchers and parents have supported their child's homework independence:

• "My philosophy is to be hands-off as much as possible in my children's homework," says parent Kathy Hernandez. "I prefer to let them be responsible for their own learning and getting their work done."

• "Because we want our daughter to develop independent learning skills," said researcher Suzanne Lane, "we let her do her homework on her own but help her if she needs it. We ask questions about her work as a check for understanding and encourage her to check her work for accuracy. We emphasize that she needs to understand the problem or the assignment, often going back to read a question or the instructions again if necessary. I will frequently ask her to explain the question back to me, or I will use probing questions to have her think about her work or her approach. In math, I may ask her if she can do a problem in different ways, using repeated addition or subtraction, or to provide a different visual representation for example. I want her to see that there are different approaches and methods to solve the problem."

- "I encouraged my kids to do their homework without any mistakes," said Meredith Reynolds, "because they had the opportunity to do it at home and spend the necessary time to get it right." She and her husband, Tom, were always available if their kids needed help.

Teacher Tracy Hughes encourages parents to allow children to do independently as much homework as possible but help out when their child gets stuck or is obviously heading in the wrong direction, or when the work is simply beyond the child's ability. If the child seems overwhelmed, then the parent needs to contact the teacher. Hughes does not grade projects done at home, knowing from personal experience that students receive differential amounts of parent assistance.

Establish Homework Routine, Find a Quiet Setting, and Provide Useful Tools

Starting in sixth grade, it was not unusual for my children to have three hours of homework every day Monday through Thursday. My wife changed from full-time employment to part-time specifically so that she could pick up the kids after school and have them start on homework, finishing as much as possible before dinner and affording some downtime in the evening. They still have a reading hour from 8:30–9:30 P.M. For our children and many other parents I know, homework is always done before television, computer games, or phone calls to friends. They have to earn electronic time by having a good day at school and successfully completing homework.

"I think the most important thing we did at home was to establish a homework routine and stick with it," said Jinny Dalbeck, former teacher and a longtime school board member. "After school my daughters would have a snack, then do homework. Or if they had an activity, they would do homework afterwards. We didn't deviate. They sat down at the kitchen table and did it. We didn't have them in their bedrooms; it was both of them at the kitchen table."

Many students are involved in after-school programs, so doing homework immediately after school every day isn't always possible. Parents can help make the most of the available time and setting.

"Because my sons have fairly busy after-school programs, we don't have a set time for doing homework," says researcher Diane Steinberg, "but completion of homework is extremely important in my family. My older child completely takes responsibility for working his homework and finishes without reminders. But it can be 5:30 P.M. before my children start their homework. Out of necessity, they do homework in different places—in the library, the car, at home, wherever we are. In Los Angeles, our children spend a lot of time in the car, so we have to be flexible."

Reenie Webb has always made sure that her daughters have a good place to do their homework and that they have the necessary resources, including encyclopedias, trips to the library, and Internet access. "We try to stay in the background," said Webb, "and let them do homework themselves."

Homework often requires a lot of space, especially on a large assignment. My children do their homework at the dining room and kitchen tables, one kid at each table. This gives them the space they need, allows my wife or me to monitor their work, and gives us ample space for textbooks, dictionaries, agendas, and papers. Our dining room table has two leaves in it, and we long ago stopped removing them because our kids need the whole table to spread out their materials.

Wherever your child's homework setting is, keep noise and distraction to a minimum, forgoing the phone and music and fostering a place that is away from younger children making noise. Some children might be soothed by soft music during homework, but it probably isn't a good idea for most. Children themselves may realize and express their need for quiet. A good friend once called about whether an after-school program was conducive to homework, and my daughter unexpectedly said she wanted to talk to our friend. She said, "Mrs. J., you can't study there because it's too noisy and kids can't concentrate."

A minimum list of tools includes sharpened pencils (lots of them), dictionaries, encyclopedia (in book form or electronic), calculator, thesaurus, rulers, White-Out, highlighters, paper (lined, typing, and graph), a three-hole punch, and an atlas. When our children were just starting school, we bought a large National Geographic atlas that continues to be very useful. We have a separate atlas of just the United States. A computer with Internet access has become virtually an essential tool for finding information—and is now even required for some assignments. Most libraries offer Internet access if you don't have access at home. An inexpensive copy machine or scanner with a printer is very helpful. We copy almost all of our children's final assignments in case they get lost in a backpack or go missing in action.

You don't need to spend a lot of money equipping your child with the tools needed for school. You can find inexpensive office products—even computers. Or your office may occasionally dispose of older computers or scanners that could still be useful at home. Generally, purchase only the supplies that you expect to need and use during the year. Public schools are often required by law to furnish the supplies students use at school, although parents frequently pitch in to help.

Other Tips on Homework

At home and sometimes even at school, instant messaging, cell phones, Web surfing, blogging, television, video games, and e-mail can all become electronic barriers to learning. One parent told me that while her daughter appeared to be working on a school paper that was due the next day, she was actually spending most of the evening instant-messaging friends. The daughter panicked when she realized how little time was left to finish her paper. Keep close tabs on any of your child's electronic habits that distract from homework. You most likely pay the bill for each of these items; therefore you can and should control their use.

Here are a few more ideas to help your child with homework:

- Take advantage of others' expertise—your spouse, friends, relatives. "We had a nice separation of duties at home with our two daughters," said parent Scott Tracy. "My wife, Mary, worked with them in areas of creativity and art. I was more the math, English–language arts, and science. That was complementary, and I think it worked very well."
- Allow children to do as much as they can before you step in. If and when you do step in, be patient, count to ten, and promise yourself and your child that you will not raise your voice.
- If your child is a multisensory learner, use manipulatives or hands-on tasks. Many children need more than classroom instruction and a textbook, so give them methods that work for them.
- Connect homework to your child's own interests and the real world whenever possible. Give your child specific examples of how you use math, reading, writing, history, science and the arts in your own life.
- Use tools that work. If flashcards and note cards help your child remember the many facts needed in school, don't hesitate to use them. My wife and I use notecards frequently, especially to help our children learn vocabulary or a foreign language. "I was a strong believer in note cards," said Meredith Reynolds. "If a child is just reading a chapter of text, for example, most of what they read the first time just passes right through." Reynolds would have her children take notes on key chapter ideas. At the top of each note card, she had them place the chapter title. "Then when they would study, the note cards made their review much easier and they retained a

lot of information that would otherwise just pass through their brain," said Reynolds.

Organizational Skills

Children usually thrive on structure and organization. With effort, parents will find a balance that helps their children without overhelping them.

"Our older daughter was very organized and didn't need our guidance," said Ann Mastergeorge, "but our younger daughter was not. One of the things we did was get her a large desk calendar that helped her map out her entire weekly schedule: what is due that week, assignments, tests, everything. The large calendar is color-coded for assignments and tests. She has notebooks too for each class and file folders by subject for her work when it is finished and returned to us. We emphasize to her that being organized saves time in the long run."

You may already have discovered the value of checklists in your own life, making a simple to-do list and checking off items as you complete them. Just seeing what you can accomplish in a single day can be a motivating experience and a good habit. Checklists or graphic organizers work equally well for your child, helping to ensure that assignments are completed and turned in when due. Beginning in about the fourth grade, many students are required to keep a daily agenda to help them organize, track, and return their work. Make strong use of one.

"On Monday each week, we review my children's assignments," said parent Karen Mathison, "and I ask them what they need to do that week and in the next few weeks. I always encourage them to ask their teachers for information and for planning ideas. The Monday review helps my children see how to manage their assignments, especially big ones, together with their extracurricular activities, such as church. We put everything down in writing on a project-planning sheet with assignments on one side and a calendar on the back."

A benefit to detailed planning is that children know exactly what has to be done and when it is due. "One of the things I try to do as a parent is to emphasize my son's organizational skills," said researcher Hilda Borko, "especially given my son's tendency to procrastinate. I try to help him structure his time, especially his homework."

Children and adults alike underestimate the amount of time it takes to do just about everything. A general rule in our home is that to be done well every assignment will take twice the amount of time of our original estimate. Emphasize to your child that he or she needs to start out well ahead of time on all assignments, but especially on long-term projects.

Test Preparation

Students take several types of tests in school, primarily state tests and classroom tests. Although this is discussed in greater detail in Chapter Eight, states must test students in mathematics and English–language arts in grades three to eight and one high school grade. States will begin testing students in science in the 2007–08 school year, once in elementary, middle, and high school. Some states test more grades and subjects, but the preceding are the minimum required by the No Child Left Behind Act. Most students take college entrance exams in high school, including the SAT or ACT, and they may take an advanced placement exam if they are enrolled in an AP course. But students take far more classroom tests than any other type, and even though state tests seem to get the lion's share of attention in the newspapers, classroom assessments are plentiful: quizzes, end-of-chapter tests, end-of-quarter tests, end-of-semester tests, and sometimes district tests. In middle and high school, it is not unusual for students to take as many as three or four classroom tests or quizzes each week.

Regardless of the type of test, students may be anxious about at least some of them. Several education researchers shared with me their suggestions, based on their own experiences and research, for how parents might help their children prepare for tests.

Eva Baker, former chair of the National Research Council's Board on Testing and Assessment, emphasized that kids differ. "Anxious kids need to be guided to reduce their anxiety." She also pointed out that tests differ. Consequently, children should prepare for the specific type of test they are taking.

"I think the goal is to motivate but not freak children out, and to help kids see that their performance is not tied to parental love," added Baker. "The other big idea," said Baker, "rather than a gimmick—is to help kids understand that effort, not smarts, makes the difference."

"Doing well on tests ultimately means knowing the test content," says Joan Herman, codirector of CRESST and author of several books on evaluation and assessment. "Getting good at format and knowing the tricks of test taking only take you so far," says Herman, "if you don't know the relevant content and skills."

"If I were to advise parents," said Robert Mislevy, "I would say they should ask their kids, 'What are the big ideas in a topic, and how does that connect to what you already know?'"

To help her children prepare for their tests, Reenie Webb drew from William K. Estes, who conducted pioneering learning research in the 1950s and 1960s. Prior to Estes's research, the prevailing view was that learning was incremental; each practice or review of material produced a small improvement in learning or retention. But Estes theorized that as humans solve problems they become more effective at solving other similar problems, using what they have already learned. Webb used Estes's research to help her children study.

"In preparing for tests, I found that my kids would review everything endlessly, starting from scratch and then covering it multiple times. I emphasized to them that they didn't need to study what they already knew. Review your materials once and cross off what you know, then concentrate your remaining time on what you don't know." Webb says that applying Estes's research increased her children's study efficiency and learning.

Estes's results have implications beyond study skills, says Webb. They suggest, among other things, that the current American practice of recycling through the same or similar material year after year (especially in math but in other areas too) is wrongheaded. "Repeated exposure by itself will not help students learn fractions, for example," says Webb, whose research includes how students learn mathematics in small groups.

"One of the things that I encourage for my children," said Jody Priselac, "which is hard for kids, is to plan ahead. In studying for a test, for example, my kids, like most, would just read over material and think that they knew it. They would look at a math problem and think, 'That's easy.' I always encouraged them—in fact, we would do it together—to review specific questions, starting a few nights before a big test. In that way, my kids developed good study habits that serve them well even today."

"The basic idea is to have a strategy for studying," said parent Meredith Reynolds, "not necessarily that one strategy is any better than another." About two weeks out from final exams, Reynolds says that she reviewed the finals schedule with her children and the material they had covered during the semester. "Then I would have them estimate about how much time they needed to put into studying for the final," said Reynolds, "say ten hours for each final." They developed a study plan, backing out from the actual date of the final exam.

"On assessments and assignments," said Mislevy, "I sometimes referred to the game nature of teaching and learning. I told my daughters that they have to figure out what their teacher is looking for. What do you need to know, to do well? My older daughter says that her hardest college classes are the ones with just a mid-term and a final, because you go into the tests without knowing what to expect. Further, the stakes are very high when there are just a few tests each semester. So understanding and clarifying what a teacher expects is very important to doing well in every class," Mislevy added.

Here are some other tips for helping children perform well on tests.

Use the Inertia Effect to Your Advantage

The physical laws of inertia can also be applied to classroom tests, which means that the first test will probably be similar to the remainder of the tests that a teacher gives during the year. Use this to your child's advantage. For example, a teacher who starts out with end-of-unit multiple-choice tests is likely to follow the pattern. The teacher might throw in short answers or an essay test every now and then, but generally speaking there won't be much variation. Teachers are usually very clear about the content to be covered and have little if any desire to trick students, although a few teachers may give a harder test to see if children are ready to move on to a new unit or determine if students can apply what they have learned to a more difficult problem or assignment.

Create Your Own Tests

As mentioned earlier, school is still largely dependent on memory, especially spelling and vocabulary; consequently, some parents (my wife and I included) create simple tests to help our children. (Recall Exhibit 6.1 as an example of a parent-made test.) Others go further.

"We created sample tests for our children using released test questions from the National Assessment of Educational Progress," said researcher Jamal Abedi. "The assessments helped us understand our children's strengths and weaknesses," he added. NAEP is a national test in a number of subjects given to a sample of students to measure national progress.

In addition to released NAEP test questions, sample questions are available from the Third International Mathematics and Science Study (TIMSS) test and from state tests. Be cautious about drawing too many conclusions from these tests, however, unless you're a test researcher like Abedi. Released test questions are not complete tests and seldom permit accurate comparison to other student performances. They don't always cover every grade level either. Appendix F has a number of suggestions on where released test questions are available on the Internet.

Other Tips

Some students benefit by reviewing material just before they go into class to take a test, but generally the best idea is to start early.

"Sometimes studying in small groups at home would work for my children," says Meredith Reynolds, "if it was the right group of students. It does take more time and scheduling, though, compared to studying by yourself," adds Reynolds.

It's also important to review tests when they come home. "My wife and I reviewed our children's tests with them," said Mislevy, "and on a poorly designed test, I would ask them what they thought would have been a better way to evaluate their own knowledge. I think that this process, combined with my own research into improved assessments, helped my daughters to recognize differences in the quality of tests and helped them in school."

If a teacher makes available a test review prior to an end-of-quarter or end-of-semester exam, by all means encourage your child to attend.

College Entrance Exams

As mentioned in Chapter Four, the SAT was revised several years ago to make it a more accurate gauge of what students learn in school. Key changes included replacement of the analogies section with critical-reading passages, and addition of a new writing essay. The critical-reading passages include reading comprehension and sentence completion, making the SAT verbal section closer to what is assessed on a state test. The writing essay requires students to develop and support a specific point of view that is based on a writing question, again similar to what is often examined on a state writing assessment.

The SAT changes were prompted by Richard Atkinson, who was then the president of the University of California and also a member of the National Research Council's Board on Testing and Assessment (BOTA). Atkinson and others felt the SAT was not linked to state standards or closely tied to university curricula. The possibility that the massive University of California system might drop the SAT as part of its admissions process helped to produce the changes, with the idea that all college entrance exams more accurately reflect state education standards. The ACT, another major college entrance exam used by many universities, was already considered to be a relatively good measure of the content taught in schools and better tied to college curricula than the SAT. The ACT assesses high school students' general educational skills and their ability to complete college-level work. Consisting of 215 multiple-choice questions, the ACT assesses student ability in English–language arts, mathematics, reading, and science.

Because the SAT or ACT is used by many U.S. universities as part of their admissions process, changes to either test are significant, especially as they influence test-preparation courses or programs. These programs come in a variety of methods, lengths, and costs. They may be a regular instructional program or Web-based. Many high schools either offer their own SAT or ACT test preparation program or free student access to a Web-based program. An unresolved debate in the education research field has been over (1) whether or not such test preparation courses actually produce higher SAT or ACT scores and (2) the relationship between the scores and college success. Parents and students seem to care little about the research. As long as tests are used to make college entrance decisions, parents and students will look for tools that may increase their child's college entrance test scores. I encourage parents to talk to their high school counselors about test preparation programs available at no cost or low cost. Be skeptical of promises or claims of large SAT or ACT score increases, especially through a short-term training system. If your child has always struggled with math, a Web-based two-hour test preparation program is unlikely to help in making significant improvement. The best way to prepare your children for college entrance exams is to start today, helping them master the skills in their current educational program.

Tutors

Regardless of how much effort children and parents put into learning, there may be times when effort alone isn't enough. A child's grades or test scores may be slipping, or a child doesn't progress at the same rate as other students over an extended period. If talking to the teacher doesn't result in a strategy that leads to improvement, or if your child frequently struggles on homework assignments, it may be time to consider a tutor. How children do on homework is a good way to know if a child needs extra help, because homework is something you can personally observe.

Sometimes parents hesitate to get a tutor, thinking their child is just going through a phase. Other parents blame a teacher or the school for their child's lack of progress. But it may be that their child just needs extra help, another type of instruction, instruction with just a few students, or one-on-one assistance. To use a medical metaphor, if your child had an illness that couldn't be remedied by your general practitioner you would ask for referral to a specialist. In many ways, hiring a one-on-one tutor or enrolling in a small-group tutoring program is the same as seeing a specialist.

"My daughter reached the point where she knew how she was doing in school," said parent Kathy Hernandez. "She felt that she wasn't doing as well as she could in math, so when she asked for a tutor, we found her one." Hernandez also noticed that her daughter wasn't able to do some problems she felt she should be able to do. Like others her age, she doesn't accept help from her parents as well as she does from a tutor.

Research indicates that tutors frequently help children improve. In some countries, such as Japan, having your child attend a special after-school tutor class is a widely recognized practice. Estimates are that more than 50 percent of Japanese students attend what are known as *juku* classes to help them in a variety of subjects. In this country, state budgets for the foreseeable future are likely to keep the student-to-teacher classroom ratio high, further pushing the need for students to seek outside help.

There may be other reasons for getting a tutor. Friction might arise between a parent and child, or in some cases the content could be beyond a parent's knowledge. Another time to consider a tutor is if you don't have the necessary time to make sure homework is completed and done well. If both parents work, doing homework late at night can be difficult. If hiring a tutor results in improvement, then it is a worthwhile investment.

Math tutor Laurie Candelora shared some signs for when a tutor might be needed:

- *Academic*—not understanding assignments. Children frequently comment that they "can't do this." Other symptoms are dropping scores on classroom tests, especially when low results occur consistently from one test to another, and declining grades.
- *Emotional*—changes in emotional state. For example, a child might start having a meltdown from struggling with homework. Attitude toward school in general changes from positive to negative. Self-esteem begins a long-term downward spiral, or the child loses confidence in abilities that used to be strengths.
- *Social*—a child becoming withdrawn. He may be spending more time alone in his room, or more time talking to friends on the phone.
- *Self-diagnosis*—asking for a tutor. Sometimes a child will recognize that she is struggling and request that you get her a tutor. She wants to have an easier time of it and may not feel comfortable asking for help in the classroom.

"Parents should recognize the difference between a short-term and a long-term learning need," says Candelora. A short-term need could be difficulty in understanding a particular concept or method. Once the child breaks through the barrier, she is back to her usual level of performance. Short-term needs can frequently be addressed through extra help from a teacher or a few visits to a tutor.

"However, if a child struggles consistently with a specific topic," Candelora adds, he may need a long-term tutor. In many cases, a long-term need stems from a child's lack of an adequate foundation or understanding in a subject and often results in lack of confidence and avoidance of the subject.

Convincing a child that a tutor might be helpful can be a challenge. Here is how Denise (previously met in Chapters Two and Three) successfully resolved the issue:

> How you feel about yourself and your abilities is as critical to success as anything in life. My daughter tends to be a "glass half empty" per-

> son. I told her I wanted to get her a little extra help to make sure she was starting junior high out on the right foot. She fought me. She told me she was not stupid, that only dumb people needed extra help. Instead of building her confidence, I feared that perhaps I was destroying it. Nothing I said could dissuade her from that belief, but I kept putting the idea into her head that it may be just what she needed to give her confidence in attacking math problems or in reading comprehension. One day, riding home from school in our carpool, a bright young lady happened to mention that she went to a tutor last year for math and that it really helped her. That did the trick. My daughter was now open to the idea of getting extra help. We started a few weeks ago, and she now loves going to these sessions.

It may be helpful to have a general tutoring session covering one subject, but your child is likely to benefit more if he has a focused need, which he or you clearly communicate to the tutor. Is he having problems with math factors? remembering a sequence of key historical dates? repeatedly failing on spelling tests? Before the tutoring session, encourage your child to identify a specific problem area or need first so the tutor doesn't just review general skills and material that your child may already know. Focus on the greatest need, the big hurdle that allows your child to perform well on an upcoming test and move on to the next challenge. Make sure your child always arrives at a tutoring session prepared and has finished any tutoring homework from the last session.

Your child's school may offer tutoring services or have a list of high school students who tutor at a nominal cost. Other parents are an excellent source of information about tutors, especially if you need a tutor in a specific topic or if your child has a learning disability. Sometimes it takes a bit of experimentation on your part to find the right match.

Candelora suggested a number of criteria to look for in a good tutor:

- *Deep content knowledge in the subject.* A tutor should not only know the content area extremely well but should have the big picture for other grades. What should your child already know, and what will he need to know next year, and the year after that? A good tutor will quickly analyze if your child's foundation needs to be reinforced and how to get there.

- *Knowledge of the school district curriculum.* Although state content standards help to make curriculum somewhat uniform, there is still great difference among school districts. A tutor who knows your district's curriculum may help your child learn your specific district or school requirements.
- *Communication.* How well does a particular tutor work with your child? Do you and your child have a favorable impression of the tutor? Does your child come away from a tutoring session with a positive attitude? Does the tutor sincerely care about your child? Does she successfully communicate your child's progress to you?
- *Results.* By the end of a full month, your child should be showing some signs of progress. By this time, she should have had four tutoring sessions, completed a full unit of work, and probably taken at least one classroom test if not two. You should observe positive changes in both confidence and attitude as well as improvement in test results.

Although student tutors may not have the instructional background or deep content expertise of an adult tutor, they may be a good alternative. My daughter's student tutor had the same math teacher a few years ago. Consequently, the student tutor knows the teacher's expectations extremely well and even designs practice tests according to the areas where she thinks my daughter needs extra help.

Avoid getting a tutor for the wrong reasons. A few kids may want a tutor because their friends have one, or they want to avoid putting forth the necessary effort in school, warns Candelora. "One student told me that because he knew he would be getting help from me, he did his Spanish assignment during his geometry lesson," said Candelora. "Obviously he wasn't paying attention in his geometry class."

Another problem, she says, is that some parents allow their child's schedule to become so full that there isn't time at home to do the work he should be doing. Going to a tutor helps him stay up with the work, but it may have a long-term negative consequence of making him tutor-dependent.

Like most aspects of education, no one size fits all, but if your child displays the signs of needing a tutor then talk to the teacher and to other parents. Meet with tutors before making a long-term commitment.

Other At-Home Learning Strategies

Many of the parents I interviewed for this book use some type of supplemental learning materials to help their child in school. In most cases, the purpose is to strengthen a weakness in a specific topic. Websites such as Ask Dr. Math (http://mathforum.org/dr.math) may be helpful. "Many publishing companies have online help available tied to a specific textbook," said Laurie Candelora.

Some parents use supplemental materials to prevent their children from falling into what is often called the summer learning gap. Others, like Suzanne Lane from the University of Pittsburgh, want their children to see various approaches to learning:

> I have used some of my involvement in research to help our daughter at home. For example, Project QUASAR focused on improving middle school students' mathematics problem-solving and reasoning skills by requiring students to solve problems in more than one way and explain how they arrived at their answer. Our research found that by explaining their answers, students would often reveal misunderstandings, even when they had correct answers. When solving a math or science problem at home, we ask our daughter to explain how she arrived at the answer or to explain her answer based on the context of the problem. This has enabled her and us to better understand what she knows and doesn't know. I think that my daughter has improved her reasoning abilities by doing these types of assessments.
>
> I have also used mathematics and reading tasks from some research and curriculum programs that I am aware of from my work

> such as the Balanced Assessment math tasks. The math tasks from Balanced Assessment reflect quality content and require students to show their solution processes and explain their answers. Tests should have high content quality, measure student learning accurately, and require students to think and reason about the content—key purposes of the Balanced Assessment tasks [see Appendix F for a link to the Balanced Assessment Website].

When children get older, they naturally want greater independence. As Hilda Borko described it, a parent's role in the learning process changes.

> As a researcher and parent, it's hard to share what you know about teaching and learning with your child in a way so that you aren't imposing it. I ask my teenage son, for example, if he wants me to review some of his work and give him feedback, but I don't insist on it. Sometimes he accepts and sometimes he doesn't. As with many adolescents at this age, my son wants to control his life. I've tried to help him identify areas of weakness, such as organizational skills or procrastination, then help him make improvements by structuring his time on homework and major assignments. I have also gone over the state test results with him so that he understands how the scoring works. What is a percentile? How are test scores used and why they are important? My advice to parents is to continue to offer help, even if it is often rejected.

Music and Art

In recent years, there has been an attempt to link music education and music listening to student achievement. The most well-known example was a study conducted by the University of California, Irvine, which showed that college students who listened to Mozart increased performance on a spatial reasoning test (although the increase lasted fifteen minutes or less). Nevertheless, these results were enough to encourage the governor of Georgia to freely distribute compact discs of classical music to parents of every child born in the state. The research evidence, however, remains thin—especially in younger children, where any increase, as with college students, is short-lived. Interestingly, monkeys who listened to Mozart while taking a memory test actually performed worse than a control group not doing so.

CRESST evaluations of several music programs, including the Los Angeles Music Center and the Artful Learning program of the Grammy Foundation's Leonard Bernstein Institute, offer some evidence that music education benefits other subjects beyond music. Further, learning a musical instrument at a young age clearly increases thinking activity (compared to, say, watching television), so the case for music and arts education in school remains respectable. But the current push to increase achievement in more traditional topics of reading, writing, science, and mathematics is likely to dominate state curriculums and district resources for some time to come. The saying that what gets tested gets taught suggests that music and the arts are likely to remain back-burner programs for schools which will increasingly be pressured to meet the math, science, and language arts rigors of No Child Left Behind.

Fortunately, outstanding music and art programs survive, in many cases thanks to dedicated teachers and parents. Parent Susan Pascale, who studied at the Mannes College of Music in New York City, moved to South Pasadena, California, in 2001, only to find that her child's school didn't have an elementary orchestra. So she created one (Glazier, 2005). Pascale became the South Pasadena Middle School's orchestra director, and under her direction the orchestra went on to play at Carnegie Hall. Parents hold a key role in developing not only their own child's music and artistic abilities but support for school programs that have in many cases been cut back owing to tight budgets. Parent Andrea Terry explained how she encouraged her children to develop their artistic abilities in and outside of school:

> When my girls were very little, Lindsay Epstein, the art consultant for Palm Crest Elementary School, trained me to be an art docent, helping in the classroom. Lindsay told me not to go around the room

telling every kid that their work was "good" or "great." These types of nondescript comments tell a kid: "My work is like everyone else's. I'm mediocre." They don't really believe you. You are just saying that to all the kids. Then, she gave examples of the encouragement I should give, like "I love how you used purple in the sky . . . it really draws my eyes to your picture and it reminds me of many beautiful sunsets."

Lindsay said that it is also important to point out their progress: "I can see that you are getting much better at drawing faces. I like how you have drawn these eyes. They look real."

Then, when you add "good job" it means something. It's genuine. They will draw more and better because the feedback is constructive. Practicing her advice at home, not just at school, really helped me to develop my children's creative abilities.

Technology

The January 2006 launch of NASA's Pluto Mission was an important reminder of the new knowledge that is possible thorough technology. Swinging around Jupiter for a gravity assist, the *New Horizons* Pluto spacecraft is speeding along at thirty-six thousand miles per hour. It will travel three billion miles before it reaches Pluto and its moon Charon in the summer of 2015. "Right now, what we know about Pluto could be written on the back of a postage stamp," said Colleen Hartman, deputy associate administrator for NASA's Science Mission Directorate. "After this mission, we'll be able to fill textbooks with new information," she added.

Technology not only advances our knowledge but also improves our lives, with benefits ranging from faster computers to robotic surgery. A comprehensive study from the NCES shows that students with strong technology skills reach higher achievement in mathematics, reading, and writing (Hedges, Konstantopoulos, and Thoreson, 2003). As with most aspects of learning, parents play a key role in supporting their children's technology abilities. Enhancing your child's enthusiasm for technology serves her well throughout her education.

The frequently dropping prices of computers in recent years and the competition for low-cost home Internet access have greatly increased the opportunities for virtually every parent to use technology to augment a child's learning at home. In addition to supporting specific classroom assignments, the Internet gives parents and children access to online school information, including assignments, grades, and supplemental classroom assignment information. At the same time, it permits ready communication among parents, teachers, and students. Parents may also find that learning software is helpful. They should find technology resources specific to their children's needs. "My son has a very strong interest in computers," said Eckhardt Klieme, "and we have supported that at home, especially in making sure he has books on programming that reinforces leaning."

Many universities offer a summer camp program for K-12 children, frequently with courses to enhance children's technology fluency. Your school, district, community college, or community center may have useful summer or after-school technology programs. A growing number of universities offer online technology training programs or self-assessment of technology skills. Although there are fees associated with some of these, and they are of varying quality, they are worth your time to investigate.

Help Your Special Needs Child Get Smart!

The tips in this chapter are equally applicable to students with special needs. Appendix A, Get Smart! Strategies for Students with Special Needs, presents extra tips on helping a child with learning disabilities in school.

Help Your Child Be Great in One Thing He or She Loves

When my daughter was struggling with reading in fourth grade, teacher Shannon Burke suggested that my wife and I try to help her become good at one thing in which she had a strong interest.

Excelling in one area often increases a child's confidence in other subjects as well, said Burke. At a minimum, it improves the child's self-esteem, which contributes to learning. For some children, this one thing might be music; for others it might be writing, acting, or volleyball. Find an activity that your child is passionate about and help her become very good at doing that one thing.

For Mrs. Burke's own daughter, it was horses. Our daughter, Markie, had a strong interest in horses as well. We took her to a Saturday school program where young girls learn how to take care of horses and have an opportunity to ride them. For Markie it was very motivating, and she has taught me more about horses than I ever knew before. On vacations, we always make sure that she has an opportunity to ride a horse; this year she participated in a summer program involving horses. Her eighth grade Civil War research project contained a major section on the role that horses played during the Civil War.

"I try to involve my kids in music and sports," said Diane Steinberg, "so that they can develop specialized skills that many of their peers don't have. My older son has been doing karate since he was five years old and should earn his black belt by age twelve. Being good at something athletic really improves his self-esteem. Participation in competitive gymnastics for my youngest son has given him a skill he likes and excels in, which has increased his self-confidence."

"Sports are helpful to children because it's usually the first time that a child wears a uniform and sees himself or herself as part of something outside of the family," said Meredith Reynolds, whose three children were all active in sports at an early age. Reynolds said other benefits are that children learn how to compromise their wants and needs for others, learn how to give up their free time for something greater than just themselves, and discover that there are choices in life they can make.

"My kids all made lifelong friends from the sport programs that they were involved in," concluded Reynolds.

8

MEASURE YOUR CHILD'S SUCCESS

> We are a nation obsessed with evaluating our children, with calibrating their exact distance from some ideal benchmark. In the name of excellence we test and measure them . . . and we rejoice or despair over the results. The sad thing is that though we strain to see, we miss so much. . . . Those harshly affected . . . possess some of our greatest unperceived riches.
>
> —*Mike Rose*

Children are evaluated from the moment they set foot onto school property. Teachers, administrators, and other students observe our children's language, actions, and learning. In many cases they quickly form an opinion, which may become everlasting. By the end of kindergarten, certainly by the first and second grade, social and academic information come together in what can be an enormous decision. As one parent of a second grade boy found out, the news is not always pleasant.

> I recently had a parent conference with my child's teacher. At the conference, now six weeks into the school year, I was told that my son might be retained. I was told he can be retained without my consent. All of his work this entire year is smiles, stars, 80 percent to 90 percent, yet the teacher insists that he is not performing as well as the other children. She also stated that he is in the lowest reading group. Why am I being told this now? Is there anything parents

> can do? Please let me know. I am very concerned and troubled by this trend in education.

As this mom realized, the consequences for not measuring up to school expectations can be enormous. With student achievement a hotly debated topic in virtually every state and national election, the push to increase test scores will continue. Parents need accurate information to help monitor their child's progress and to know what they can do to help. Test scores are one part of the process of knowing how your child is doing in school, but they are not the only factor. This chapter also covers how to evaluate your child's progress on the basis of assignments and grades, teacher conferences, informal strategies, and report cards.

Understanding Test Scores

Norm-referenced tests. Criterion-referenced tests. Performance assessments. Standards-based reporting. Achievement levels. Percentile ranks. Age-equivalent scores. Test lingo can drive a parent crazy. Appendix E is an Assessment Glossary that can help you understand basic assessment terms.

Complicating matters is that state educational tests are changing all the time. Many changes are driven by federal or state policymakers who pass legislation requiring more tests in the hope of higher achievement. Other changes are driven by new tests that may in fact do a better job of measuring state standards than a current test. In some cases cost may be a factor, although as Robert Linn says, tests are relatively inexpensive compared to such other educational costs as implementing a new program or curriculum.

Though many state tests have similarities, most differ enough that the best way to understand them is to read the information that comes with your child's scores. Treat it as you would medical information on a drug prescription for your child. Responsible test publishers want their tests to be used correctly and make a great effort to help parents understand their child's scores. They usually include cautions about accuracy and test use. The media are also helping the public better understand test scores. Professional organizations including the Education Writers Association and The Hechinger Institute offer workshops to help reporters better communicate test results to the public.

Here are some specific points to know about tests.

Tests Can Be Used Inappropriately

Most uses of state and classroom tests are appropriate, but a few schools and groups misuse tests. One of the most prevalent misuses is the kindergarten admissions exam. Many private schools, and even a few public schools, use achievement or aptitude admissions tests because they cannot accommodate all the children who apply. Admissions tests screen out children and help promote the school as a selective institution. A test is simple to administer, cheap, and the results quickly available. Most parents accept the test results as an objective measure of their child's abilities, making the exclusion appear justified. The negative effect is that a disproportionate number of African American and Latino and Latina children (especially boys) are excluded from selective kindergarten or other grades. Tests at a very young age are less accurate and more influenced by demographic or behavioral factors than by a child's ability to learn. Additionally, such tests are seldom (if ever) developed with the intended goal of preventing school entry. Despite the fact that national standards warn against the use of a single test for this type of purpose, many selective schools continue this practice.

You are unlikely to have much recourse if your child is excluded from a school for not making the cut score on an admissions test. If your child was close, you could ask for a retest, arguing some of the points made in this chapter. If your child performed well on other criteria, you might argue that overall performance should be the determining factor, not test performance. But if the only way your child will be admitted to a school (or to, say, a gifted program) is by excluding another child, then my advice is usually to accept the decision. You and your child made the best effort and there may well be other schools or programs that will be better for your child.

Tests Are Not Perfect

Research by David Rogosa at Stanford University has shown that a student may have only a 30 to 50 percent chance of scoring within five points on the same test if taken a second time. A score change of even as many as ten points or more may be completely attributable to the test, not the student. Consequently, if high-stakes decisions are to be made, such as high school graduation, use of other criteria in addition to a single test score is encouraged. Selective universities, for example, base their admissions decisions on many student factors, among them the rigor of the courses a student takes in high school, a student's grade point average, SAT or ACT scores, and sometimes a personal essay describing a child's unique skills or challenges.

"Normative comparisons are irrelevant," says Reenie Webb, "and can be very inaccurate." Webb, who teaches a university course in testing, said of her own daughters: "We work hard to make it easier for our kids to not make comparisons. Unfortunately, schools are really about comparisons, especially once you enter middle school. We see it especially with our twin girls. Teachers and even people in the grocery line are always comparing my girls to each other. We have tried to focus on individuation. My husband and I help each of our children realize that they are unique and important people."

Understand the Basic State Test Reports

Tests of large numbers of students can be traced back to the Boston Survey of 1845, which was perhaps the first use of printed tests for large-scale assessment of student achievement in the United States (Worthen and Sanders, 1987).

The Elementary and Secondary Education Act (ESEA) of 1965 was the true impetus for statewide tests. Under the 1965 ESEA, of which No Child Left Behind (NCLB) is the most recent version, the federal government requires an objective measurement of whether or not federal funding (often called Title I) is improving the achievement of children living in poverty. For some states, it became easier to simply test all students, not just those receiving Title I federal funds. Many states too wanted to know how well their educational programs were working.

In general, achievement did not substantially improve despite the additional Title I funding and the increase in testing. Amid growing concern with the quality of American education, the ESEA of 1994, the Improving America's Schools Act, mandated statewide standards and tests for the first time. In the years that followed, a number of states were slow to implement the required standards and tests, leading to the No Child Left Behind Act, which set a firm deadline of 2005–06 for states to test statewide or forfeit substantial federal funds. Virtually all states are on track to comply with at least the standards and assessment provisions of No Child Left Behind, which, as mentioned earlier, requires states to test in both math and English–language arts in grades three to eight and once in high school.

Schools must make adequate yearly progress (AYP) or risk losing some of their Title I funds, which may make up a critical part of a school's budget. Consequently, state test performance is extremely important to schools and school districts. Schools that fail to make adequate yearly progress for two consecutive years are classified as needing improvement. If they continue to fail to improve, they face additional sanctions. In severe cases, they may be forced to close down.

State test reports usually come in one of two forms. A national norm-referenced test, such as the Stanford Achievement Test, Iowa Tests of Basic Skills, California Achievement Test, or Comprehensive Test of Basic Skills, reports student scores as a percentile rank. Percentile ranks range from 1 to 99, with a midpoint of 50. The midpoint is set so that 50 percent of the original group of students who took the test—that is, the norm group—score above the midpoint and the other 50 percent score below it. The attractiveness of percentile ranks is that they are easy for parents to understand.

Standards-based reporting is the second major way in which state test results may be reported. For example, the Massachusetts Comprehensive Assessment System uses "achievement levels" of four broad performance categories: warning or failing, needs improvement, proficient, and advanced. California uses five categories: far below basic, below basic, basic, proficient, and advanced. Like an A-F grading system, achievement levels give parents a broad measure of how their child is performing in school.

Performance or achievement levels are set with at least a fair amount of human judgment, and research by CRESST and other organizations indicate that the levels are prone to wide variation. Despite this shortcoming, they are the predominant state reporting method today.

Most parents I know like to see their children performing at the 70th percentile rank or higher on national norm-referenced tests, or at the proficient or advanced achievement level in every subject of a state standards-based test. Obviously, a norm-referenced test, which by its design requires that half of all children perform below the 50th percentile, entails not all students performing above the midpoint. Similarly, states sometimes set advanced performance levels on standards-based tests extremely high, meaning that a performance of "basic" may not necessarily be a poor performance. The whole process can be very confusing. Here is my own personal approach to using test scores for my children.

On norm-referenced tests, my hope is that my children will be in the upper range, the 50th–99th percentile, although I know that by design not every child can be above the midpoint on a norm-referenced test. (California uses the CAT/6 test.) I compare my children's scores to performance across our school district and look for small or modest individual increases from one year to the next. A small drop of a few percentile points from last year to this year doesn't bother me, as I know that student performance varies from one year to the next. I also keep in mind that students take a new test each year, developed in nearly all cases by a new group of people and measuring new content. I would be concerned with more than a drop of 10 percentile points, but other than that I realize no single test can perfectly measure my child's achievement.

On standards-based tests, I like to see my children at the proficient or advanced level. (Our state test is called the California Standards Test and has quite rigorous achievement levels.) I would be concerned if my son or daughter dropped from a higher category into a lower category from one year to the next. I know, however, that a student near the lower part of a category in one year—say, proficient—might only need to miss one or two test questions next year to drop to the top of the basic category. My child's true performance may not have changed at all. I also know that the tests from one year to the next year differ. Because my children have moved up a grade, they take a different test, so the tests they might take in eighth grade are not perfectly comparable to the tests in ninth grade. In my opinion, a drop of two full categories—say, from proficient to below basic, is substantial enough to warrant a teacher discussion. Again, I look for improvement over several years, or at a minimum for my children to be proficient or above.

Unfortunately, like most parents, by the time I receive my children's scores in the late summer they are about to enter the next grade. Nevertheless, if I see a substantial drop in their scores compared to the previous year, I discuss this with their incoming teachers and monitor my children's progress during the year, especially after they are tested the next year.

I encourage parents to ask themselves if state test scores support their child's performance on graded tests and assignments. Do the scores reflect teacher observations, grades, and your own knowledge of your child's abilities? A child with special needs or an English language learner will likely have lower performance, on average, than other children. The primary use of state test scores on the part of parents, in my opinion, is to develop an overall picture of a child's achievement. The more evidence one has, the more detailed and accurate the picture.

During the year, my wife and I closely review our son's and daughter's classroom test results. If we see a long-term weakness in a particular topic, we talk to their teachers. In sixth grade, for example, I e-mailed my daughter's language arts teacher because a classroom test—supported by our own observations—showed that she didn't fully understand some grammar concepts. The next day, the teacher reviewed the concepts with her, and we reinforced her learning at home.

Waiting for too many signs that a child needs help may allow him to fall behind. If an existing instructional strategy doesn't work, then a new strategy may be helpful. Oftentimes giving students more of the same instruction that didn't work in the first place doesn't lead to improvement.

According to test researcher Robert Mislevy, "We looked at the state tests, but they usually just confirmed what we already knew from working with our daughters at home or what their teacher had told us. For some parents, test scores are very important, especially if they see a big divergence in grades and state test scores."

Why We Don't We Have a Single National Test

A recurring question that I receive from reporters and parents is, Why does each state have its own test? Wouldn't it be less expensive and better educationally to have a single national test, similar to many countries? The answer is rooted in the U.S. Constitution. You may recall that rights not covered in our Constitution or Bill of Rights are rights retained by states. The word *education* does not appear in the Constitution or the Bill of Rights; consequently, education is a state right. Viewing a national test as an intrusion of federal government, states have strongly opposed a national test for many years. George Bush, Sr., in the early 1990s and Bill Clinton in the mid-1990s tried unsuccessfully to convince Congress to pass a national test.

A national test would result in a national curriculum, as states, schools, and districts would quickly align their instruction to a national test. A national test could produce a narrower curriculum with fewer topics covered. But the biggest factor working against a national test, in my opinion, remains the desire on the part of states to retain control of their own educational programs—and tests. It seems unlikely, though not impossible, that Congress will pass legislation creating a national test in the future. NCLB has reinforced the well-known weaknesses of a system that uses fifty state tests.

Evaluating Performance on Assignments and Grades

Many researchers and parents have at least one dismaying story about tests, assignments, or grades. Harvard researcher Daniel Koretz recalled a teacher who actually deducted points from his daughter's assignment because the staple was placed horizontally instead of vertically. Jamal Abedi described the time when his son received zero points out of one hundred on a sociology assignment in which he had closely followed all directions. One parent said that he could not understand how his son, who had received A's in every math class before sixth grade, was given B's by a math teacher throughout his sixth grade year. His son went on to score at the 99th percentile rank on the sixth grade CAT/6 test, the highest possible score.

"I think to some extent that [classroom] grading can be arbitrary," says Reenie Webb. "In some cases, points are deducted based on something that is trivial. Alternately, even if my kids get an A on an assignment, it doesn't mean that they really understand the material."

Every teacher is different, and as a result no evaluation system is perfect, said veteran teacher Lani Moore.

A major contributing factor to the issues over classroom grades mentioned by Webb is the quality of many classroom assignments and tests. Lindsay Clare Matsumura and others at CRESST (2000) have examined the quality of classroom assignments in their research and found that many assignments are of poor quality, and that teachers give little feedback (in some cases, none) to students on their mistakes or how to improve their performance the next time. Many classroom tests are heavily dependent on memory, with far less emphasis on problem solving or application of knowledge.

Most classroom tests, assignments, and grading practices have not substantially changed from those we encountered in school. An A given to a student who answers 93 percent or above is still based on no factor other than a long tradition of doing so. The 93 percent cut score does not take into account the difficulty of the test or how well the teacher has taught the course. In most cases, the grading practice can be justified because students take numerous tests during the semester, and other factors such as homework and assignments are included in the final grade. Further, many teachers will make adjustments when they see that students overall performed less well than expected, especially on a new classroom test. Therefore, classroom test accuracy is less critical than accuracy on a state exit exam, where failure may result in a student not receiving a high school diploma.

In the early 1990s many schools, districts, and states started to use new types of assessments, often called performance assessments but also referred to as authentic or alternative assessments. Performance assessments include portfolios (a collection of student work), journals, multistep problem-solving questions, extended essays, and almost anything that is not a traditional assessment (that is, multiple-choice, true-false, fill in the blank, or any type of select-a-response question). Performance assessments arose because of a general concern that traditional tests (usually multiple-choice) measure only a limited range of skills, mostly memorization of facts or the use of basic formulas. Performance assessments were designed to measure application of knowledge and skills to real-world problems. Another impetus for performance assessments was that student performance was usually quite stagnant on most state tests, in addition to performance on the National Assessment of Educational Progress. The hope was that performance assessments would not just measure learning but improve achievement by requiring students to use higher-order thinking skills.

Knowing that teachers teach what is tested, many educators and policymakers were quick to develop and use performance assessments in the 1990s. Some states dropped their existing state multiple-choice tests and created entirely new state tests using performance assessments. However, research (a substantial amount of it conducted at the center where I work) showed that performance assessments were expensive to accurately score on a large-scale basis and that students had to take quite a few performance assessments to produce a dependable score. It wasn't long before most states dropped performance assessments as a state assessment, but they remain relatively popular for classroom assessment, especially in elementary school. Your child's teacher, for example, may ask her to keep her math or language arts assignments in a portfolio, occasionally grading the portfolio as a whole, or asking your child to select her best work and put it into a "best-work portfolio," which may then be graded. Journals also remain popular because they support a child's writing at school and at home, but they may or may not be scored. Other types of classroom performance assessment include exhibitions, presentations, and performance assignments, this last of which may include multistep problems and essays. The CRESST Website has a number of language arts performance assignments developed as part of a Los Angeles Unified School District project (see www.CRESST.org).

Most teachers are quite conscientious about their assignments, tests, and grading practices. They often allow students with special needs, for example, to complete fewer parts of an assignment or retake a test. As with all educational issues, talking to your child's teacher is the best way to help your child when questions arise.

Teacher Conferences

Research by Lorrie Shepard and others at the University of Colorado has shown that many parents value teacher feedback on student performance more than information from norm-referenced tests. Formal teacher feedback is usually presented during a parent-teacher conference, but it may occur at specific meetings during the school year. Here are a few strategies on using a parent-teacher conference to evaluate your child's progress:

- Interact with your child's teacher well ahead of time. A teacher conference should be primarily an update on your child's progress, because you and the teacher have talked frequently and built up a trusted relationship.
- Get input from your child before the meeting, and if the school and teacher permit it, include your child in the conference. If your child is not included in the conference, talk to him before the conference about his own perceptions of his academic strengths and weaknesses. There is often a high correlation between your child's self-perception and that of his teacher. Former Principal Donna Elder encourages parents to talk with their child after the conference as well.
- Write down specific questions you have for your child's teacher and send them ahead of time. You focus your own thoughts, give the teacher time to answer your questions, and are more likely to have your questions answered. Finally, you convey to the teacher the value you place on this meeting.
- Ask about your child's attitude toward school. As discussed in Chapter Three, children with a positive attitude toward school usually perform better and have stronger social skills.
- Make a plan. Before you leave the meeting, have a follow-up plan to address any weaknesses or problems. Make sure that you, the teacher, and your child follow up on any commitments made.
- Stay in touch. Keep in contact with the teacher and call another meeting if necessary to reevaluate your child's progress.

"Our middle school doesn't have regular parent conferences," said Ann Mastergeorge, "but we meet with one of her teachers every year." Quarterly progress reports are helpful, as is getting back just about every assignment and test, plus report cards and state test scores. Mastergeorge reviews her daughter's textbooks and assignments and receives informal feedback from her daughter's teachers regularly.

Informal Strategies to Obtain Feedback

E-mail between parents and teachers has become an effective supplement to the telephone for communicating informally about a child's progress, especially because e-mail can be transmitted at any time. It is usually fine for short questions and answers, but longer discussion is usually done best in person or on the phone.

Spending time at school gives you better access to teachers and staff. If you can help as a classroom volunteer, you establish yourself not only as a willing partner in your own child's education but also as a contributor to the learning of other children. It gives you the added benefit of observing your child's performance in comparison to other children. Don't turn volunteer work into a conference about your child, however; they are two distinct roles.

Use a Student Report Card to Identify Overall Progress

Driven by a perceived need to furnish parents with more comprehensive information about their child's strengths and weaknesses, many schools and districts have adopted new standards-based student report cards (Exhibit 8.1). It usually reports how well your child has reached the state content standards in various subjects, reflecting the desire to align report cards with state and district standards. Though usually prevalent more at elementary schools, standards-based report cards may also be found in some middle and high schools; high schools generally maintain the traditional A–F format owing to college entrance requirements.

Newer formats, however, may provide so much information that they confuse parents. Terms such as *emerging*, *progressing*, or *exceeds the standard* may be unclear compared to an A, B, or C. The new report cards are often designed with the goal that students will

Exhibit 8.1. Standards-Based Student Report Card, Third Grade Language Arts Section, La Cañada Unified School District

THIRD GRADE PROGRESS REPORT

Student: ____________________

Explanation of Markings (for details see reverse side)

4 Achieving district grade level exit standards with excellence
3 Achieving district grade level exit standards
2 Approaching district grade level exit standards
1 Not achieving district grade level exit standards
NA Not assessed this reporting period; Not applicable
✔ Indicates an area of curriculum focus for science and social science
(+) Plus indicates an area of strength
(-) Minus indicates an area of difficulty
( ) Blank indicates adequate skills reflected by grade

	2nd	3rd	4th
CITIZENSHIP			
Exhibits self-control			
Arrives in class on time			
Respects the rights and property of others			
Shows kindness and consideration			
Follows classroom rules			
Follows school, safety and playground rules			
Listens without interrupting			
WORK HABITS			
Transitions well from one activity to another			
Takes pride in quality of work			
Displays good organizational skills			
Works independently			
Follows directions			
Makes effective use of class time			
Completes assignments in a timely manner			
Returns homework on time			
Works well with adults			
Works well with peers			

Detailed Explanation of Markings

4 Achieving district grade level exit standards with excellence
Student consistently meets and frequently achieves with excellence the district standards. The student grasps, applies and extends key concepts, processes and skills for the district grade level standards. The student's work is comparable to the student models and district rubrics that are labeled advanced.

3 Achieving district grade level exit standards
Student meets the district standards. The student demonstrates proficiency in the vast majority of district grade level standards. The student, with limited errors, grasps and applies the key concepts, processes and skills for the district grade level standards. The student's work is comparable to the student models and district rubrics that are labeled proficient.

2 Approaching district grade level exit standards
The student is beginning to meet and occasionally does meet the district grade level standards. The student is beginning to grasp and apply the key concepts, processes and skills for the district grade level standards. The student's work may frequently contain errors. The student's work is comparable to the student models and district rubrics that are labeled approaching.

1 Not achieving district grade level exit standards
The student is not meeting the district grade level standards. The student is working below grade level. The student's work is comparable to the student models and district rubrics that are labeled below grade level.

Language Arts Standards

Reading: Word Analysis, Fluency and Systematic Vocabulary Development

LANGUAGE ARTS

Effort:			
Reading Grade:			
Decoding/word analysis			
Fluency/expression			
Comprehension			
Literary response			
Reads independently			
Writing Grade			
Organization and focus			
Clear and coherent			
Developed ideas			
Descriptive vocabulary			
Punctuation and capitalization			
Proofreading, editing and revising			
Grammar			
Paragraphing			
Neatness and legibility			
Penmanship-formation of letters and words			
Spelling Grade:			
Spells high frequency words			
Assessment activities			
Applies spelling rules in daily written work			
Listening and Speaking Grade:			
Listens Critically			
Responds Appropriately			
Expresses self clearly			
Orally summarizes			
Speaks with proper grammar			
Makes effective oral presentations			

Decoding and Word Recognition: Students know and use grade appropriate phonics patterns when reading. They read aloud fluently, accurately and with expression.

Vocabulary and Concept Development: Students use various strategies to determine the meaning of words, such as context, a dictionary, knowledge of word parts and knowledge of synonyms, antonyms and homophones.

Reading Comprehension

Structure of Informational Materials: Students use text features such as glossaries and indexes to locate information in text.

Comprehension and Analysis: Students read and understand grade-level-appropriate material. They use a variety of comprehension strategies such as asking questions and making predictions. They distinguish the main idea and supporting details in expository text.

Literary Response and Analysis

Students read and respond to a wide variety of children's literature. They understand plot and setting, analyze characters and determine the author's message in classic and contemporary stories. They distinguish poetry, drama, fiction and nonfiction.

Writing Strategies

Organization and Focus: Students write paragraphs with a topic sentence and include simple supporting facts and details. Their writing reflects a consideration of audience and purpose.
Penmanship: Students write legibly in cursive, using margins and spacing correctly.

Writing Applications

Students write narratives and descriptions using many details. They write letters, thank-you notes and invitations using standard formatting.

show progress during the year. Consequently, your child might not receive the highest marks during the first quarter or semester because he has not mastered those skills. Parents and students who have been accustomed to receiving mostly A's and B's may be in for a bit of a surprise if the new report card shows the child suddenly receiving ones or twos on a scale of one to four. Usually, when new report cards are introduced a school or district has a parents' meeting to discuss the new reporting system. As with most aspects of education, talk to your child's teacher if you need clarification or have concerns.

It appears that once parents become accustomed to standards-based report cards, they indicate a deeper understanding of their child's progress. According to a study by KSA-Plus Communications, parents also say that they have better knowledge of what their children are learning in school through the new report cards. Here are some strategies for using a student report card, regardless of type:

- Ask for a midterm grade or progress report before the end of a semester. Midterm grades or ratings can be helpful in knowing how your child is doing and what needs to be done to improve the final grade.
- Study the report cards thoroughly. If you don't understand the ratings, talk to your child's teacher. Don't wait until the next parent-teacher conference.
- Discuss the report card with your child. Ask how she would grade herself, and compare those ratings to grades or ratings from your child's teacher.
- Ask for a commitment from your child, if there are areas that need to be improved. Work with your child on assignments or projects that will improve any areas of weakness, and monitor her progress.

Regardless of the format, compare the ratings or grades to other information, including test scores, assignments, and your own observation of your child's performance. Strengths or weakness are more dependable if they are consistent across multiple measurements. Meredith Reynolds describes her approach: "If one of our child's grades wasn't as high as we thought it should be, we encouraged him or her to improve. Together, we developed a written plan for getting there: 'How are you going to do this? How much time do you have, and what other commitments?' Together we would write down on a calendar how they were going to improve and then work on it. Having a specific plan helped them to focus their efforts and time and made them accountable."

"We don't overemphasize report cards," said researcher Ann Mastergeorge. "Our motto is to do your personal best." But her daughter was struggling in eighth grade honors English, despite having a great teacher. So Ann promised her daughter a ticket to see *Phantom of the Opera* if she could turn her grade around, beginning with making sure all of her assignments were turned in on time. Her daughter went from an F to a B- and finally an A, earning the theater ticket and finding herself anxious to take another honors English class next year in ninth grade.

"I don't think she would have gotten the A otherwise," said Mastergeorge, "but again we emphasized to do her personal best, which she now knows can be an A if she really works hard."

Evaluate Technology Skills

Many states and districts have developed technology standards for students, but children have varying opportunities to develop technology fluency at school and at home. Although most parents and educators agree that technology skills for their children are important, few evaluation methods exist to measure student progress. Given these challenges, here are a few ideas on how parents might evaluate their child's technology skills:

- How well does your child handle basic computer operations, such as opening and using software? Can he or she transition between programs and solve basic computer problems when they arise?
- Can your child use software as a tool to assist in classroom work—typing, writing, and eventually preparing formal

presentations, graphics, desktop publishing, and even Website development?

- How efficient is your child in acquiring information needed to support classroom learning? Does he effectively use search terms and bookmarks and find content of high quality? How well does your child use the content to support his paper, presentation, or project?
- Sharon Sutton from Corinne Seeds asks, "Do young children go to the computer and use it without prompting? Do they perceive it as a useful tool that helps in their learning?"

Help with Self-Monitoring and Evaluation

As discussed in Chapter One, self-monitoring contributes to a student's learning ability and enhances a child's feeling of competence and personal control. According to Barbara McCombs (1991), self-evaluation also contributes to "understanding of the self and the learning task, learning outcomes, one's own and other's expectations, the importance of the task and of doing well, and the cost or effort required." Parents who can help their children evaluate their own learning processes are likely to contribute to their child's learning.

Michelene Chi found that high-performing students generate more self-explanations than low-performing students, offer higher-quality explanations, and effectively self-monitor their learning (Chi and Bassok, 1989). Reenie Webb put that same knowledge to work for her children. "Having my kids explain to me what they were thinking really helped them understand the material better," said Webb. "Until you can explain it, you don't really know it," added Webb.

Parents can encourage their children to self-monitor their work by asking how well they think they did on a given assignment or test. Make sure your child is familiar with the teacher's criteria for evaluating student work, and suggest that she use the same criteria to evaluate her own performance. If you see other ways to improve your child's work, suggest that she try it on her next assignment.

Create a Portfolio of Student Performance

I encourage parents to put all performance-related information into a folder at home, creating a portfolio of student performance. The folder should contain the state academic standards for that grade, report cards, major student assignments, a scoring rubric if it is used for multiple assignments, test score results, and notes from parent-teacher conferences. Ambitious parents might even keep a small journal about their child's performance. Review the portfolio in preparation for parent-teacher conferences and at other times during the year to gauge student progress. It also will be helpful in providing a year-to-year review of student improvement. Another advantage of keeping a portfolio of student work is that it may help a younger child who will soon be in the same grade. Jamal Abedi (2004) describes his approach to knowing how his two children were doing in school:

> We talk a great deal with teachers to know how our children are doing in school. Usually at the beginning of the year my wife, Feri, makes an appointment and meets with our daughter's teachers. Feri asks the teachers to send any information home in addition to the usual tests and assignments, anything that might show us how our children are doing. We stay in contact with teachers during the year by e-mail, phone, or conferences. Our district has a computerized reporting system, which lets us know how our daughter is doing on classroom assignments and tests. The state test score results are also very helpful, especially when compared across several years. We noticed one year that Sarah's scores dropped in reading, so we talked to the teacher, who encouraged her to do more reading at home, which she did and which helped her increase her scores the next year. We also hired a language arts tutor who helped Sarah to read for conceptual understanding and who encouraged her to keep reading. Receiving encouragement from someone other than her parents was very helpful.

9

GET SMART! COMMUNICATIONS

> Every one of us gets through the tough times because somebody is there, standing in the gap to close it for us.
>
> —*Oprah Winfrey*

To focus only on the academic aspect of learning would be to ignore some startling statistics about the emotional part of school and being a youth:

- A young person takes his or her own life every hour and forty-five minutes in the United States ("Suicide . . . ," 2005).
- A survey of San Diego City School students found that one in ten children had attempted suicide in a single year ("San Diego City Schools . . . ," 2005).
- Depression, a main cause of suicide, is often seen in children who are under stress and who have attention and learning problems in school ("Teen Depression Warning Signs . . . ," n.d.).
- In 2003, 29 percent of students in grades nine through twelve reported that someone had offered, sold, or given them an illegal drug on school property in the twelve months before the survey (NCES, 2005).
- Nearly five hundred thousand children drop out of school every year. According to NCES, nearly 40 percent of Hispanic students drop out of school before completing twelfth grade.

- Low IQ, learning disability, poor attitude toward school, and school failure are strongly related to delinquent behavior (Juvenile Delinquency, 1997).

According to psychologist Pete Gero, poor communication between children and their parents is a key factor that puts children in today's society at risk. In too many cases, we communicate "at" our children and not with them. Gero described a counseling session this way:

> One day a father came in to my office for counseling with his daughter. The dad, who was rich—and told me he was rich—quickly launched into a lecture directed at his daughter about how she wasn't communicating with him and how irresponsible she was. He went on and on for a very long time. When he finished, I asked his daughter what her father had said. 'He's mad at me,' was her reply. Did she not hear what her Dad said? Yes, she heard everything, but the only meaning he conveyed to her was anger.

Gero went on to discuss the value of listening deeply to our children and finding the right time and place for important conversations. Researcher Hilda Borko described what worked for her: "I've learned that there are good and bad times for communication with my teenage son. Early morning and late night don't work for us. We found that going out to dinner one night each week is a good time and place for us to communicate. As a single parent, it has also been very important for me to communicate effectively with his dad, especially in developing a consistency in our messages to him."

What we say to our children has more power and influence than we usually realize. One day I was skiing with Coty when I witnessed a young girl, about eight years old, taking a skiing lesson. She was sobbing because she didn't want to take the lesson and her father was threatening her—most likely angry that the money he paid for the lesson would be wasted. I will always remember his words: "If you don't get out there, I am going to spank the shit out of you." The anger in his voice only caused the poor girl more grief and more crying. I told the father that this was not a good way to talk to his daughter. He told me to mind my own business. The young girl eventually complied with her father's demands, but she was still in tears when I saw her on the slopes a few minutes later. The ski instructor, who had not heard the father's comments, was attending to the girl, but I will long be haunted by the grim reality of the cruel words (and sometimes actions) that parents use, which can damage—if not destroy—a child's self-esteem and motivation.

This chapter covers *Get Smart!* strategies to improve your child's social development, decision making, and communications.

Social Development

Bullying remains a key issue at most schools today, but fortunately there are a growing number of programs to reduce bullying behaviors. For example, teachers at UCLA's Corinne Seeds University Elementary School, led by Ava de la Sota, developed the Safe Schools social and character development program, to improve students' communication skills in early ages. Every Safe Schools classroom has a toolbox filled with a set of Cool Tools used to reduce verbal put-downs and bullying type behavior. A teacher asks students, for example, to squeeze toothpaste out of a tube and then asks them to put the toothpaste back in. When the students can't, they are told that the toothpaste is similar to the words we sometimes use to put down another person, easy to get out of our mouth, but virtually impossible to put back in. Another tool is a small stop sign, symbolic of how students can exit a bad situation such as name calling on the part of another student. The stop sign reminds us that we can decide to end the conflict simply by stopping and leaving. Safe Schools helps children make smart social decisions, avoid conflict, and create an atmosphere of trust and support.

Another component of the Safe Schools program uses Cool Tools such as a traffic signal to teach young children about decision making. A red light represents a decision made by adults, not children (a five-year-old child, for example, may not cross a busy street without an adult or older student to walk with him). A yellow light is a decision where a child has input but must ask a parent for permission ("May I have a sleepover for my birthday, Mom?"). A green light is a decision that children make themselves (during free play on the playground, a child may select from any of the available activities without asking an adult). The stoplight tool helps young children transfer what they know about one symbol, a traffic signal, to a new and more complex topic, decision making. That both can be related to safety further reinforces the learning. Find out if your school has a social development program and what activities you can carry out at home to reinforce your child's social development. Appendix F has more information about the Safe Schools program.

Improved Decision Making

Education Spectrum, a nonprofit organization in Pasadena, California, created a child development program that includes physical activities to help socially challenged children. One of their goals is to help children become more responsible for the decisions they make. Good decisions lead to positive consequences, while poor decisions lead to negative results. If a child doesn't put water into the dog's dish, for example, the dog suffers from thirst and a child may lose a privilege. Focusing on one critical aspect of behavior at a time, such as decision making, emphasized at school, home, and play is more realistic than a host of remedies that may overwhelm you and your child.

"Our oldest son was having a difficult time socially," said one parent, "so we discussed it with his teacher and the school psychologist, who recommended a specific therapist. He attended a social skills group from age five to age eight, which helped him a great deal. Making friends really comes easy to him now. This was one of the wisest choices that we have made as parents because our son's life is so much more fulfilling."

"We had natural and logical consequences for the decisions our daughters made," said school board member Jinny Dalbeck, who used what she called the Get out of Jail card if her girls made a less-than-perfect decision.

"If our girls made a bad choice, we stated why it was bad and asked, 'What did you learn?'" This was their Get out of Jail card. Talking about it, instead of immediate punishment, "allowed our girls to feel that they could always discuss things," said Dalbeck, "that they weren't in mortal fear of us, and helped to keep communications open." If they repeated the same mistake, then they knew there would be major consequences.

Some things children do are nonnegotiable. Dalbeck's daughters knew, for example, that coming home with alcohol on their breath would cost them all driving privileges.

"We tried to give our kids choices in life," said parent Lani Moore, "and encouraged them to talk about what they were thinking. I think as a result that they became independent thinkers; they don't follow the herd. Our daughter in college now is secure enough in herself that she makes good choices. For example, she sees kids in college who drink too much, and she knows that that isn't for her."

"You have to be careful in talking with your children," said parent Kathy Hernandez. "I've learned what not to say to them and what not to say about them to others. It is tempting to share details of my children's lives with good friends, but it is more important for them to trust me."

Tips for Enhancing Communications

Parents can support communication at home by eating meals together and talking about their day. If your children are like mine and don't automatically chirp up about their day at school, follow Karen Mathison's method and talk about your own day. Once a conversation gets started on almost any topic, they eventually join in.

"My kids were always ones who, if you asked them how their day went or what they learned, said their day went fine or that they didn't learn anything," said researcher Marilyn Cochran-Smith. "Although I never gave up asking them how things were going or what they were learning, I found out about how they were doing by staying in close contact with their teachers. Notes were helpful, and e-mail was really useful to me because of my schedule. Parents need to find a teacher communication strategy that works for them," added Cochran-Smith.

Making the time for communications means setting limits on some of the things our children like to do. "We had a rule that there were no televisions or telephones in our daughter's bedrooms," said school board member Scott Tracy, "and we closely monitored television content as well. Certain programs like "The Cosby Show" were family time rituals that we eagerly anticipated."

Some parents, like Meredith and Tom Reynolds, set rules where television and electronics were not allowed from Sunday through Thursday night. "Tom and I wouldn't watch television either on those nights," said Reynolds, "and one of the positive outcomes was that we talked more as a family than we might have done otherwise."

"Children need opportunities to make mistakes," noted Lani Moore, "and when they make them, to have the opportunity to try again. That's part of the learning process."

Kids can also learn from mistakes that parents have made in their lives. During one dinner conversation, I told my children about the time when I, and a group of other fifth grade kids, verbally bullied three girls. We referred to the girls as gorgons, and one of them as Medusa. It was the cruelest thing I have ever done in my life. One day, the teacher overheard us and gave the entire class a well-deserved lecture. Though our bullying stopped, the damage to those three girls was already done. At our ten-year high school reunion, I recounted with one friend how awful we had been and how much we wanted to say we were sorry. Of course, none of the three girls were there; two of them never graduated with our class. I learned from that lesson, and by sharing this story with my own children I hope that it might help them to realize the awful consequences that our words can have on other people.

In his book *The Explosive Child*, Ross Greene describes a communications strategy that parents can use to foster communications at home (1998), especially when communications are strained. Greene suggests that parents use three baskets, A, B, and C, to set priorities that they have for their children. Here is my suggestion for how to apply his strategy to school.

Reserve the A basket for items that are absolutely essential, such as "Yes, you must go to school today even if you are bored in social studies." The C basket is for items of the lowest priority, for example making a child complete every extra credit assignment that comes her way. If a child is struggling in school, parents can start out with most items in the C basket. Some items may just stay there, especially if they are beyond a child's ability, such as "Only A's and B's on every report card." Others may gradually be moved higher, as with extra-credit assignments.

The B basket is for the in-between issues and is often where compromise is appropriate. Let's say that your child wants to play soccer, which will consume two days per week after school—a time when he currently does his homework. A reasonable compromise is to set parameters on soccer. For example, your child may play soccer, but on those days he must complete all homework by 8:30 P.M. and there is no television or electronics on those evenings.

The idea is that parents don't need to draw a line in the sand on every issue, fearing that compromise will result in erosion of their authority. Very few decisions in life are clear-cut (as with selection of just the right prom dress, or college). Compromise doesn't mean that a parent gives up the right to make a final decision. It means we are willing to share responsibility and consequences with our children. We also acknowledge that we are not always right. Transfer of good decision making to children through guidance and flexibility is a key goal for parents.

Before he passed away, Harry Handler, a former UCLA adjunct professor and retired superintendent from the Los Angeles Unified School District, shared with me his and his wife's strategies for effective communication with their daughter when she was in school:

- *Avoid pressure*. According to Handler, their daughter was under ample pressure just by being the child of a deputy superintendent at the second largest school district in the nation. "In everything we did, we tried to be nonjudgmental," said Handler.
- *Emphasize effort, not achievement*. Both Handler and his wife, Kay, valued achievement, but they emphasized to their daughter that a grade was not as important as the effort she put into it. Also important were the skills she developed and the content she learned.
- *Communicate*. "We talked a lot about school and our jobs," said Handler. "We encouraged her to realize that we all had jobs in life. Her job was school. Do the best you can at your job."
- *Be constructive*. "Our approach," said Handler, "was always that she should do her homework herself, but if she wanted us to review it, we would. If we did, however, she needed to know that we would have constructive suggestions. She could use our suggestions or not. Our idea was to get her to keep coming back. Even now, at the age of thirty-five, she will ask us for feedback."
- *Offer choice*. There are some things that were nonnegotiable and others where their daughter had complete choice. "Building family traditions was very important to us," Handler said, "such as having a birthday and letting that person choose the place to have dinner. It is a tradition we follow to this day."

There are many things we can do to create a strong environment that supports positive communications, as third grade teacher and parent Lani Moore explains:

> When our kids were growing up my husband and I liked to take each child on a special activity on a weekend, one parent with one child separately. The next time, we switched kids. They were the prince

> or the princess for the day and could choose what they wanted to do. My husband, Jess, would usually take the kids camping, hiking, or fishing. With me, we would often go to museums or play miniature golf. When camping, Jess would set the camera on a remote and take a picture of the two of them, which made for great scrapbook memories. Our daughter enjoyed traveling to Santa Paula to pick out a large Halloween pumpkin in the fields where they were grown, about an hour from home. As they got older, we still tried to do these special weekends, especially as they were getting ready to leave for college. Just before our son went into the Navy, my husband Jess took him on a tour of the Grand Canyon. We have many great memories of these times we spent together.

Parents can't force communication with their children, but they can foster opportunities, as the Moores did, to create a time where both communications and lasting relationships develop.

"My advice to parents is to set high expectations," said Jinny Dalbeck, mother of two children. "Encourage them to do the things that they *need* to do before things they *want* to do, and be consistent in all that you do. The other suggestion is to keep the lines of communication open, starting well before kindergarten. I always talked to my children as adults, never talked down to them. We didn't set unrealistic expectations and always had natural and logical consequences. If you do X, then Y is likely to happen."

Here are some suggestions from Meredith Reynolds:

- Always be available for your child. Don't look busy; just kind of hang out, and they will talk to you.
- Always know where your kids are. Even today, with two kids in college, we call them a lot. Call, call, call.
- Know their friends, and go to football and basketball games; just being there is important.
- Have kids to your house. When our kids have someone over, we are always there; we don't leave. After all, it's our house and we live there too. We don't bother them, but we greet their friends

when they arrive and we insist that they say good-bye when they leave.

- Avoid becoming involved in your child's disagreements with their friends because as a parent it is really hard for you to sort those disagreements out. Don't keep a bad image of any kid.
- Kids need different styles at different times. Our approach was always that we are raising adults, not children. They are our responsibility.
- My husband, Tom, was fully with me in our children's education, either coaching or with scouts. Even today he does a lot of camping with them. In academics, he stood as a role model, overcoming dyslexia to graduate from Stanford. I was more of the taskmaster; Tom was the heart and inspiration.

Involving your children in organizations that have strong social components can help them develop both communications and self-confidence, as described by parent Andrea Terry: "For us, Girl Scouting had a profound effect on our daughter's lives. The girls learned organization, time management, leadership, and to care for their fellow man. All the while, they just thought they were having fun and being trusted with more responsibility. Their self-confidence blossomed with each accomplishment. It forced them to try things they never would have without the encouragement of the group."

There are dozens of organizations that nurture the social side of our child's education. Terry credits volunteer organizations and the YMCA for helping her daughters "learn teamwork, and find themselves more confident and successful." She said that her daughters took these experiences into other parts of their lives. "I think having your child work in some volunteer capacity for those less fortunate is essential to their perception of the world, and their humanity," said Terry.

"We felt strongly about the arts and about giving back to the community," said Ann Mastergeorge. Her daughter collects books for a children's hospital and this past holiday season helped a family in need. "Learning about giving back to the community also gives back to your child," said Mastergeorge, "and can help them to make important career choices."

Children don't always have to have dozens of friends in school; most will have time to develop deep friendships with only a few students.

"I understood how important it is for a child to have one good friend," said Denise. "Not every child needs to be part of the popular social group. But I read that just having one good friend can make all the difference in keeping your child from being picked on and help them to get through school. I encouraged my middle daughter's friendship with another child at school who was extremely different from her but complemented her nature. My daughter was quiet and a bit withdrawn, while this other child was very outgoing and a bit bossy. They clicked and have been best friends for several years."

The saying that you can't pick your child's friends is not entirely true. Again, parents can make a difference by associating with other families who share their own values. Here are some other strategies for improving communications with our children:

- *Recognize the warning signs of a communications meltdown.* They typically include prolonged discussion back and forth on one topic, voices getting louder, emotional temperature rising—all this often followed by an ultimatum from you, tears from your child, or the silent treatment, both you and your child feeling miserable. No one wins.
- *Know that it's OK to lose an argument.* Actually, it is better to avoid arguments, but if you have missed the warning signs then just stop talking, or say, "OK, I agree." "Uh-huh" works very well for me because it isn't total capitulation. I cannot tell you how many arguments I have lost and how happy I have been to lose them. This method works equally well with many adults, especially family members. I tell myself this is not important; I love this person too

much to have an argument. So I just shut up and say, "Uh, huh. May I get you something from the kitchen?"

• *Use diversion effectively.* For any of the warning signs given here, you can say that you will discuss the issue later, or completely switch the topic. When my kids were very young and in the midst of a back-seat "debate," I would say, "Did you see that bear over there?" Of course they caught on pretty quickly that we don't have too many bears in Los Angeles, so I became more creative. Try asking them what they want for their birthday and see if that doesn't switch their attention. In many cases, you will find little or no need to discuss the debate topic later because it wasn't very important in the first place.

• *Give your child and yourself a second chance.* If your child's voice suddenly increases an octave or if she blurts out something rude, which would warrant a punishment under most conditions, try giving her one more chance. In a very calm voice, ask, "Would you like to say (or try) that again, Honey?" Chances are that these few seconds will give your child enough time to think through her words or actions and come back in a calmer voice. You may have helped your child put the toothpaste back into the tube, avoided a meltdown or punishment, showed that you are a forgiving parent, and let your child really think about what she said or did. Finally, you made your child model the tone of voice, choice of words, or actions that she should be using all the time. Practicing the right behavior often helps more than punishment.

• *Time-out for adults.* Others have said this, but time-out for adults is very helpful. If you are stressed to the point that it impairs your own decision making, it's a good idea to pause, walk away if necessary, and think before you speak or act. Both children and adults tend to make better decisions if they have more time to make them. In most cases, our decisions are not so urgent that stepping away for one minute, perhaps talking with our spouse, will produce a better outcome. In the Safe Schools program, the color blue is used to encourage children to cool down, ice, or chill, before they make a decision they may later regret.

• *Take time for yourself as well.* Everyone needs a break from the stresses of life, including those that arise from our children's education. They will benefit from parents who are emotionally and physically fit. Get exercise, eat properly, and involve yourself in a hobby or activity that you enjoy. Tennis and photography work for me.

• *Keep yourself and your children organized.* Getting everyone to school and work in the morning is, for most parents and students, a time of at least a little stress, and in some cases morning madness. Set the table the night before, have clothes for everyone laid out (better: have everyone do their own), and keep decision making to the minimum. Morning is usually no time to give your kids a choice between pancakes, waffles, or French toast. You are not a restaurant. At our house, we have a morning checklist of what must be done, and we stick to it. When our kids were younger, we sometimes used a kitchen timer instead of multiple verbal reminders. Do what you need to do to reduce morning stress and make everything work.

• *Manners count.* Teach your child how to answer the phone and to have good table manners. Instill the idea that there are appropriate and inappropriate ways to do things. Teacher Ron Clark (2003) suggests fifty-five essential lessons to help children become not just good students but good people. Among them are to "say thank-you within three seconds of receiving something."

• *Avoid big mistakes.* Some mistakes have drastic consequences. Drug or alcohol abuse is one of them. My wife and I recently shared an Oprah Winfrey program with our children on drug use to reinforce what they have learned in school about the dangers that drugs pose to them. Two young women had become methamphetamine drug addicts after friends offered them free drugs. The Oprah program graphically showed how methamphetamines destroy brain tissue and caused one of the young women to lose her car, her home, her husband, and her young child. (See Appendix F).

• *Learn from mistakes.* Being able to learn from mistakes and not repeat them is a defining maturation point in children. When a child makes a mistake, use it as a learning tool to avoid the same mistake in the future. Tell your child of similar mistakes you have made in your own life and how you avoided making the same mistake twice.

• *Hug your kids*. When our daughter came to live with us as a foster child, she was ten months old, having been taken away from her mother because of neglect. For nearly the first six weeks in our home, she cried whenever we didn't hold her. Even a toy would not stop the crying. Once picked up, Markie was happy. "A hug, a gentle stroke on the back, a kiss on the cheek, a tousle of hair, all say to your child 'I love you,'" say Andrea Frank Henkart and her daughter Journey (1998). For Markie, being held was an emotional attachment that told her she was loved.

• *Be able to let go*. School principal Cindy Keech (2004) reminds parents that our kids are not us. They may not want to go to our alma mater but instead have their own goals and lives. We need to nurture and guide, but ultimately they will find their own path.

Pioneer educational researcher Robert Glaser shared with me his approach to the social education of his two daughters when they were growing up:

> My wife used to ask our daughters about their relationships with other kids, and they learned to talk to us freely. Sylvia would ask them, for example, "How do you nurture a relationship? What are the critical components of a friendship?" We tried to instill in them a sense of values and how to evaluate friendships, a sense of friendship and caring for others.
>
> Another thing we did was to use time after dinner to discuss news and affairs of the day. The news was usually national, two sides of a story; a debate was a good example. If an election was coming up, our girls would ask us whom we were voting for and why. They would share their opinions with us too, and we would also discuss people who had made new inventions or discoveries, like Francis Crick and James Watson, who were DNA pioneers, for example.

Many years ago, Gordon Pader, a good friend of my parents when I was growing up, gave me an excellent piece of advice on my upcoming marriage. He said, "Never go to bed mad at your wife." I try to apply his same wisdom to my children as well and hope that they too will forgive me when I am less than perfect. Whatever transgression may have occurred during the day, of which a fair number are my own fault, I always kiss them good night and say, "I love you." And they always answer, "I love you too, Daddy."

Conclusion: Getting Started Today

> Education has opened many, many doors. However, there are still innumerable doors shut tight—unopened yet. These are the doors of the future. Perhaps one of my children will open one of these doors—I shall help give him the key.
>
> —*Unknown*

Children are not ingredients in a recipe. Some may need more sugar; others may need more spice. Parents too are different, creating a dynamic family unit where multiple learning strategies are usually better than any single method. Experimentation and flexibility are important, as well as accepting the fact that implementation will not be perfect. Above all, we must model the same passion for learning and communication that we hope to teach our children.

We can start by analyzing our child's strengths and areas where he or she needs improvement. Going a few steps at a time to address the most pressing needs is a better approach than trying to do everything at once, which will most likely overwhelm our children and us. From the many suggestions given in this book, pick one or two to start with, and then pick one or two more as soon as the first ones seem to be working. If your child has specific weaknesses, pick the parts of the Get Smart Learning Model that address his or her needs. Whatever you do, get started today.

"School is a bit of game to get through," said researcher Robert Mislevy. "It's an opportunity for our children to learn how to learn what they need to know for the rest of their life."

Teacher Tracy Hughes (2004) reminds us that:

- You are one strand of a three-strand chord.
- Don't ever give up if you think something is important.
- Be consistent, patient, and flexible.
- Be enthusiastic and have a positive attitude.
- Shower with love.

"Nag and nurture," suggests Mary Maushard from Johns Hopkins University, summarizing her own parenting approach. Learning is a journey that lasts forever.

Drop the guilt that comes from being a less-than-perfect parent. We are good parents already and making a substantial difference in our children's lives.

"None of us got where we are solely by pulling ourselves up by our bootstraps," said Supreme Court Justice Thurgood Marshall. "We got here because somebody—a parent, a teacher, an Ivy League crony, or a few nuns—bent down and helped us pick up our boots."

Our role is to be that somebody for our children.

Appendix A: *Get Smart!* Strategies for Students with Special Needs

> Do not let what you cannot do interfere with what you can do.
>
> —*John Wooden*

If your child has a learning disability, you are far from alone. According to the National Center for Education Statistics (2005), 8 percent of students enrolled in public schools, almost four million children, have been formally diagnosed with a learning disability. Many school districts report a substantially higher percentage, sometimes reaching 12–15 percent of their total student population. The percentage of students with autism in particular has risen dramatically. The U.S. Department of Education reported a fivefold increase in the number of students diagnosed with autism and being served under the Individuals with Disabilities Education Act (IDEA) during the 1990s. In the same decade, the California Department of Developmental Services estimated a 273 percent increase in children with autism (Dybvik, 2004).

Disabilities vary substantially regarding their impact on learning; however, when viewed as a whole, students with disabilities perform far lower on state and national assessments, have more behavioral problems in school, and drop out of school at a substantially higher rate than their nondisabled peers. Parent involvement and support is helpful to virtually all students, but it is crucial for students with disabilities, who can benefit substantially when their parents work closely with teachers to create strong school and home learning environments. Here are some specific Get Smart! suggestions to help your special needs child: diagnosis, coping, action, and resources.

Diagnosis

If there is one area of agreement among educators, it is the value of early diagnosis of a child's learning disabilities. Early identification and intervention can help a child maximize learning potential and reduce stress for both parents and child. Your child's pediatrician can guide you in identifying possible disabilities while your child's preschool or regular school teachers can offer helpful day-to-day behavioral or performance information that may support the need for a formal evaluation.

There are, of course, many types of learning disability, varying in type, severity, and capacity of being diagnosed accurately. In many cases, children may have multiple disabilities, which interact in ways that create an almost child-specific disorder. Further complicating assessment of learning disabilities is the fact that few formal assessments are designed for the sole purpose of diagnosing specific learning problems. Consequently, even though tests play a critical role in diagnosing learning disabilities, they should be only one part of a comprehensive evaluation process. IDEA recommends that multiple measures be used in evaluating a child's potential disability and that the tests be validated for the specific use. School psychologists normally use a series of assessments to evaluate learning disabilities in addition to rating scales from parents and teachers.

Parents, who may be in a state of disbelief or disappointment that their child has a disability, are not always satisfied with a school's evaluation or treatment plan for their child. Because diagnosis is more difficult than for many physical illnesses, parents may want to seek a second opinion. Your child's pediatrician is usually a good first step.

Coping

Learning that your child has a disability can be one of the most heart-wrenching experiences in a parent's life. Denial is common, and grieving may last a lifetime if your child's disability has long-term effects. The severity of the disability may influence the degree of pain that a parent feels, but regardless, the process is not an easy one. In my own son's case, his diagnosis of high-functioning autism was preceded by a series of less serious disabilities, including Asperger's syndrome, pervasive development disorder, and attention deficit disorder. Each diagnosis brought new pain and required a healing period before my wife and I felt even modestly ready for the new challenge.

Support groups are usually plentiful and helpful. In many cases, they can be an excellent source of local information, to help you in developing an action plan and deal with the stress often associated with being a parent of a special-needs child.

Action

One of the positive attributes of the No Child Left Behind Act is that it requires all students, including students with disabilities, to reach "proficient or above" levels on state tests. Prior to NCLB, many students with disabilities were excluded from state testing. Because NCLB mandates testing of nearly all students, most schools are focusing more efforts and resources to help students with learning disabilities.

Having a child with a disability requires more work on the parent's part. You will probably have more frequent contact with your child's teachers as well as a school psychologist, counselor, and possibly the principal. Each will work with you as part of a team to develop an individualized education program (IEP) for your child. It is natural for parents to advocate for their child's needs, which may stretch or surpass a school's ability to afford or provide. Parents want to somehow make their child normal, or at least create the opportunity for their child to reach maximum learning potential. This is especially true in the first few months after a child has been diagnosed with a disability, when parents have yet to realize that a child's special needs will prevent him or her from attaining the high achievement of other children. Parents may go to excruciating lengths in the early stages of the special education process, believing and hoping that there is something the school can and must do to make their child succeed equal to others. Consequently, IEPs can be an enormous time of stress in which parents bring in advocates for their children and battle lines are drawn. Even under the best of circumstances, tension exists.

Prepare for an IEP as you would for a parent-teacher conference. Review your child's records, including state test scores, report cards, recent assignments, and classroom test results. Become familiar with your child's specific disability by reading or talking to other parents. Prior to your IEP meeting, consider sending specific questions to your child's teacher or to the IEP team. For our own son, we have a standard one-page list of his specific characteristics, briefly describing his disability plus strategies that have been successful in the past. We share the page with his teachers when we meet. You may be inclined to write a multipage essay on your child; I encourage you to make it no longer than one page if you expect it to be read and used. Otherwise, it may quickly work its way to the bottom of the many memos and notes that teachers receive daily. You might consider printing it on bright paper and laminating it.

During the IEP, each teacher, the school psychologist, a special education teacher, counselor, and principal will likely take turns speaking. Make sure that you ask how much time is available for this meeting and that you are provided ample time to speak. Bring the questions you submitted ahead of the IEP meeting and any others that have arisen since then. Again, having your questions in writing helps ensure that they are answered before you leave the meeting. Send follow-up questions after the meeting to the appropriate individual, usually the special education teacher. In some cases, the meeting must be extended to another date and time in order to address all of your child's needs.

Your action plan developed during the IEP meeting should address instructional and testing modifications that may be necessary for your child. Students with disabilities usually need additional support in the classroom, depending on the severity of their special need. Accommodations or adaptations may include sitting in the front of the classroom, extra time to complete assignments, fewer assignments (or exemption from assignments that are substantially hindered by the child's special need), modified grading, opportunity to retake assessments if the first score falls below a specific threshold, or use of a classroom computer to take notes. Homework is often reduced or a time limit set so that students with disabilities are not spending an excessive amount of time on homework. Students with major needs may require a classroom aide at all times. A behavior or classroom management plan may also be part of the IEP depending on your child's needs.

Students with disabilities may be allowed to take different classroom tests, complete fewer questions, dictate their answers, or have more time to complete the test. More than one accommodation is often helpful, but close monitoring and changes may be necessary to find an assessment strategy that works best for your child. On state tests, students with severe disabilities may be allowed to take a completely different test made specifically for students with disabilities and usually have as much time as is necessary to complete it.

Instruction and assessment accommodations or adaptations have some drawbacks. Reducing assignments, homework, or the number of test questions ultimately has an impact on a child's learning. Reducing vocabulary requirements in a foreign language, for example, means that a student with disabilities is unlikely to achieve the same skills as his or her nondisabled peers. Other accommodations, such as sitting in the front of the classroom, are less likely to have an instructional effect. Harvard Professor Daniel Koretz points out that any change to the test or its administration changes the test validity, including the conclusions that you can draw from the test results. In one study, Koretz found that disabled students were outperforming their nondisabled peers on the Kentucky state test—possibly a result of providing more accommodations than necessary to students with just mild disabilities. Working closely with the IEP team can help achieve a balance that best serves your child.

Students or adults with disabilities may have specific strengths or gifts. In the movie *Rain Man*, Dustin Hoffman played the role of an autistic savant with mathematics abilities far above those of the average person, able to multiply large digits in his head and memorize cards played in a game of black jack. At the same time, he had enormous difficulty with basic communication (a typical autistic trait) and had lived in a mental institution for many years. Similarly, students with disabilities may have special skills and talents. Researcher Susan Baum (1990) developed categories of giftedness within learning disabilities. The former ERIC Clearinghouse on Disabilities and Gifted Education created a checklist of characteristics often associated with gifted students who have learning disabilities (Willard-Holt, 1999), among them:

- High abstract reasoning ability
- Advanced vocabulary
- Good mathematical reasoning ability
- Good problem-finding and [problem]–solving skills
- Supersensitivity
- Imaginati[on] and creativ[ity]

Evaluating the talents of a student with disabilities is a challenging task, complicated by the fact that many learning-disabled children express themselves less effectively than their nondisabled peers. Additionally, some learning-disabled children's negative behavior may hide their talents. A comprehensive evaluation by medical professionals combined with your input to your child's IEP team can help identify special needs and talents.

A final word about your action plan. If this is your first IEP meeting, or even your fifteenth, you are likely to be overwhelmed during the meeting itself, as each teacher, psychologist, or counselor offers test score information, grades, or other feedback. Don't feel that you have to make major decisions right away. Your child's disability is unlikely to change in the course of the next week or month. Take the time you need to understand the information presented at the IEP meeting, and then make the important decisions that become an effective action plan. As you monitor the effectiveness of the plan and your child's learning, you will make changes that lead to improvement. Education is a journey, not a footrace, especially in helping a child with special needs.

Resources

Here are useful resources for helping your child with disabilities succeed in school.

National Dissemination Center for Children with Disabilities (NICHCY). www.nichcy.org/. Excellent source of information for parents of children with learning disabilities. The center has a toll-free number to help answer individual questions: 800/695–0285. E-mail questions may be sent to nichcy@aed.org.

National Center for Learning Disabilities. www.ncld.org. Contains many online resources for parents of children with learning disabilities, including a Parent Center, free newsletter, online discussions, and resources from preschool through high school.

National Center on Educational Outcomes. www.education.umn.edu/ceo/. Has useful information about educational assessment of students with disabilities and accommodations. The Special Topics of this Website may be especially helpful to parents.

UCLA School for Mental Health Project. www.smhp.psych.ucla.edu. Publishes a free quarterly newsletter, *Addressing Barriers to Learning*. Furnishes information to improve outcomes for young people by enhancing the field of mental health in schools.

Educational Resources Information Center. www.eric.ed.gov/. Gathers and disseminates professional literature and information on educating individuals of all ages, including children with disabilities, English language learners, and gifted.

Appendix B: Using a School Report Card

Although most states have had school report cards for a number of years, the No Child Left Behind Act (2002) made school report cards mandatory. You can usually find school report cards through your state department of education's Website or on your school district's site. Several independent organizations, such as www.greatschools.net, also have reports and data on many schools across the nation. State laws may require more information than mandated by NCLB to be included in school report cards; consequently, some school report cards fill as many as twenty pages. This appendix presents some of the factors commonly found and supported by research as indicators of school quality. A sample report card from Polytechnic High School in the Long Beach (California) Unified School District shows many of these factors in a school report card.

Test Scores

In reviewing test scores, look for an increase over a number of years, not just the current score. Is the school showing a steady pattern of progress? How does this progress compare to other schools in the same or nearby districts? Many school test scores are increasing, especially in elementary schools, so it is important to compare a prospective school's scores against state and district improvements. An increase of 2 percent at an individual school may look quite good, but not so good if the average state increase that year was 4 percent.

Make sure comparison is made between the same tests, since different types are not directly comparable. Generally, scores from the Stanford Achievement Test, the Iowa Tests of Basic Skills, and California Achievement Test should not be directly compared to each other because they assess different content and are often developed using substantially different groups of students.

Here are selected sections from Polytechnic High School in Long Beach. For complete LBUSD report cards, see www.lbusd.k12.ca.us/. My thanks to Lynn Winters, Chris Dominguez, and James Suarez of the school district for their permission to use this report card.

The report card for Polytechnic High School offers three test result types (Exhibits B.1 and B.2). First, the Academic Performance Index (API) is a composite index of test scores in various grades and subjects using student performance on the California Standards Test. Polytechnic shows consistent API gains during the past three years. Second, the school reports performance on the CAT/6, a nationally norm-referenced test using percentile ranks. Third, Polytechnic reports separate subject performances on the California Standards Test, the state standards-based assessment used to report progress under NCLB. The schoolreports percent proficient or advanced in four subjects: English–language arts, mathematics, science, and history–social science.

Student Attendance Rate

Obviously, higher attendance is better than lower attendance. Some school districts may have 15 percent of students or more absent from school every day, with as many as 50 percent of these students truant. Other school districts average a 5 percent student absentee rate. Not surprisingly, schools with a lower absentee rate tend to be higher-performing than those with more absenteeism.

Exhibit B.1.

Polytechnic High School

A California Distinguished School -- Shawn Ashley and Gwen Mack, Co-Principals

School Accountability Report Card 2005 - 2006

School Wide API

	API Base Data		
	2002-03	2003-04	2004-05
Percent Tested	97	98	98
Base API Score	686	697	696
Growth Target	7	6	5
Statewide Rank	7		
Similar Schools Rank	9		

	API Growth Data		
	2002-03	2003-04	2004-05
Percent Tested	97	98	98
API Growth Score	686	697	715
Actual Growth	31	11	19

Source: California Department of Education, Policy and Evaluation Division

2004-05 Adequate Yearly Progress

Content Area	Met 2003-04 AYP Criteria	School wide % Proficient or Above
English Language Arts	yes	53.1%
Math	yes	54.3%

Source: California Department of Education, Policy and Evaluation Division

Our School's Test Scores

The data below represent school averages in percentiles. Data not comparable for the 3-year period. SAT 9 (01-02) norms differ from CAT6 (02-03, 03-04) norms. No comparisons should be made between the CAT6 and SAT9 tests.In 2004-05, the CAT 6 was not administered in high schools.

Grade	Reading			Language			Mathematics		
	01-02	02-03	03-04	01-02	02-03	03-04	01-02	02-03	03-04
	SAT9	CAT6	CAT6	SAT 9	CAT6	CAT6	SAT9	CAT6	CAT6
9	41	57	58	57	56	58	65	59	60
10	38	61	56	47	61	58	56	60	58
11	46	58	59	56	57	58	61	59	60

Source: California Department of Education, Policy and Evaluation Division

Exhibit B.2.

Standardized Testing and Reporting (STAR)

Through the California Standardized Testing and Reporting (STAR) program, students in grades 2 through 11 are tested annually in various subject areas. Currently, the STAR program includes California Standards Tests (CST) and a norm-referenced test (NRT). The CST tests English-language arts and mathematics in grades 2 through 11, science in grades 5, 9, 10, and 11, and history-social science in grades 8, 10, and 11. Prior to 2005, the NRT tested reading/language arts and mathematics in grades 2 through 11, spelling in grades 2 through 8, and science in grades 9 through 11. Beginning in 2005, the NRT tests reading/language arts, spelling, and mathematics in grades 3 and 7 only, and no longer tests science in any grade.

California Standards Tests (CST)

The California Standards Tests (CST) show how well students are doing in relation to the state content standards. Student scores are reported as performance levels. The five performance levels are Advanced (exceeds state standards), Proficient (meets state standards), Basic (approaching state standards), Below Basic (below state standards), and Far Below Basic (well below state standards). Students scoring at the Proficient or Advanced level meet state standards in that content area. Students with significant cognitive disabilities who are unable to take the CST are tested using the California Alternate Performance Assessment (CAPA). Detailed information regarding CST and CAPA results for each grade and proficiency level can be found at the California Department of Education Web site at http://star.cde.ca.gov or by speaking with the school principal. Note: To protect student privacy, scores are not shown when the number of students tested is 10 or less.

CST - All Students

Data reported are the percent of students achieving at the Proficient or Advanced level (meeting or exceeding the state standards).

Subject	School			District			State		
	2003	2004	2005	2003	2004	2005	2003	2004	2005
English-Language Arts	43	43	45	32	33	38	35	36	40
Mathematics	31	26	28	34	34	38	35	34	38
Science	30	32	34	21	20	23	27	25	27
History - Social Science	34	36	39	27	28	34	28	29	32

Graduation Rate

There is wide variation in how states and school districts report the graduation rate, making this statistic somewhat ineffective at this time. The Education Trust (2003) noted that South Dakota reported a statewide graduation rate of 97 percent, while Nevada reported 63.7 percent—figures so far apart as to question their accuracy. Recent efforts to reach common methods for measuring high school graduation rate should produce more accurate comparison in the future. Naturally, a higher graduation rate is better than lower. Relatively precise comparison can be made between schools in the same school district where the probability is high that the reporting system is the same. The next most accurate comparison is between school districts in the same state. Polytechnic High School reported a 91.3 percent graduation rate in 2005 (Exhibit B.3).

Advanced Placement Classes

Large differences exist in the number of advanced placement courses offered by high schools. Generally, more is better, but some schools are actually deemphasizing their AP program because many of the courses have become little more than studying the content covered on the AP test. Passing the test at the end of the course is a more accurate indicator of student achievement, so look at the percentage of students who passed the AP test and compare that to the national average. In the 2002–03 school year, 437 Beverly Hills High School students took 773 advanced placement classes, with a 74.2 percent passing rate. The national passing rate was approximately 64 percent that year. For 2005, Polytechnic High School reports an overall passing rate of 70 percent in nineteen subjects.

Like other California high schools, Polytechnic reports the percentage of students who completed all courses required for entrance into the University of California or California State University system. This is a relatively consistent indicator of high school quality for the state of California.

Exhibit B.3.

School Completion (Secondary Schools)

Beginning with the graduating class of 2006, students in California public schools will have to pass the California High School Exit Examination (CAHSEE) to receive a high school diploma. The School Accountability Report Card for that year will report the percent of students completing grade 12 who successfully completed the CAHSEE.

These data are not required to be reported until 2006, when they can be reported for the entire potential graduating class. At that time, the data are expected to be disaggregated by special education status, English learners, socioeconomically disadvantaged status, gender, and ethnic group.

Dropout Rate and Graduation Rate

Data reported regarding progress toward reducing dropout rates over the most recent three-year period include grade 9 through 12 enrollment, the number of dropouts, and the one-year dropout rate as reported by CBEDS. The formula for the one-year dropout rate is (grades 9 through 12 dropouts divided by grades 9 through 12 enrollment) multiplied by 100. The graduation rate, included as one of the requirements of California's definition of Adequate Yearly Progress as required by the federal No Child Left Behind (NCLB) Act, is calculated by dividing the number of high school graduates by the sum of dropouts for grades 9 through 12, in consecutive years, plus the number of graduates.

Grade	School			District			State		
	2003	2004	2005	2003	2004	2005	2003	2004	2005
Enrollment (9-12)	4638	4684	4779	26790	27489	28140	1772417	1830903	1876927
Number of Dropouts	82	119	125	771	856	1005	47871	58189	61253
Dropout Rate (1-year)	1.8	2.5	2.6	2.9	3.1	3.6	2.7	3.2	3.2
Graduation Rate	89.6	91.0	91.3	85.2	84.8	82.6	87.0	86.7	86.7

Some high schools report the percentage of students entering postsecondary education, usually as the percentage of students attending either a two-year or four-year university or college. Unfortunately, this figure has several limitations. First, it is only useful for high schools. Second, it does not account for students who may have dropped out of school, possibly creating a higher percentage of college-bound seniors than is really the case. Third, in some situations, percentage of college-bound students relies on self-reported student data instead of actual college enrollment. Finally, this school quality indicator may not differentiate between the types of college that students attend. Let's say that 80 percent of Smith High School seniors are college-bound, but of that amount 75 percent enroll in a two-year college. Meanwhile, let's say that the same proportion, 80 percent, of Garcia High School seniors are also attending college, but of that amount 75 percent are attending a four-year college. Although they have the same 80 percent college-bound percentage rate, Garcia High School appears to be more successful in preparing its students for a four-year college (Exhibit B.4).

Average Class Size

The research is quite mixed on how class size affects student achievement. Smaller class size seems to have a more positive effect for schools with less-disciplined or less-motivated students. If all students are motivated to learn, class size seems to make little difference in achievement. Class size also appears to have a greater effect on younger children than older, and usually the size (student-to-teacher ratio) needs to be reduced to approximately fifteen to one or less to make a substantial difference. Regardless of the research, smaller class size permits more interaction between students and teachers; consequently, parents continue to use class size as a factor when making a choice of school. Middle and high school class size is usually larger than in elementary schools. The report card for Polytechnic High School reports class size in four key subject areas, allowing comparison across three years (Exhibit B.5).

Exhibit B.4.

Postsecondary Preparation (High Schools Only)

Advanced Placement and International Baccalaureate Courses

Data reported are the number of Advanced Placement (AP) and International Baccalaureate (IB) courses and classes offered, and the enrollment in various classes. The data for fine and performing arts include AP Art and AP Music, and the data for social science include IB Humanities.

Subject	*Number of Courses*	*Number of Classes*	*Enrollment*
Fine and Performing Arts	3	3	56
Computer Science	1	1	13
English	2	10	345
Foreign Language	3	4	116
Mathematics	3	9	273
Science	5	12	358
Social Science	4	19	605

Student Enrollment in Courses Required for University of California (UC) and/or California State University (CSU) Admission

Data reported are the number and percent of student enrollment in courses required for University of California (UC) and/or California State University (CSU) admission. The percent of student enrollment is calculated by dividing the total student enrollment in courses required for UC and/or CSU admission by the total student enrollment in all courses. Note: Each student is counted in each course in which the student is enrolled. As a result of these duplicated counts, the student enrollment in all courses will, and the student enrollment in courses required for UC and/or CSU admission may, exceed the actual student enrollment figure for the school.

Student Enrollment in All Courses	*Student Enrollment In Courses Required for UC and/or CSU Admission*	*Percent of Student Enrollment In Courses Required for UC and/or CSU Admission*
27146	18450	68.0

Graduates Who Have Completed All Courses Required for University of California (UC) and/or California State University (CSU) Admission

Data reported are the number and percent of graduates who have completed all courses required for University of California (UC) and/or California State University (CSU) admission. The percent of graduates is calculated by dividing the total number of graduates who have completed all courses required for UC and/or CSU admission by the total number of graduates.

Number of Graduates	*Number of Graduates Who Have Completed All Courses Required For UC and/or CSU Admission*	*Percent of Graduates Who Have Completed All Courses Required For UC and/or CSU Admission*
990	520	52.5

Exhibit B.5

Average Teaching Load and Teaching Load Distribution (Middle and High Schools Only)

Data reported are the average class size and the number of classrooms that fall into each size category (i.e., number of students), by subject area, as reported by CBEDS. (MIDDLE AND HIGH SCHOOLS ONLY)

Grade Level	Avg. Class Size	2003 Number of Classrooms			Avg. Class Size	2004 Number of Classrooms			Avg. Class Size	2005 Number of Classrooms		
		1-22	23-32	33+		1-22	23-32	33+		1-22	22-32	33+
English	27.7	60	51	85	30.3	31	47	99	30.7	19	59	92
Mathematics	34.0	7	22	83	32.4	13	28	75	33.1	12	28	78
Science	32.8	7	26	59	33.6	5	24	65	33.7	6	17	69
Social Science	32.6	5	40	65	34.3	4	16	76	33.0	5	32	61

Suspension and Expulsion

Discipline rules vary substantially among states, school districts, and even schools, making this a less accurate indicator than some other factors. However, a fair amount of consistency normally occurs across schools in the same school district, allowing reasonable comparison between district schools. Polytechnic High School reports suspensions and expulsions across three years, which may help detect trends. However, the numbers can be highly variable and should be cautiously interpreted. The presence of a dress code or uniforms may also indicate a school or districtwide approach to maintaining safe schools (Exhibit B.6).

Percentage of Students Taking State Tests

In past years, states and school districts excluded a large number of special education and English language learning (ELL) students from their state tests, thereby inflating true student achievement. However, NCLB requires that a minimum of 95 percent of students take the state test, including special education, ELL, and significant subgroups such as Latinos and Latinas, African Americans, whites, and Asians. For a school you may be considering, the higher the percentage of students included in testing the more closely the test score represents the performance of all students at the school. Polytechnic High School reports an increasing percentage of students taking the California Standards Test, with a minimum of 95 percent growing to as high as 98 percent (Exhibit B.7).

Average SAT or ACT Scores

The SAT and ACT are used by many colleges as part of their admissions criteria and are therefore quite important for most college-bound students (Exhibit B.8). The average school scores are often used as a measure of high school quality and are of interest to parents. As one example, for the 2003–04 school year the average

Exhibit B.6.

Our Suspensions/Expulsions

	2002-03 (ADA 97,550)		2003-04 (ADA 96,317)		2004-05 (ADA 96,319)	
	School	District	School	District	School	District
Suspensions (number)	158	4,110	480	4,478	350	5,110
Suspensions (rate)	3%	4%	10%	4.6%	7.3%	5.3%
Expulsions (number)	0	40	6	67	4	24
Expulsions (rate)	0%	.04%	.1%	.06%	.08%	.02%

Exhibit B.7.

Schoolwide API

Data reported are API Base and Growth scores, growth targets, statewide and similar schools ranks, and percent tested.

	API Base Data				*API Growth Data*		
	2002	*2003*	*2004*		*2002*	*2003*	*2004*
Percent Tested	95	97	98	Percent Tested	97	98	98
API Base Score	655	686	696	API Base Score	696	697	715
Growth Target	7	6	5	Actual Growth	41	11	19
Statewide Rank	6	7	7				
Similar Schools Rank	8	9	7				

Exhibit B.8.

SAT 1 (Scores of High School Seniors)

	School			District			State		
	2004-05	2002-03	2003-04	2004-05	2002-03	2003-04	2004-05	2002-03	2003-04
Grade 12 Enrollment	1,132	1,149	1,151	6,506	6,220	6,424	409,576	385,181	395,194
% of Grade 12 Taking Test	45	49	44	31	33	30	36	37	35
Average Verbal Score	507	491	499	476	471	472	499	494	496
Average Math Score	537	518	533	498	495	499	521	518	519

combined national SAT score was 1026 out of a possible 1600. The average North Carolina combined SAT score for high school seniors was 1006 and for Wake County Public Schools the average was 1063, with three high schools above 1100 (WCPSS, 2004).

However, in 2005, the SAT underwent major changes, adding a third section of the test—a writing essay—and thus adding 800 more possible points for a combined total of 2400 points. Consequently, if using the SAT as a measure of school quality, be sure you are not comparing scores from 2004 and before to scores from 2005 and beyond.

The ACT has a scoring range of 1–36, with a combined average national score of English, math, reading, and science of about 21 in the year 2004. Both the reporting scales and reporting methods vary considerably between the SAT and ACT, so be cautious. Also, be aware that many schools report just one of these average scores, either the ACT or SAT, and that the scores reflect the performance only of those students who take the tests (usually college-bound seniors).

Student Mobility

The student mobility figure, although not often available on school report cards, affords a basic estimate of the rate of student turnover each year. In some urban schools, the percentage has exceeded 50 percent in a single year (Lasley and Bainbridge, 2001). Usually, a higher student mobility rate is associated with lower achievement, although parents should again realize that most public schools have no control over who enrolls and who leaves. This rate may become more widely available in the future, but it should be a key question to ask school administrators and other parents.

Other Information

School report cards contain a wealth of other useful information. Polytechnic High School, for example, reports that it was a California Distinguished School, offers internal academy programs, hosts an 900-plus-member PTA, has many parent booster clubs, and recently modernized several buildings. Effectively knowing how to use a school report card can simplify your search for finding a high-quality school district or school, but it should still not take the place of actually visiting the school before purchasing a new house or enrolling your child in a new school.

Appendix C: What to Look for in High-Quality Classrooms

If you are selecting a school for your child, make sure you visit classrooms in addition to the school buildings, and talking to the principal. Margaret Heritage, whom we met in Chapter Four, is now a researcher at CRESST. She devised the checklist presented here to help parents and others evaluate the quality of school classrooms. My thanks to Margaret for allowing me to use her guide.

Learning Context

Research shows that the teacher is the most important school factor in student learning. The role of the teacher is to create situations in which students learn. In this section, we highlight what an observer in a classroom might look for to indicate the quality of the learning situation for students. The observation criteria are by no means exhaustive, but they offer a guide for focusing a brief visit to a classroom.

Organization

- Is the classroom well ordered, or is it untidy and disorganized?
- Is the classroom set up for a range of instructional approaches (whole class teaching, small group work, individual work)?
- Is the classroom set up for independence? Are a range of materials and equipment readily accessible? Are there places for students to store their materials and backpacks? Are there charts with instructions that support routines, behavior and learning?

• Does the circulation of the classroom permit students to move about without interrupting the work of others and with a minimum of time wasted?

Resources

• Are there resources that support a variety of ways of explaining ideas and representing thinking (different types and sizes of paper, a range of writing tools, things to manipulate and build with, computers)?

• Are there objects and materials that reflect the cultural commonality, diversity, and richness of society (images that show people of diverse race and ethnicity, book displays and artifacts that reflect U.S. history and culture, and information on achievement of citizens, especially from underrepresented groups)?

• Are there resources and artifacts to encourage students to find information and investigate research questions (newspapers, maps, measuring tools, the Internet, videos, a range of reference books, posters, photographs)?

• Are there objects and materials that attract attention, arouse curiosity, and promote discussion because they are challenging, unusual, intriguing (objects from various time periods, primary source documents, cultural artifacts from many peoples, objects from the natural environment such as rocks, minerals, interesting plant life, and machines)?

• Is the curriculum mediated solely through a textbook?

Climate

• Are the students behaving in an orderly way?

• Do the students display interest and enthusiasm?

• Are the students listening to each other and to the teacher?

• Are there positive, supportive relationships between teachers and among peers?

• Are the values of care and respect taught and modeled? Is the teacher respectful to the students? Are the students respectful to each other?

• Is the noise level in the classroom conducive to learning?

Wall Displays

• Is there evidence of work in progress (brainstorms, graphic organizers, student questions)?

• Is there work that can be referred to as part of ongoing activity and used as sources of new ideas and new learning (charts, student problem-solving strategies, research notes)?

• Is there a range of final products of student work (diagrams, explanations, narratives, three-dimensional work)?

• Is the work displayed in a way that values and illustrates learning (for example, the work samples are accompanied by the standards they meet or by a description of the process; the work is mounted carefully and is displayed aesthetically)?

Lessons

The lesson the teacher has designed is an important indicator of quality. In this section, we pose questions to help guide observation of a lesson. Sometimes classroom observers have the opportunity to talk to the teacher and the students; we also include questions that an observer can ask to assist in evaluating the quality of a lesson.

Teacher

• Is the purpose of the lesson clear? Are the objectives stated at the beginning of the lesson?

• Can the teacher tell you what she is doing, and why? What is the lesson's purpose? Where it is leading the students?

• Is there a match between the stated objectives and what the students are doing?

- Does teacher feedback support learning? Is the feedback specific and substantive? Does the feedback help students move forward and take the next step? (For example, "You've got the right idea about trying to explain your rule. Now think: Does it apply to all triangles?" "You've described the author's intent very clearly. Now, can you identify some of the literary devices the author uses to achieve his intent?")
- Are the teacher's responses mainly managerial and procedural?
- Is the majority of the lesson time focused on learning, or is it spent mainly on organization and discipline?
- If the students are working independently, does the teacher engage with groups or individuals for instructional purposes, or does the teacher spend all the time monitoring the students while they are completing assigned tasks?
- If the students are working in groups, are they cooperating, sharing roles, discussing the topic, and listening to each other, all actively involved?
- Are transitions from one activity or from one grouping situation to another smooth?
- Who is doing all the work in the classroom: the teacher, or the students?

Student

- Can the students tell you what they are doing, and why? Do they know what the purpose of their activity is, or do they say they are doing the activity because they were told to? Do the students know how the particular lesson fits into a program of study?
- Is there a high level of participation from all students (equal participation from girls and boys, from students of various ethnicities and language proficiency)?
- Do the students say the task is easy? hard? interesting?
- Do the students looked interested in the lesson, or do they appear bored?

- Do they have all the materials they need with them, or do they waste learning time looking for materials?
- Are the students focused on what they are doing, or are they distracted?
- Do students waste a lot of time waiting for the teacher's help?
- Do the students help each other?
- Do the students give each other positive and constructive feedback ("I like the way you wrote about your experience, but one part wasn't clear to me. I'd like to suggest that . . . .")?
- Does what the students are doing seem *worth* doing?

Questions

If you can spend some time in a classroom, a good way to assess the quality of the classroom is to listen to the kind of questions the teacher and students ask during the lesson. Part of the skill of effective instruction is use of questions that directly affect the thinking of students. In this section, we guide you in focusing on questions in the classroom.

Teachers' Questions

- Are all the teachers' questions centered on discovering whether students know the "right" answer? (For example: "Who was the first man to step onto the moon?" "How many natural elements have been found on earth?") Or are questioning strategies used strategically to support development of students' thinking ("Can anyone add to John's idea? What is the difference between John's and Carrie's approaches to solving the problem?" "How does this give you an idea about how the plant carries on the process of photosynthesis?")?
- Are the majority of questions centered on instruction ("Can you show me what you have been working on today and describe what you are doing?"), or are they mainly procedural and behavioral

("Who needs time to finish the assignment? Can you keep your voices down?")?

• Do the questions show that teachers value students' thinking ("What might be another explanation for that?" "What prediction can you make about what is going to happen? Why do you think that?")?

• Does the teacher give sufficient wait time after asking the question to allow students to think and formulate an answer?

Students' Questions

• Do the students ask thinking questions (for example, "I wonder why . . . ?" "How does that compare with . . . ?" "Can you clarify your statement about . . . ?"), or are all the questions procedural ("How many pages do I need to write?")?

• Do the students initiate discussion ("Can I share my strategy with the group?")?

Lasting Impressions

At the end of the observation, what is the impression you take away from the classroom? If you were a student, would you say it is a place where you want to be? Is it a place that you are sorry to leave and would enjoy spending time in again? Most important, are you pleased that your child has or will have the opportunity to learn in this classroom? These are important questions to ask yourself at the end of your visit and will help you gauge the quality of the teaching and learning in the class.

Appendix D: Tips on Writing a Paper

Here is one method for writing a short paper of three hundred to six hundred words, but it can easily be adapted to longer writing assignments. (See Figure 7.1, Sample Graphic Organizer: Writing a Paper.) The organizer is based on a paper written during a five-day timeframe, but it can be adapted to the length of available time. I've written this Appendix as suggestions to a student, but parents may use it as a guide for their children.

Before You Start

Read the assignment from your teacher carefully. Then answer these questions:

1. What is the purpose of the report?
2. Who is the audience?
3. How long does the report have to be?
4. When is the report due? How much should I write each day in order to leave a full day for a final proofing and review?
5. Do I need any clarification from the teacher? (If so, get clarification the next time you see your teacher. Or send the teacher an e-mail message.)
6. Do I have all the resources that I need? (It's good to have everything gathered before you write, but in some cases you will need to do additional research to fill in the gaps. Get started early and stay with your schedule.)

Organize

- Brainstorm what you know about the topic. Write down details, even if it is just somewhat related to the topic. Don't worry about the order, and don't judge whether each detail will be included in the final report. If you can, write a full sentence about each detail (for example, "Alfred Wegener was a key figure in plate tectonics.").
- Review your other resources and add more details about the topic. Resources may include your classroom notes, textbooks, library books and magazines, Internet sources, and electronic encyclopedias. Some computers are preloaded with an electronic encyclopedia.
- Group what you know into categories. For example, you are doing a report on plate tectonics. Your categories might be the *key figures* associated with plate tectonics, the four fundamental plate tectonic *processes*, and three *uses* of plate tectonics today. Using notecards can help you move things around.
- Outline the report. Your first paragraph introduces the topic and the subtopics. The middle section describes each of the main categories. The final paragraph should summarize your report. If a category or your entire paper follows a chronological order, arrange your outline accordingly. Chronological order is easy to follow. In this illustration, the key figures in plate tectonics would be introduced in the order in which they lived.

Write the Paper

If you have written a sentence for every detail, the writing process should primarily be putting those sentences in order and adding transitions between sentences and paragraphs. Each paragraph should begin with a topic sentence that leads into the rest of the paragraph. Here is an example of a draft.

> Three key figures in the development of a theory of plate tectonics were James Hutton, Charles Lyell, and Alfred Wegener. In the 1700s, James Hutton, a Scottish chemist and geologist, theorized

> that the earth was much older than previously thought, setting forth the concept of uniformitarianism. Described in his book *Theory of the Earth*, Hutton theorized that present geologic processes were responsible for the development of the earth over millions of years, countering beliefs that the earth was only 6,000 years old. Charles Lyell, a British geologist in the 1800s, built upon Hutton's theory . . . .

Review and revise several times until the paper seems to flow smoothly. Run a spelling and grammar review. Use active verbs and subjects. Don't worry if your paper isn't perfect; save that for the rewriting process.

Rewrite

Review your grammar, spelling, vocabulary, and sentence structure. Check especially for run-on sentences and words that repeat too frequently. Ask your parents to read it over. If the paper is submitted to your teacher in sections—such as an outline, first draft, and final paper—make sure that you have made the required changes. As your writing improves, you will try new techniques. You may include quotes, pose questions that you then answer, or use storytelling devices (See also Writing, Chapter 7).

References

If this is a research report, check your citations and references closely. There are quite a few styles available, among them MLA (Modern Language Association of America), APA (American Psychological Association), and Chicago Manual of Style, to name a few. Whichever style guide your school uses, buy a copy of the manual as an essential reference for future papers. In addition to covering research citations and references, each style guide covers many important writing topics such as selecting a topic, taking notes, where to find information, and plagiarism. A useful Web site for helping to properly format references is citationmachine.net.

Finally, go back and read your teacher's instructions that may cover such details as the title page, a specific font to use, or placement of page numbers. Check your paper for each of these and make sure you have followed the directions precisely. Although properly formatting your paper won't make up for poor writing, an improperly formatted paper sends a red flag to the teacher that the entire paper deserves a closer look.

Teachers require different types of writing assignments so that you become proficient in multiple formats, but some assignments may give you options such as a book report, movie review, newspaper article, or research report. As a student, try different types of writing assignments, build your skills in each format so that you will be prepared for any type of future writing.

Appendix E: Assessment Glossary

Accommodations: Changes in a test's administration or design that help to compensate for a student's disabilities or limited English proficiency while maintaining the integrity of the test. An accommodation is a change to the test administration, such as allowing a student more time to take the test; an *adaptation* usually changes the test itself (as with simplifying the wording of the test).

Alternative assessment: (also authentic or performance assessment) Usually, an assessment of student skills or knowledge by any method other than multiple-choice, true-false, fill-in-the-blank, or short-answer. When scored and used as an assessment, any of the following are often considered alternative assessments: exhibitions, science experiments, demonstrations, written or oral responses, journals, and portfolios. Ideally, alternative assessments require students to "show what they know" rather than have the opportunity to guess at an answer. Well-made alternative assessments may also help children learn from the assessment.

Achievement level: Performance standards that define broad categories of performance on a test, usually set by a state or the federal government. The National Assessment of Educational Progress uses four achievement levels: below basic, basic, proficient, and advanced.

Anchor(s): A sample of student work that represents a specific performance level or grade. For example, a teacher gives students a sample essay that received a grade of A. The sample essay is an anchor paper. On performance assessments administered to many students, raters usually have previously scored anchors for each possible grade or score to help them score all assessments consistently. On classroom assignments or assessments, anchors can help students understand a teacher's expectations for a specific grade.

Assessment: Measurement of a student's knowledge, skills, performance, or ability.

Assessment system: Multiple assessments combined into a comprehensive reporting format that produces accurate information about student or school performance. A student assessment system, for example, might include a state standards-based test, a norm-referenced test such as the Iowa Tests of Basic Skills, a district test (often called a *benchmark assessment*), and a combination of classroom tests.

Classroom assessment: Teacher- or textbook-developed measurements of student knowledge or skills, usually in a specific subject. In addition to being used to assign grades, classroom assessments allow the teacher to inform and influence their own instruction and to diagnose student or classroom strengths and weaknesses.

Content standards: Clearly defined requirements of what students should *know and be able to do* in specific subjects and grades, usually developed and set by the state. The content standards form the basis of what should be taught in the classroom and what will be measured on state tests.

Criteria: Well-defined performance guidelines used to evaluate the quality of student work. A criterion in a student essay on World War II, for example, might be "the main causes and effects of World War II," with points awarded for the quality and number of causes and effects mentioned. Criteria are often consolidated into a scoring rubric, which produces a score for each criterion and a combined score. Criteria, when well defined and effectively communicated to students, afford valuable guidance on how a particular assignment or assessment will be scored.

Criterion-referenced test: Measurement and reporting student performance on a specific standard, goal, or criterion. On criterion-referenced tests, the test developer or state usually sets a cut score for a specific achievement level. It is possible that all or no children will reach a specific achievement level. Bar exams, medical exams, high school graduation tests, and so forth usually require the test taker to attain a minimum criterion to pass the test. No Child Left Behind requires that all students reach the proficient or advanced level of their state tests by the 2013–14 school year.

Grade equivalent score: The report of a student performance based on a child's age, and usually based on a school calendar. A fifth grade child receiving a grade equivalent score of 5.5 on a math test would be considered to have performed at about the level of other students in the fifth month of the fifth grade on this particular math test. Though easy to understand, grade equivalents are only a rough estimate of children at particular years and months. Parents should be extremely cautious about grade equivalent scores because they suggest more accuracy than is usually the case. In this example, there is no guarantee that any child at the fifth grade and fifth month actually took the test.

Item: An individual question or problem on an assessment.

Norm-referenced assessment: An assessment where student performance is reported in comparison to a larger group. The larger group, called a "norm group," is often a national sample representing a wide and diverse cross-section of students. On a norm-referenced test, 50 percent of students perform above the midpoint of the test and 50 percent perform below it, regardless of how skilled the students are as a total group. A test can be both norm- and criterion-referenced.

Percentile rank: On a norm-referenced test, the norm group performance range is divided into 100 equal parts, with 50 percent of the scores above the midpoint and 50 percent below the midpoint. A score at the 77th percentile rank means that 77 percent of the students in the norm group scored below that student.

Performance assessment: See alternative assessment.

Performance standards: Explicit definitions of what students must do to demonstrate proficiency at a specific level on the content standards. For example, the performance level "exceptional achievement" on a dimension "communication of ideas" is reached when the student "examines the problem from several positions and provides adequate evidence to support each position."

Portfolio assessment: A collection of student work scored with well-defined criteria and used to measure student knowledge and skills, frequently over a period of time.

Standards-based assessment: Usually an assessment that measures student, school, or state progress in achieving a set of content standards. Achievement is usually reported as a specific achievement level for students, and as a percentage of students reaching a "proficient or above" achievement level for schools, districts, and states.

Appendix F: Supplemental *Get Smart!* Resources

The resources described in this appendix were accurate at the time of this writing. Because many of them -are Internet-based, they may not necessarily be available now or in the future if their Internet addresses change.

Resources Mentioned in *Get Smart!*

SWRL Reading Program: The SWRL (Southwest Regional Laboratory for Educational Research) reading program has been adapted into the Reading for All Learners Program. (www.usu.edu/teach/read.htm; www.usu.edu/teach/text/Scientific.pdf)

Balanced Assessment Tasks: The math Balance Assessment problems may be found at two Websites: http://balancedassessment.concord.org/ and http://balancedassessment.concord.org/aboutprogram.html.

Math Replacement Units: The math replacement units produced by the California Department of Education are no longer available; however, Rebecca Corwin and Susan Russell wrote several of the books used in the original program, including *Measuring: From Paces to Feet* and *Sorting: Groups and Graphs*. There is information about the *Mathematics Teacher Education and Resource Place* at http://www2.sjsu.edu/depts/mathed/syllabi3.html.

Released Test Questions: Many test questions in math and science are available from the Third International Mathematics and

Science Test of 1995 and 2003. TIMSS released test questions in fourth and eighth grade math and science may be found at timss.bc.edu/timss2003i/released.html. Released test questions in elementary, middle, and high school math and science are available from TIMSS (timss.bc.edu/timss1995i/Items.html).

State Released Test Questions: Many states have released test questions from their state tests. Check your state department of education Website. For example, released questions from the California High School Exit Exam may be found at www.cde.ca.gov/ta/tg/hs/resources.asp.

SAT: Information about the new Scholastic Aptitude Test, including sample questions, may be found at www.collegeboard.com/newsat/index.html.

ACT: Comprehensive information about the ACT may be found on the ACT Website, www.act.org. Sample questions from the main ACT may be found at http://www.actstudent.org/sampletest/index.html. Sample writing questions may be found at www.act.org/aap/writing/sample/index.html.

Oprah Program on the Effects of Crystal Methamphetamines: Websites indicating that the Oprah video program on Crystal methamphetamines may be ordered through them is http://hs.boisestate.edu/radar/videos/meth.pdf.

Suggested Publications

The following books, magazines, and Websites are useful resources for parents.

Books

- *A Mind at a Time*. (2002). By Mel Levine. Pediatrician Levine shares more than thirty years of his experience in helping children whose minds are different from others'. He offers many suggestions for parents to improve their child's learning in school.

• *In Schools We Trust: Creating Communities of Learning in an Era of Testing and Standardization*. (2002). By Deborah Meier. The legendary founder of Central Park East School in Harlem and Mission Hill School in Boston, Meier writes with passion and experience about her own trust in public schools. Chapter 3, "Parents and Schools," gives invaluable insight into the critical relationship between these most important partners.

• *Motivated Minds: Raising Children to Love Learning*. (2001). By Deborah Stipek and Kathy Seal. The authors offer a practical and useful guide on how to motivate children to succeed in school.

• *Schools That Learn: A Fifth Discipline Fieldbook for Educators, Parents, and Everyone Who Cares About Education*. (2000). By Peter Senge, Nelda Cambron-McCabe, Timothy Lucas, Bryan Smith, Janis Dutton, and Art Kleiner. Practical advice to parents and educators on how to improve our nation's schools, with dozens of innovative examples of ideas that work.

• *Spark Your Child's Success in Math and Science: Practical Advice for Parents*. (2002). By Jacqueline Barber, Nicole Parizeau, and Lincoln Bergman. Winner of a Parent's Guide Award, *Spark Your Child's Success* offers dozens of research-based methods for parents to help their children in both math and science.

• *Testing Students with Disabilities*. (2002). By Martha Thurlow, Judy L. Elliott, and James Ysseldyke. Written by many of the best-known experts on learning disabilities, Testing Students with Disabilities covers its topic in depth and provides many useful tools to support professional development.

• *Improving Test Performance of Students with Disabilities . . . on District and State Assessments* (Second Edition). (2006). By Judy Elliott and Martha Thurlow. Provides many strategies for improving instruction and learning for students with disabilities including test accommodations, goals alignment, and practical applications.

Magazines

• *Our Children: the National PTA Magazine*. Each issue contains parenting articles by experts on children's education, health, and well-being; information on advocacy efforts; the latest news that affects children and youth; and updates from National PTA, and state and local PTAs (http://www.pta.org/pr_our_children_magazine.html).

• *Edutopia*, published by the George Lucas Educational Foundation. *Edutopia* covers a broad variety of topics on current educational issues. Also has an e-newsletter. Although written primarily for teachers, the articles cover many school topics of interest to parents. Has a special focus on technology to support learning (http://www.edutopia.org/magazine/index.php).

Recommended Websites

The U.S. Department of Education has many helpful publications for parents who want to support their children's learning. Here are just a few.

- Help My Child with Academics (www.ed.gov/parents/academic/help/edpicks.jhtml?src=ln)
- Knowing More About Learning Disabilities (www.ed.gov/parents/needs/speced/edpicks.jhtml?src=ln)
- Helping Gifted Children (www.ed.gov/parents/needs/gifted/edpicks.jhtml?src=ln)
- Helping Children with English Language Learning Needs (www.ed.gov/parents/needs/english/edpicks.jhtml?src=ln)

The Links to Better Education site has links to hundreds of sites on dozens of diverse education topics, ranging from speech anxiety to studying physics. Some of the links were not active at the time of this writing, but there are so many that it is well worth your time to take a look. Most of the sites have suggestions for students to help them perform well in school (http://www.chemistrycoach.com/linkstoa.htm).

The Monroe County Public Library in Indiana has many links for parents to other Websites on diverse topics ranging from children's software to helping your child use the Internet (http://www.monroe.lib.in.us/childrens/parents.html). Other useful links from the Monroe County Public Library may be found at www.monroe.lib.in.us/ childrens/pmags.html, including links to home schooling resources.

The Center on School, Family and Community Partnerships helps families, educators, and members of communities work together to improve schools and enhance student learning and development (http://www.csos.jhu.edu/p2000/center.htm).

The Southwest Educational Development Laboratory has helpful research and tools about family involvement in schools (http://www.sedl.org/work/family_community.html).

A few Websites that my children use regularly are www.Wikipedia.org, a free encyclopedia with nearly one million entries; and Dictionary.com (at http://dictionary.reference.com), Thesaurus.com (at http://thesaurus.reference.com), and www.reference.com. Each of these last three web sites contains what its name implies and supports children's learning on a variety of school subjects and research projects.

References

Abedi, J. (2004). The No Child Left Behind Act and English language learners: Assessment and accountability issues. *Educational Researcher, 33*(1), 4–14.

American Psychological Association Board of Educational Affairs. (1997, November). *Learner-centered psychological principles: Guidelines for school redesign and reform*. Washington, DC: American Psychological Association. [http://www.apa.org/ed/lcp2/lcptext.html]; retrieved May 8, 2006.

American Educational Research Association, American Psychological Association, and National Council on Measurement in Education. (1999). *Standards for educational and psychological testing*. Washington, DC: American Educational Research Association.

Aschbacher, P. R. (1999). *Developing indicators of classroom practice to monitor and support school reform*. (CSE Technical Report 513). Los Angeles: National Center for Research on Evaluation, Standards, and Student Testing.

Asimov, N. (2003, May 5). Hakuta argues teachers of English learners are underqualified. *San Francisco Chronicle*. [http://ed.stanford.edu/suse/news-bureau/displayRecord.php?tablename=notify1&id=121].

Atkinson, R. C., & Jackson, G. B. (1992). *Research and education reform: Roles for the office of educational research and development*. Washington, DC: National Research Council.

Bailey, D. (2000). From the directors: Long-term consequences of childcare. *Early Development*, 4(1), 1.

Baker, E. L. (1999, Summer). *Technology: Something's coming, something good*. (CRESST Policy Brief 2). Los Angeles: National Center for Research on Evaluation, Standards, and Student Testing.

Baker, E. L., Aschbacher, P. R., Niemi, D., & Sato, E. (1992). *CRESST performance assessment models: assessing content area explanations*. (CSE Technical Report 652). Los Angeles: National Center for Research on Evaluation, Standards, and Student Testing.

Baker, E. L., Niemi, D., Herl, H., Aguirre-Muñoz, Z., Staley, L., & Linn R. L. (1999). *Report on the content area performance assessments (CAPA): A collaboration among the Hawaii Department of Education, the Center for Research on Evaluation, Standards, and Student Testing (CRESST) and the teachers and children of Hawaii*. (Final Deliverable). Los Angeles: National Center for Research on Evaluation, Standards, and Student Testing.

Banner, J., & Cannon, H. C. (1999). *The elements of learning*. New Haven, CT: Yale University Press.

Barber, J., Parizeau, N., & Bergman, L. (2002). *Spark your child's success in math and science: Practical advice for parent*. Berkeley, CA: Great Explorations in Math and Science.

Barnett, Steven. (1995). Long-Term Effects of Early Childhood Programs on Cognitive and School Outcomes. *The Future of Children*, 5(3), 25–50.

Baum, S. (1990). *Gifted but learning disabled: A puzzling paradox*. (ERIC EC Digest #E47). Reston, VA: ERIC Clearinghouse on Disabilities and Gifted Education. [http://www.kidsource.com/kidsource/content/Gifted_learning_disabled.html].

Becher, R. (1986). *Parents and schools*. ED269137. ERIC Digest. ERIC Clearinghouse on Elementary and Early Childhood Education. [http://www.ericdigests.org/pre-924/parents.htm].

Bennett, W. J. (1986). *What works: Research about teaching and learning*. Washington, DC: U.S. Department of Education.

Black, P., & Wiliam, D. (1998). Inside the black box: Raising standards through classroom assessment. *Phi Delta Kappan*, 80(2), 46-48. [http://www.pdkintl.org/kappan/kbla9810.htm].

Bloom, B. S., Englehart, M. D., Furst, E. J., Hill, W. H., & Krathwohl, D. R. (1956). *Taxonomy of educational objectives: The classification of educational goals*. New York: Longmans, Green.

Briggs, M., Safaii, S., & Lane Beall, D. (2003). Position of the American Dietetic Association, Society for Nutrition Education, and American School Food Service Association—Nutrition Services: An essential component of comprehensive school health programs. *Journal of the American Dietetic Association*, *103*, 505–514.

Boehner, J. (2004, April). *No Child Left Behind implementation station*. [http://edworkforce.house.gov/issues/108th/education/nclb/nclb.htm].

Brophy, J. (1987, October). Synthesis of research on strategies for motivating students to learn. *Educational Leadership*, 40–48.

Butler, D. L. (1998, August). *Promoting self-regulation in the context of academic tasks: The strategic content learning approach*. Paper presented at annual American Psychological Association meeting, San Francisco.

Chi, M.T.H., & Bassok, M. (1989). Learning from examples via self-explanations. In L. B. Resnick (Ed.), *Knowing, learning and instruction: In honor of Robert Glaser* (pp. 251–282). Mahwah, NJ: Erlbaum.

Choi, K. C., Seltzer, M., Herman, J. L., & Yamashiro, K. (2004). *Children left behind in AYP and non-AYP schools: Using student progress and the distribution of student gains to validate AYP*. (CSE Technical Report 637). Los

Angeles: National Center for Research on Evaluation, Standards, and Student Testing.

Choi, K. C., & Shin, E. (2003). *What are the chances of getting into a UC school?* (CSE Report 623). Los Angeles: National Center for Research on Evaluation, Standards, and Student Testing.

Clare Matsumura, L. (2000). *Using teachers' assignments as an indicator of classroom practice*. (CSE Technical Report 532). Los Angeles: National Center for Research on Evaluation, Standards, and Student Testing.

Clare Matsumura, L., Garnier, H. E., & Pascal, J. (2002). *Measuring instructional quality in accountability systems: Classroom assignment quality and student achievement*. (CSE Technical Report 582). Los Angeles: National Center for Research on Evaluation, Standards, and Student Testing.

Clark, R. (2003). *The essential 55*. New York: Hyperion.

Clark, R. (2005). Instructional strategies. In H. F. O'Neil (Ed.), *What works in distance learning: Guidelines* (pp. 89-109.) Greenwich, CT: Information Age.

Clowes, G. A. (1998, April 1). *U.S. twelfth-graders flunk international math and science test*. School Reform News: The Heartland Institute. [http://heatland.org/ Article.cfn?artld=13402].

Conaway, M. S. (1982). Listening: Learning tool and retention agent. In A. S. Algier & K. W. Algier (Eds.), *Improving reading and study skills* (pp. 51–63). San Francisco: Jossey-Bass.

Cooper, S. J. (2002, April 10). Selectivity rises in ivy league schools. *Daily Princetonian News*. [http://www.daily princetonian.com/archives/ 2002/04/10/news/4852.shtml].

Costa, A. L. (2000). Describing habits of mind. In A. L. Costa & B. Kallick (Eds.), *Discovering and exploring habits of mind* (pp. 21–40). Alexandria, VA: Association for Supervision and Curriculum Development.

Costa, A. L., & Kallick, B. (2000). Teaching the habits of mind directly. In A. L. Costa & B. Kallick (Eds.), *Activating and engaging habits of mind* (pp. 72–97). Alexandria, VA: Association for Supervision and Curriculum Development.

Cotton, K., & Wikelund, K. R. (2001). Parent involvement in education. *School improvement research series: Research you can use*. Portland, OR: Northwest Regional Educational Laboratory. [http://www.nwrel.org/scpd/sirs/3/cu6.html].

Darling-Hammond, L., & Loewenberg Ball, D. (1998). *Teaching for high standards: What policymakers need to know and be able to do*. New York: National Commission on Teaching and America's Future and Consortium for Policy Research in Education.

Dembo, M., & Gubler Junge, L., (2005). Learning strategies. In H. F. O'Neil (Ed.), *What works in distance learning: Guidelines* (pp. 41–64). Greenwich, CT: Information Age.

Dobyns, L., & Crawford-Mason, C. (1994). *Thinking about quality: Progress, wisdom, and the Deming philosophy*. New York: Random House.

Dominowski, R. 1998. Verbalization and problem solving. In D. J. Hacker, J. Dunlosky, & A. C. Graesser (Eds.), *Metacognition in educational theory and practice* (pp. 25–46). Mahwah, NJ: Erlbaum.

Duckworth, A. L., & Seligman, M.E.P. (2005). Self-discipline outdoes IQ in predicting academic performance of adolescents. *Psychological Science, 16*(12), 939–944.

Dweck, C. (2000, February 7). How can teachers develop students' motivation and success? Website interview by Gary Hopkins. *Education World.* [http:/www.educationworld.com/a_issues/chat/chat010.shtml].

Dybvik, A. C. (2004, Winter). Autism and the inclusion mandate. *Education Next*, pp. 42–47.

Edmonds, R. R. (1979, March/April). Some schools work and more can. *Social Policy*, 28–32.

Edmonds, R. R. (1981, September/October). Making public schools effective. *Social Policy*, 56–60.

Education Trust. (2003, December). Telling the whole truth (or not) about high school graduation rates. Washington, DC: Education Trust [www2.edtrust.org/NR/rdonlyres/4DE8F2E0–4D08–4640-B3B0–013F6DC3865D/0/tellingthetruth gradrates.pdf].

Eisner, E. W. (2000). Benjamin Bloom: 1913–1991. *Prospects: The quarterly review of comparative education*. Paris: UNESCO, International Bureau of Education, *30*(3).

Epstein, J. L. (1994). Theory to practice: School and family partnerships lead to school improvement and student success. In C. Fagnano & B. Werber (Eds.), *School, family, and community interactions: A view from the firing line*. Boulder, CO: Westview Press.

Epstein, J. L., Sanders, M. G., Simon, B. S., Salinas, K. C., Jansorn, N. R., & Van Voorhis, F. L. (2002). *School, family, and community partnerships: Your handbook for action* (2nd ed.). Thousand Oaks, CA: Corwin Press.

Fasko, D., Jr. (2000–01). Education and creativity. *Creativity research journal. 13*(3&4), 317–327.

Fawcett, A. E. (1965). *The effect of training in listening upon the listening skills of intermediate grade children*. Doctoral thesis. Pittsburgh, PA: University of Pittsburgh, p. 237. (Abstract: Dissertation Abstracts 25: 7108–7109; November 12, 1965).

Foorman, B., Francis, D., Beeler, T., Winikates, D, & Fletcher, J. (1997). Early interventions for children with reading problems: Study designs and preliminary findings. *Learning Disabilities: A Multi-disciplinary Journal*, 63–71.

Gall, M. D., Gall, J. P, Jacobsen, D. R., & Bullock, T. L. (1990). *Tools for learning: A guide to teaching study skills*. Alexandria, VA: Association for Supervision and Curriculum Development.

Gallagher, T. *Thomas Edison, ADD poster child.* [http://borntoexplore.org/edison.htm.]; retrieved August 23, 2005.

Gardner, H. (1993). *Creating minds*. New York: HarperCollins.

Gerber, B. L., Cavallo, A., & Marek, E. A. (2001). Relationships among informal learning environments, teaching procedures and scientific reasoning ability. *International journal of science education, 23*(5), 535–549.

Gerstner, L. V. (2001, October 9). Remarks as delivered at the 2001 National Education Summit. [http://66.102.7.104/search?q=cache:OjJeC0UvwQAJ:www.ibm.com/lvg/1009.phtml+&hl=en].

Glazier, B. "Pascale Honored by State Legislators." *South Pasadena Review* [http://www. southpasadenareview.com/aroundtown.html]; retrieved March 26, 2005.

Greene, R. W. (1998). *The explosive child*. New York: HarperCollins.

Haydel, A., & Roeser, R. (1992). On motivation, ability, and the perceived situation in science test performance: A person-centered approach with high school students. *Educational Assessment,* 8(2), 163–189.

Hedges, L. V., Konstantopoulos, S., & Thoreson, A. (2003, April). *NAEP validity studies: Computer use and its relation to academic achievement in mathematics, reading, and writing*. (Working Paper 2003–15) Washington, DC: National Center for Education Statistics.

Henkart, A. F., & Henkart, J. (1998). *Cool communication*. Novato, CA: Family Freedom.

Herman, J. L., & Yeh, J. P. (1980). *Some effects of parent involvement in schools*. (CSE Technical Report 138). Los Angeles: UCLA Center for the Study of Evaluation.

Hiatt-Michael, D. (2001). *Preparing teachers to work with parents*. (ERIC Digest ED460123). Washington, DC: ERIC Clearinghouse on Teaching and Teacher Education. [http://www.ericdigests.org/2002-3/parents.htm].

Higbee, K. L. (2001). *Your memory: How it works and how to improve it*. New York: Marlowe.

Howe, A. (1996, December 9). *Adolescents' motivation, behavior and achievement in science*. [http://www.educ.sfu.ca/narstsite/publications/research/Adolescent.htm].

Hughes, T. (2004, June 27). *How do you help your child succeed?* Presentation to 2004 National PTA Convention, Anaheim, CA.

Jackson, D. N. (1998). *An exploration of selected conative constructs and their relation to science learning*. (CSE Technical Report 467.) Los Angeles: National Center for Research on Evaluation, Standards, and Student Testing.

Josephson, M. (2005, February). *Live backwards*. [http://www. charactercounts.org/knxwk398.htm (347:5)].

Journal of the American Dietetic Association. (2003). 103, 505–514. [http://www.eatright.org/cps/rde/xchg/ada/hs.xsl/advocacy_1729_ENU_HTML.htm].

Juvenile delinquency. (1997). *Prevention Researcher,* 4(2). [http://www. tpronline.org/read.cfm?ID=22].

Karnes, M. B., McCoy, G. F., Zehrbach, R. R., Wollersheim, J. P., Clarizio, H. F.,

Costin, L., & Stanley, L. S. (1961). *Factors associated with underachievement and overachievement of intellectually gifted children*. Champaign, IL: Champaign Community Unit Schools.

Keech, C. (2004, June 27). *Help your child succeed in middle school and high school*. Presentation to 2004 National PTA Convention, Anaheim, CA.

Kupermintz, H. (2002). *Levels of affective and conative constructs* (pp. 123–137). Mahwah, NJ: Erlbaum.

Lasley, T. J., & Bainbridge, W. L. (2001, November 11). Black students lag behind white counterparts: Urban schools must close the achievement gap. Dayton, OH: *Dayton Daily News*.

Lemke, M., Sen, A., Pahlke, E., Partelow, L., Miller, D., Williams, T., Kastberg, D., Jocelyn, L. (2004, December 6). International outcomes of learning in mathematics literacy and problem solving: PISA 2003 results from the U.S. perspective. [http://nces.ed.gov/pubsearch/pubsinfo.asp?pubid=2005003]; retrieved May 8, 2006.

Lerner, R. (2004, December 6). *Statement on the release of the program for international student assessment (PISA)*. [http://www.nces.ed.gov/commissioner/remarks2004/ 12_6_2004.asp].

Levine, M. (2002). *A mind at a time*. New York: Simon and Schuster.

Lewis, A. (1999, June). *1998 CRESST conference proceedings: Comprehensive systems for educational accountability and improvement*. (CSE Technical Report 504.) Los Angeles: National Center for Research on Evaluation, Standards, and Student Testing.

Linn, R. L. (2005). *Fixing the No Child Left Behind Act*. (CRESST Policy Brief 8). Los Angeles: National Center for Research on Evaluation, Standards, and Student Testing.

Lundsteen, S.W.R. (1965, November). Critical listening: Permanency and transfer of gains made during an experiment in the fifth and sixth grades. *California Journal of Education Research, 16*, 210–216.

Lutkus, A. D., Daane, M. C., Weiner, A. W., & Jin, Y. (2003). *The Nation's Report Card: Writing 2002, Trial Urban District Assessment*. U.S. Department of Education, Institute of Education Sciences. Washington, DC: National Center for Education Statistics.

Maltin, L. (1995). *Leonard Maltin's movie encyclopedia: Career profiles of more than 2000 actors and filmmakers, past and present*. New York: Penguin Press.

Martin, D. (2006, March 29). Hawaii schools' progress slides. *Honolulu Star Bulletin*. [http://starbulletin.com/2006/03/29/news/story06.html].

Marzano, R. J. (2003). *What works in schools: Translating research into action*. Alexandria, VA: Association for Supervision and Curriculum Development.

Marzano, R. J., Pickering, D. J., & Pollock, J. E. (2001). *Classroom instruction that works: Research-based strategies for increasing student achievement*. Alexandria, VA: Association for Supervision and Curriculum Development.

Mastergeorge, A. (2000, December). Presentation to the Education Writers of

America, Los Angeles. [http://www.cse.ucla.edu/products/ overheads_set.htm].

McCabe, M. P. (1991). Influence on creativity and intelligence on academic performance. *Journal of creative behavior, 21*, 271–282.

McCombs, B. L. (1991). The definition and measurement of primary motivational processes. In M. Wittrock & E. L. Baker (Eds.), *Testing and cognition* (pp. 62–81). Mahwah, NJ: Erlbaum.

McGowen, M., & Tall, D. (2001). *Flexible thinking, consistency, and stability of responses: A study of divergence*. [http://www.warwick.ac.uk/staff/ David.Tall/drafts/dot2001-mcgowen-tall-draft.pdf].

McLean, H. (2004, February 23). *Schools chief Jack O'Connell sponsors legislation to improve high school student performance*. (CDE News Release #04–17). [www.cde.ca.gov/nr/ne/yr04/yr04rel17.asp.] Sacramento: California Department of Education.

Mead, N. A., & Rubin, D. L. (1985). *Assessing listening and speaking skills*. (ERIC Digest ED 2632626). Urbana, IL: ERIC Clearinghouse on Reading and Communication Skills. [http://ericae.net/edo/ED263626.htm].

Meier, D. (2002). *In schools we trust*. Boston: Beacon Press.

Misra, R., & McKean, M. (2000). College students' academic stress and its relation to their anxiety, time management, and leisure satisfaction. *American Journal of Health Studies, 16*, 41–51.

Mondale, S., & Patton, S. B. (2001). *School: The story of American public education*. Boston: Beacon Press.

National Center for Education Statistics. (2001). Fathers' and mothers' involvement in their children's schools by family type and resident status. (NCES 2001–032). Washington, DC: U.S. Department of Education.

Gerald, D. E., & Hussar, W. J. (2003, October). *Projections of education statistics to 2013*. (NCES Report 2004–013). Washington, DC: National Center for Education Statistics, United States Department of Education. [http://nces.ed.gov//programs/projections/ch_1.asp#1].

National Center for Education Statistics. (2005, June). *The condition of education*. (NCES Publication 2005094). Washington, DC: United States Department of Education. [http://nces.ed.gov/programs/coe/2005/section1/indicator06.asp].

National Commission on Excellence in Education (NCEE). (1983). *A nation at risk: The imperative for educational reform*. Washington, DC: U.S. Government Printing Office.

National Research Council. (2000). *How people learn: Brain, mind, experience, and school* (expanded edition). Committee on Developments in the Science of Learning (J. D. Bransford, A. L. Brown, & R. R. Cocking, Eds.). Washington, DC: National Academy Press.

Nelson, J. R., Martella, R. M., & Marchand-Martella, N. (2002). Maximizing student learning: The effects of a comprehensive school-based program for preventing problem behaviors. *Journal of Emotional and Behavioral Disorders, 10*(3), 136–148.

No Child Left Behind Act of 2001, Pub. L. No. 107–110, 115 Stat. 1425 (2002).

O'Neil, H. F., Jr., & Abedi, J. (1996). Reliability and validity of a state metacognitive inventory: Potential for alternative assessment. *Journal of Educational Research, 89*, 234–245.

Ouchi, W. (2003). Making schools work: A revolutionary plan to get your children the education they need. New York: Simon and Schuster.

Peterson, P. L. (1997, April). *Learning to talk with new audiences about educational research.* Presidential address presented at annual meeting of American Educational Research Association Conference, Chicago.

Piaget, J. (1959). *The language and thought of the child* (3rd ed.). London: Routledge and Kegan Paul.

Pinzur, M. (2003, February 15). *Builders grade Dade school district.* [http://www.miami.com/mld/miamiherald/news/photos/5187193.htm?1c].

Quick Facts. (2005, August). *UCLA news.* Los Angeles: University of California, Los Angeles. [http://newsroom.ucla.edu/page.asp?menu=mediaserv & submenu=background].

Rafoth, M. A., Leal, L., & DeFabo, L. (1993). *Strategies for learning and remembering: Study skills across the curriculum.* Washington, DC: National Education Association.

Renzulli, J. S. (1992). A general theory for the development of creative productivity in young people. In F. J. Monks & W.A.M. Peters (Eds.), *Talent for the future: Social and personality development of gifted children. Proceedings of the Ninth World Conference on Gifted and Talented Children* (pp. 51–72). Assen/Maastricht, The Netherlands: Van Gorcum.

Rosenau, J. S. (1998). Familial influences on academic risk in high school: A multi-ethnic study. [Doctoral dissertation, Temple University, (1998). UMI No. 9911056]. Cited in Marzano, R. (2003). *What works in schools: Translating research into action*, p. 130.

Rothstein, R., Carnoy, M., & Benveniste, L. (1999). *Can public schools learn from private schools?* Case studies in the public and private non-profit sectors. Economic Policy Institute.

San Diego City Schools releases youth risk behavior survey: Biennial survey shows 10-year trend. (2002, February 26). San Diego: San Diego City Schools media release. [http://www.sandi.net/news-releases/news-releases/2002/020226YRBS.html].

San Marino (CA) High School Report Card (2004). San Francisco: School Wise Press.[http://www.schoolwisepress.com/pdf-vault/19/19–64964–1937754h.pdf].

Sanders, W. L., & Horn, S. (1994). The Tennessee Value-Added Assessment System (TVAAS): Mixed-model methodology in educational assessment. *Journal of Personnel Evaluation in Education, 8*, 299–311.

Schwendiman, J., & Fager, J. (1999, January). *School programs: Good for kids, good for communities*. Portland, OR: Northwest Regional Educational Laboratory. [http://www.nwrel.org/request/jan99/article4.html].

Seiler, J. S. (2004). *High school math level and its influence on science achievement*. Master's thesis, Webster University [http://www.mrseiler.org/thesis.pdf].

Stecher, B. M., & Barron, S. I. (1999). *Quadrennial milepost accountability testing in Kentucky*. (CSE Technical Report 505). Los Angeles: National Center for Research on Evaluation, Standards, and Student Testing.

Sternberg, R. J. (2002). Beyond g: The theory of successful intelligence. In R. J. Sternberg & E. L. Grigorenko (Eds.), *The general factor of intelligence: How general is it?* (pp. 447–479). Mahwah, NJ: Erlbaum. Stevenson, H. W., & Stigler, J. W. (1992). *The learning gap: Why our schools are failing and what we can learn from Japanese and Chinese education*. New York: Summit Books.

Stipek, D. (1988). *Motivation to learn: From theory to practice*. Upper Saddle River, NJ: Prentice Hall.

St. James, E. (1997). *Simplify your life with kids*. Kansas City, MO: Andrews McMeel.

Suicide and America's Youth. (2005, August 25). Seattle, Washington. [http://www.1-teenage-suicide.com/].

Sweller, J. (2004, April 20). *Human cognitive architecture and instructional design*. Presentation to CRESST research staff. Los Angeles: National Center for Research on Evaluation, Standards, and Student Testing.

Teen depression warning signs, information, getting help. Focus Adolescent Services. [http://www.focusas.com/Depression.html].

Tishman, S. (2000). Why teach habits of mind? In A. L. Costa & B. Kallick (Eds.), *Discovering and exploring habits of mind* (pp. 41–52). Alexandria, VA: ASCD.

Urbanski, A. (1994). *Real change is real hard: Lessons learned in Rochester*. (CRESST Line Newsletter). Los Angeles: Center for Research on Evaluation, Standards, and Student Testing.

Vygotsky, L. S. (1982–84). *Sobrainie so_inenii* [Complete Works]. Vols. 1-6. Moscow: Pedagogika.

Wake County Public School System (WCPSS). (2004). *Three WCPSS high schools above 1100 on 2004 SAT*. Wake County Public School System. Raleigh, NC [http://www.wcpss.net/news/2004_SAT/].

Wang, M., Haertel, G., & Walberg, H. (1997). Fostering Educational Resilience in Inner-City Schools. [http://www.temple.edu/lss/htmlpublications / publications/pubs97–4.htm].

Willard-Holt, C. (1999, May). *Dual exceptionalities*. ERIC Clearinghouse on Disabilities and Gifted Education. (ERIC Digest no. 574). Washington, DC: Office of Educational Research and Improvement.

Winquist Nord, C. (1998, April). *Students do better when their fathers are involved in school*. Washington, DC: National Center for Education Statistics. (NCES 98–121. Issue Brief). [nces.ed.gov/pubs98/web/98121.asp].

Wittrock, M. C. (1990). Generative processes of comprehension. *Educational Psychologist, 24*, 345–376.

Worthen, B. R., & Sanders, J. R. (1987). Educational evaluation: Alternative approaches and practical guidelines. New York: Longman.

Wright, S. P., Horn, S. P., & Sanders, W. L. (1997). Teacher and classroom context effects on student achievement: Implications for teacher evaluation. *Journal of personnel evaluation in education, 11*, 57–67.

Zimmerman, B. J. (1994). Dimensions of academic self-regulation: A conceptual framework for education. In D. H. Schunk & B. J. Zimmerman (Eds.), *Self-regulation of learning and performance: Issues and educational applications* (pp. 3–21). Mahwah, NJ: Erlbaum.

About the Author

Ronald Dietel is the assistant director for research use and communications at the National Center for Research on Evaluation, Standards, and Student Testing (CRESST) at UCLA. CRESST conducts research on educational testing, including K-12 assessments, and evaluates the effectiveness of educational and training programs. From December 2001 to December 2005, he was a member of the La Cañada (California) Unified School District Governing Board, including one year as president and one year as vice president of the board. Dietel publishes articles on school quality and educational testing in a variety of professional education magazines, such as the National PTA's *Our Children* magazine. He has been quoted for his education expertise in a number of media, notably the *Washington Post*, *Los Angeles Times*, National Public Radio, and the Associated Press. He has written and directed a number of video programs on educational testing, prominently *Assessment Models*, which was a finalist for the Distinguished Achievement Award from the Association of Educational Publishers.

A graduate of the U.S. Air Force Academy with a B.S. in international affairs, Dietel holds a master's degree from the University of Northern Colorado in communications, an MBA from Chapman University, and a doctorate (Ed.D.) in educational evaluation from UCLA. He is a graduate of the American Film Institute's Conservatory. His two children attend high school in California.

Index

C

G

H